Communications
in Computer and Information Science 1519

Editorial Board Members

More information about this series at https://link.springer.com/bookseries/7899

Paulo Rogério de Almeida Ribeiro ·
Vinícius Rosa Cota ·
Dante Augusto Couto Barone ·
Alexandre César Muniz de Oliveira (Eds.)

Computational Neuroscience

Third Latin American Workshop, LAWCN 2021
São Luís, Brazil, December 8–10, 2021
Revised Selected Papers

 Springer

Editors
Paulo Rogério de Almeida Ribeiro 🆔
Federal University of Maranhão (UFMA)
São Luís, Maranhão, Brazil

Vinícius Rosa Cota 🆔
Federal University of São João del-Rei
São João del-Rei, Minas Gerais, Brazil

Dante Augusto Couto Barone 🆔
Federal University of Rio Grande do Sul
Porto Alegre, Rio Grande do Sul, Brazil

Alexandre César Muniz de Oliveira 🆔
Federal University of Maranhão (UFMA)
São Luís, Maranhão, Brazil

ISSN 1865-0929   ISSN 1865-0937 (electronic)
Communications in Computer and Information Science
ISBN 978-3-031-08442-3   ISBN 978-3-031-08443-0 (eBook)
https://doi.org/10.1007/978-3-031-08443-0

This Springer imprint is published by the registered company Springer Nature Switzerland AG
The registered company address is: Gewerbestrasse 11, 6330 Cham, Switzerland

Preface

The human brain is considered the most complex object in the known universe and the least understood organ in the human body. To reveal it is such a hard task that neuroscience may only be properly carried out by a multi and interdisciplinary research team, with medical doctors, psychologists, engineers, computer scientists, mathematicians, pharmacists, physicists, etc. A fruitful approach may be to gather remarkable minds from distinct scientific fields and standpoints to uncover the brain. In order to fulfill this requirement, the Latin American Workshop on Computational Neuroscience (LAWCN) was born in 2017. It is a biannual event, the first edition (LAWCN 2017) taking place in Porto Alegre (Brazil) and the second edition (LAWCN 2019) in São João Del-Rei (Brazil), that addresses topics of computational neuroscience, artificial intelligence, neuroscience, and neuroengineering.

Besides all the usual endeavors of organizing a workshop, for the third edition (LAWCN 2021) we also had to deal with a rare and tough challenge, namely the COVID-19 pandemic. Instead of a completely online event, LAWCN 2021 was held as an innovative hybrid event, i.e. both online and in person in the city of São Luís – capital and largest city of the Brazilian state of Maranhão with a stunning colonial historical center (UNESCO World Heritage Site) – during December 8–10, 2021. Six world-class scientists – from Brazil, Argentina, and the USA – kindly accepted our invitation to give keynote speeches, presenting their work either remotely or in person. Similarly, authors of accepted papers gave presentations in fifteen-minute sessions, or accepted posters in a ninety-minute session, both online and in person.

All manuscripts submitted were reviewed single-blindedly by at least three experienced reviewers from our Program Committee (PC) consisting of 61 members: 23 researchers from Brazil and 38 from abroad (Argentina, the USA, Germany, Portugal, Spain, Austria, Colombia, Switzerland, Mexico, Greece, Australia, Norway, Ecuador, Italy, Chile, the UK, and Hungary). The 16 papers you will find in this volume of Springer's Communications in Computer and Information Science (CCIS) represent the top tier of those accepted. They encompass all areas of the event, and they take forward research on interdisciplinary applications of artificial intelligence (AI) and machine learning (ML); AI and ML applied to robotics; AI and ML applied to biomedical sciences; health issues and computational neuroscience; software and hardware implementations in neuroscience; and neuroengineering (science and technology).

LAWCN 2021 was organized by the Federal University of Maranhão (UFMA – Universidade Federal do Maranhão, Brazil) with the support of Fundação Sousândrade (FSADU). Financial aid was provided Plexon Inc. and by the International Brain Research Organization (IBRO). NeuroTechX (NTX) was a major partner for the conference, contributing ideas, minds, panelists, and assisting with worldwide dissemination. Springer has become a key collaborator of LAWCN as the publisher of our top papers in their CCIS series.

We, the editors of CCIS volume 1519, would like to express our most heartfelt gratitude to all the organizations, keynote speakers, authors, PC members (reviewers), and participants involved in LAWCN 2021. You all helped us to stage an awesome event and publish this excellent book, which may aid, in a small way, the task of solving the puzzle of the brain. Thank you!

December 2021

Paulo Rogério de Almeida Ribeiro
Vinícius Rosa Cota
Dante Augusto Couto Barone
Alexandre César Muniz de Oliveira

Organization

Conference Chairs

Paulo Rogério de Almeida Ribeiro (Chair)	Federal University of Maranhão (UFMA), Brazil
Vinícius Rosa Cota (Co-chair)	Federal University of São João del-Rei (UFSJ), Brazil

Organizing Committee

Alex Oliveira Barradas Filho	Federal University of Maranhão (UFMA), Brazil
Alexandre César Muniz de Oliveira	Federal University of Maranhão (UFMA), Brazil
Allan Kardec Duailibe Barros Filho	Federal University of Maranhão (UFMA), Brazil
Dante Augusto Couto Barone	Federal University of Rio Grande do Sul (UFRGS), Brazil
Fabrício Lima Brasil	Edmond and Lily Safra International Institute of Neuroscience, Santos Dumont Institute (ISD), Brazil
Frederico Augusto Casarsa de Azevedo	Massachusetts Institute of Technology (MIT) and Harvard Medical School, USA
Jaime Andres Riascos Salas	Institución Universitaria de Envigado, Colombia
Paulo Rogério de Almeida Ribeiro	Federal University of Maranhão (UFMA), Brazil
Sen Cheng	Ruhr University Bochum, Germany
Sofia Maria Amorim Falco Rodrigues	Federal Center for Technological Education of Minas Gerais (CEFET-MG), Brazil
Vinícius Rosa Cota	Federal University of São João del-Rei (UFSJ), Brazil

Program Committee Chair

Paulo Rogério de Almeida Ribeiro	Federal University of Maranhão (UFMA), Brazil

Program Committee

Abner Cardoso Rodrigues Neto	Edmond and Lily Safra International Institute of Neuroscience, Santos Dumont Institute (ISD), Brazil
Alan Talevi	National University of La Plata, Argentina

Alex Oliveira Barradas Filho	Federal University of Maranhão (UFMA), Brazil
Alexandre César Muniz de Oliveira	Federal University of Maranhão (UFMA), Brazil
Ali Khaledi Nasab	Stanford University, USA
Allan Kardec Duailibe Barros Filho	Federal University of Maranhão (UFMA), Brazil
Ander Ramos-Murguialday	University of Tübingen, Germany
André Salles Cunha Peres	Universidade de Coimbra, Portugal
Andrea Sarasola	TECNALIA, Spain
Andreea-Ioana Sburlea	Graz University of Technology, Austria
Antônio Roque	University of São Paulo (USP), Brazil
Bruno Feres de Souza	Federal University of Maranhão (UFMA), Brazil
Carlos Campos	University of Itaúna, Brazil
Carlos Dias Maciel	University of São Paulo (USP), Brazil
Carolina Bellera	National University of La Plata, Argentina
Cesar Alberto Collazos	Universidad del Cauca, Colombia
Cristina Simon-Martinez	University of Applied Sciences Western Switzerland, Switzerland
Dania Gutiérrez	Cinvestav Monterrey, Mexico
Dante Augusto Couto Barone	Federal University of Rio Grande do Sul (UFRGS), Brazil
Dimitris Kugiumtzis	Aristotle University of Thessaloniki, Greece
Dinesh Kant Kumar	Royal Melbourne Institute of Technology (RMIT) University, Australia
Edgard Morya	Edmond and Lily Safra International Institute of Neuroscience, Santos Dumont Institute (ISD), Brazil
Edison Pignaton de Freitas	Federal University of Rio Grande do Sul (UFRGS), Brazil
Eduardo López-Larraz	Bitbrain, Spain
Erivelton Geraldo Nepomuceno	Federal University of São João del-Rei (UFSJ), Brazil
Fabrício Lima Brasil	Edmond and Lily Safra International Institute of Neuroscience, Santos Dumont Institute (ISD), Brazil
Frederico Augusto Casarsa de Azevedo	Massachusetts Institute of Technology (MIT) and Harvard Medical School, USA
Gabriel Mindlin	Universidad de Buenos Aires, Argentina
Gabriela Castellano	University of Campinas (Unicamp), Brazil
Gil Lopes	University Institute of Maia (ISMAI), Portugal
Guillermo Cecchi	IBM T.J. Watson Research Center, USA
Héctor Julián Tejada Herrera	Federal University of Sergipe (UFS), Brazil
Jaime Andres Riascos Salas	Institución Universitaria de Envigado, Colombia

Jean Faber	Federal University of São Paulo (UNIFESP), Brazil
Jessica Cantillo-Negrete	National Institute of Rehabilitation, Mexico
Jim Tørresen	University of Oslo, Norway
Jorge Parraga-Alava	Universidad Técnica de Manabi, Ecuador
José C. Príncipe	University of Florida, USA
Jose Donoso	Ruhr University Bochum, Germany
Juan Felipe Ramirez Villegas	Institute of Science and Technology Austria, Austria
Justus Alfred Kromer	Stanford University, USA
Kai Olav Ellefsen	University of Oslo, Norway
Leonardo Bonato Félix	Federal University of Viçosa (UFV), Brazil
Lilian Konicar	Medical University of Vienna, Austria
Lucas Alberca	National University of La Plata, Argentina
Luciana Gavernet	National University of La Plata, Argentina
Marcelo Pias	Federal University of Rio Grande (FURG), Brazil
Marianna Semprini	Istituto Italiano di Tecnologia, Italy
Michela Chiappalone	Istituto Italiano di Tecnologia, Italy
Nerea Irastorza	TECNALIA, Spain
Nivaldo Antônio Portela de Vasconcelos	Federal University of Pernambuco (UFPE), Brazil
Omar Andrés Carmona Cortés	Federal Institute of Maranhão (IFMA), Brazil
Patricio Orio	Universidad de Valparaíso, Chile
Paulo Rogério de Almeida Ribeiro	Federal University of Maranhão (UFMA), Brazil
Pedro Almeida	University of Lisbon, Portugal
Reinhold Scherer	University of Essex, UK
Renan Cipriano Moioli	Federal University of Rio Grande do Norte (UFRN), Brazil
Rodrigo Alejandro Sierra Ordoñez	University of Szeged, Hungary
Sen Cheng	Ruhr University Bochum, Germany
Ulysse Côté-Allard	University of Oslo, Norway
Vinícius Rosa Cota	Federal University of São João del-Rei (UFSJ), Brazil

Keynote Speakers

Alan Talevi	National University of La Plata, Argentina
André Carvalho	University of São Paulo, Brazil
Angela Wyse	Federal University of Rio Grande do Sul, Brazil
José C. Príncipe	University of Florida, USA
Kerstin Schmidt	Federal University of Rio Grande do Norte, Brazil
Peter Tass	Stanford University, USA

Organizing Institution

Federal University of Maranhão (UFMA), Brazil

Sponsors and Supporters

Contents

Interdisciplinary Applications of Artificial Intelligence (AI) and Machine Learning (ML)

Semantic Segmentation of the Cultivated Area of Plantations with U-Net 3
Walysson Carlos dos Santos Oliveira, Geraldo Braz Junior,
and Daniel Lima Gomes Junior

Use and Interpretation of Item Response Theory Applied to Machine
Learning 15
Jade Dias, Caio Maia Rodrigues, and Abner Cardoso Rodrigues

AI and ML Applied to Robotics

Towards Loop Closure Detection for SLAM Applications Using Bag
of Visual Features: Experiments and Simulation 27
Alexandra Miguel Raibolt da Silva, Gustavo Alves Casqueiro,
Alberto Torres Angonese, and Paulo Fernando Ferreira Rosa

Loss Function Regularization on the Iterated Racing Procedure
for Automatic Tuning of RatSLAM Parameters 48
Paulo Gabriel Borralho Gomes, Cicero Joe Rafael Lima de Oliveira,
Matheus Chaves Menezes, Paulo Rogério de Almeida Ribeiro,
and Alexandre César Muniz de Oliveira

Controlling the UR3 Robotic Arm Using a Leap Motion: A Comparative
Study 64
Diego A. Lopez, Manuel A. Lopez, Dario S. Muñoz, Jesús A. Santa,
David F. Gomez, Dante Barone, Jim Torresen, and Jaime A. Riascos Salas

AI and ML Applied to Biomedical Sciences

Web Service Based Epileptic Seizure Detection by Applying Machine
Learning Techniques 81
Pedro Augusto Araujo da Silva de Almeida Nava Alves,
Alex Oliveira Barradas Filho, and Paulo Rogério de Almeida Ribeiro

Health Issues and Computational Neuroscience

Machine Learning Search of Novel Selective NaV1.2 and NaV1.6
Inhibitors as Potential Treatment Against Dravet Syndrome 101
   Maximiliano Fallico, Lucas N. Alberca, Denis N. Prada Gori,
   Luciana Gavernet, and Alan Talevi

Implementation of Intra and Extracellular Nonperiodic Scale-Free
Stimulation *in silico* for the NEURON Simulator 119
   Heitor de Carvalho Barros Terra, Fernando da Silva Borges,
   Marcio Flávio Dutra Moraes, and Vinícius Rosa Cota

In silico Investigation of the Effects of Distinct Temporal Patterns
of Electrical Stimulation to the Amygdala Using a Network of Izhikevich
Neurons 132
   João Pedro Silva e Oliveira, Victor Rafael Pereira Discacciati,
   Daniel de Castro Medeiros, Márcio Flávio Dutra Moraes,
   Grace S. Pereira, Keite Lira de Almeida França, and Vinícius Rosa Cota

Software and Hardware Implementations in Neuroscience

Brain Connectivity Measures in EEG-Based Biometry for Epilepsy
Patients: A Pilot Study 155
   Bruna M. Carlos, Brunno M. Campos, Marina K. M. Alvim,
   and Gabriela Castellano

A Multiplatform Output Stage for the Development of Current-Fixed
Electrical Stimulators Applied to Neural Electrophysiology 170
   Maikon L. Santos, João D. Nolasco, and Vinícius R. Cota

Neuroengineering – Science and Technology

Physiological Self-regulation Using Biofeedback Training: From Concept
to Clinical Applicability 189
   Karina Aparecida Rodrigues, João Vitor da Silva Moreira,
   Daniel José Lins Leal Pinheiro, Ana Teresa Contier, Esper Cavalheiro,
   and Jean Faber

Movement-Related Electroencephalography in Stroke Patients Across
a Brain-Computer Interface-Based Intervention 215
   Juan C. Castro-Aparicio, Ruben I. Carino-Escobar,
   and Jessica Cantillo-Negrete

Resting-State Exaggerated Alpha Rhythm from Subthalamic Nucleus
Discriminates Freezers from Non-freezers Phenotypes in Parkinson's
Disease: Possible Association to Attentional Circuits 225
  Arnaldo Fim Neto, Maria Sheila Guimarães Rocha,
  Luiz Ricardo Trajano, Julia Baldi de Luccas,
  Bruno Leonardo Bianqueti, Tiago Paggi de Almeida, Fábio Godinho,
  and Diogo Coutinho Soriano

Effect of Hand Dominance When Decoding Motor Imagery Grasping Tasks ... 233
  Katrine Linnea Nergård, Tor Endestad, and Jim Torresen

Kinematic Responses as a Control Strategy to Visual Occlusion 250
  Carlos Eduardo Campos, Cíntia de Oliveira Matos,
  Lucas Cléopas Costa da Silva, Paulo Rogério de Almeida Ribeiro,
  Crislaine Rangel Couto, Suziane Peixoto dos Santos,
  and Herbert Ugrinowitsch

Author Index 263

Interdisciplinary Applications of Artificial Intelligence (AI) and Machine Learning (ML)

Semantic Segmentation of the Cultivated Area of Plantations with U-Net

Walysson Carlos dos Santos Oliveira[(✉)] [iD], Geraldo Braz Junior[iD],
and Daniel Lima Gomes Junior

Universidade Federal do Maranhão - UFMA, 322, São Luís, MA 65.086-110, Brazil
walysson.oliveira@discente.ufma.com.br, geraldo@nca.ufma.br,
daniellima@ifma.edu.br

Abstract. The farm tax is mainly on agricultural production. To reduce tax evasion in agribusiness, it is possible to monitor the development of plantations through the analysis of satellite images. For this, deep learning techniques can be applied in satellite images to estimate a planted area of the plantations, which, in turn, can be used to estimate the production of monitored plantations. This work aims to analyze the satellite images of plantations to predict the cultivated area of plantations using semantics with convolutional neural networks. To achieve this goal, a method is proposed, which includes the creation of a dataset for planting area data, image segmentation with U-net architecture, tests to obtain the best combination of hyperparameters, and the evaluation of network performance. The proposed methodology with the network with a U-net segmentation architecture returned mean IoU results above 80%.

Keywords: Deep learning · Satellite image · Agriculture application

1 Introduction

Brazilian agribusiness is a prosperous and profitable activity. Abundant area, regular rainfall, solar energy and a diversified climate make Brazil a country with natural requirements for planting. Agribusiness is responsible not only for a large part of the food items consumed, but also for a production chain that involves various segments of the economy. In 2019, the sector represented 21.6% of the national GDP, according to the Ministry of Agriculture, Livestock and Supply of Brazil [20].

Since agribusiness is of paramount importance in the Brazilian economy, its participation in the contribution to the functioning of the government through taxes and fees arising from its activity is natural. However, agribusiness has a high rate of tax evasion that occurs as a result of the current complexity of the Brazilian tax system, in addition to the difficulty of inspection by the State, due to the great cost that such inspection entails, making its execution unfeasible [4].

The public service has been modernizing [22], not as agilely as the private sector, but projects such as Digital Government, which aim to accelerate the

© Springer Nature Switzerland AG 2022
P. R. d. A. Ribeiro et al. (Eds.): LAWCN 2021, CCIS 1519, pp. 3–14, 2022.
https://doi.org/10.1007/978-3-031-08443-0_1

digital transformation in the public sector, have contributed to the moderniza-
tion [9]. As an example, Tax Administration bodies such as the Federal Revenue,
State and Municipal Revenues have been crossing large volumes of data such as
credit cards, electronic invoices and other tax documents to identify tax evasion.

In the context of agribusiness, the tax burden of rural establishments is calculated mainly on their agricultural production. In order to reduce tax evasion,
it is possible to monitor the development of plantations through the analysis of
satellite images. For this, deep learning techniques can be applied in satellite
images to estimate the planted area of the plantations which, in turn, can be
used to estimate the production of the monitored plantations. This would bring
contributions such as: the reduction of tax evasion in agribusiness, the reduction of State expenses in on-site audits in places of difficult access and also the
possibility of application in other areas.

In recent years, deep learning with the algorithms of convolutional neural
networks, recurrent neural networks and generative adversary networks, has been
widely studied and applied in various fields with promising results and great
potential. Specifically, increasing attention has been paid to its application in
agriculture [12, 28]. Recent studies that propose to segment land cover regions
as in [17], vegetation areas as in [27] and plantation areas as in [14], use fully
convolutional neural networks for this purpose.

Understanding that efficiency in tax inspection implies a reduction in tax
evasion, reduces costs, increases collection and may in the future bring about
qualitative changes in the tax collection mechanism in agribusiness. The present
study uses deep learning techniques to estimate the cultivated area of plantations using semantic segmentation with convolutional neural networks in satellite
images. As this application is still little explored in the agribusiness segment,
several contributions are included in this work. The main contributions can be
highlighted: (a) the construction of a satellite image dataset, which can help
other researchers, with the marking of eight classes identified in the terrestrial
coverage of plantation regions (b) the proposition of an architecture deep learning that helps to automate the inspection process of rural establishments for tax
purposes; and (c) the possibility of applying the proposed architecture to other
problems with remote sensing images.

2   Related Works

To solve segmentation problems of satellite images and aerial images of plantations, the approaches found in the literature, in general, make use of deep
learning techniques. These works focus on datasets created by companies, gov-
ernments, universities and researchers. In the general case, datasets are usually
created specifically for the particularities of the research or application. Some of
these works are discussed in this section.

The Agriculture-Vision [8] dataset contains 21,061 aerial images of US farms
captured throughout 2019. The dataset consists of six classes that are cloud
shadow, double crop, crop failure, puddle water, water path and weed block.

Agriculture-Vision is a dataset for semantic segmentation of multiple classes, where these classes can overlap, for example, a puddle of water shaded by a cloud. To solve this problem, [2] proposed a new fully convolutional neural network architecture that they called AgriSegNet. AgriSegNet uses attention ports and combines the result of segmenting the images in different resolutions reaching 47.96% of mean IoU.

The winner of the Agriculture-Vision challenge used a U-Net based architecture and combined a Residual DenseNet with Squeeze-and-Excitation (SE) [7] blocks. In addition, expert networks with the same architecture but with fewer layers were used to segment less frequent classes such as crop failure and water puddle. The result network in mean IoU was 63.9% obtaining the best average performance of the competition.

The Slovenia Dataset and Oregon Dataset datasets were used to segment vegetation regions in satellite images into three classes being trees, shrubs and grass [3]. In this approach, the DeepLabV3+ [6] convolutional neural network architecture was used, which achieved 78.0% accuracy in the Slovenia Dataset and 78.9% in the Oregon Dataset.

A U-net based architecture [19] was used in [23] to segment land cover areas in satellite images and classify them into different types of crops. The datasets used were the BigEarthNet Dataset [21] which presents 44 land cover classes and the CORINE Dataset [5] which was developed by the European Environmental Agency and presents a variety of classes including types of plantation crops. The architecture used was a modified U-net with a ResNet50 [11] in the encoder. The method had an accuracy of 77% for plantation areas and 86% for forest areas.

Even though some datasets are already available in the literature for segmentation of plantation and land cover regions, they do not present the level of detail that is sought in this research and are not related to plantations in Brazilian territory. Thus, in this study, a new dataset is built for this specific research and will be available to other researchers. Most of the works used architectures based on U-net and in this study architectures of this type are also tested.

3   Methodology

In this section, we describe the methodology proposed in this work to estimate the cultivated area of plantations using semantic segmentation with convolutional neural networks in satellite images. For this, the Building the Dataset steps will be followed, which is subdivided into Image Acquisition and Annotation, followed by the Pre-processing, Hyperparameter Adjustment, Network Model training and Performance Evaluation steps. Figure 1 illustrates the proposed methodology. Each of these steps is explained in the following sections.

3.1   Building the Dataset

From searches carried out in the literature, some image datasets were found for segmentation of plantation areas. However, none of the datasets found presents

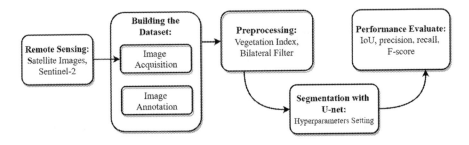

Fig. 1. Metodology

the desired level of detail for the problem addressed, nor are they from Brazilian areas with its most common vegetation and plantations. Thus, it was decided to create its own dataset.

Image Acquisition. Image acquisition is done with the aid of the *Google Earth Engine* (GEE) cloud-based geospatial processing platform. GEE is a satellite image catalog and geospatial dataset that allows the user to view, manipulate, edit and create spatial data [15]. The satellite used is Sentinel-2, which has a spatial resolution of 10m in its 4 main bands and image updates every 10 days [18].

To facilitate the acquisition of the images, a continuous area of plantations of 78,590.5 km² of total area and 1,233.8 km of perimeter was selected, as illustrated in Fig. 2 a). Point A, in Fig. 2 a), is located at coordinates 10°47'19.41"S and 46°73'36.57"W and Point B at coordinates 14°32'85.88"S and 44°90 '44.33"W. The images corresponding to this area will be downloaded with the GEE API, which allows defining the region of interest, a range of dates for the capture of images by the satellite and allowing filtering by the probability of clouds for images with better quality.

The Sentinel 2 satellite has a variety of bands that capture different information from the Earth's surface. For the purpose of this work, 4 bands of interest were selected, which are the bands B2 (Blue), B3 (Green), B4 (Red) and B8 (Near Infra Red).

The image acquisition region covers a large expanse of land, so it is necessary to fragment the region into blocks of lower resolution. The selected area was fragmented in a tabular (or grid) form, composed of several blocks of 256 × 256 resolution images, as shown in Fig. 2 c). The naming of the images will indicate their position in the image grid so that larger areas can be reassembled.

Image Annotation. After the acquisition steps, masks are created containing the marks of each class in the images. The tags will be used to carry out the training and evaluation of the networks. The marking process is carried out with the help of a tool for this purpose called *Labelme* [24].

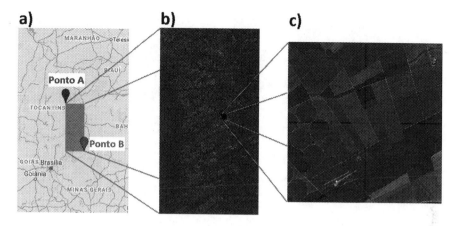

Fig. 2. a) Acquisition area. b) full image. c) 4 image blocks. (Color figure online)

The region of interest in this work is the area of cultivation of planta-tions. To define the classes, the plantation cultivation area is divided into three classes according to the plantation development stage: Plantation preparation area (class 1) which is the region of soil prepared to receive planting, Young planting (class 2) which is the initial stage of the plantation that mixes green areas with still areas of soil and mature plantation (class 3) which are regions where the plantation is developed. It was thought important to mark the paths that normally delimit the plantations and were named as Plantation division lines (Class 4). The fifth class represents areas of natural vegetation, green areas that are not cultivated, called Grassland or Forest Areas (class 5). The other classes are Areas of soil or rocks (class 6), Water (wetlands, lakes, rivers, etc.) (class 7) and Dwelling Areas (class 8) which are artificial houses or buildings in the farm regions. The definition of classes and marking of areas was based on other datasets with similar intent: *DeepGlobe Land Cover* [10], *LandCoverNet* [1] and the *EOPatches Slovenia* [3].

The image annotation process is carried out in three stages by different peo-ple, where the first one makes the tagging of all the images, the second reviews all the tags made by the first person and makes the necessary corrections. The third person is an expert in the field of agriculture who reviews a sample of the tagged images and informs them of the necessary adjustments. Figure 3 presents some examples of tagged images.

3.2   Preprocessing

Two pre-processing images are used, one being a smoothing filter and the other a color vegetation index. The smoothing filter used is the bilateral filter to pre-serve the edges of objects in the images. Colored vegetation indices are used in remote sensing of plantations and forests. These indices have the function of accentuating a specific color, such as the green of the plantation [25]. The vege-

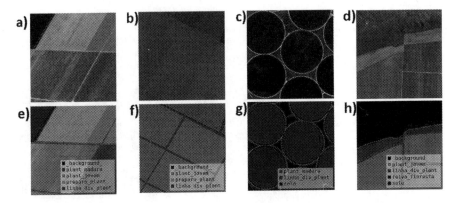

Fig. 3. a), b), c) and d) are RGB images of the dataset and e), f), g) and h) are, respectively, their annotations. (Color figure online)

tation index used was the Normalized Difference Vegetation Index (NDVI) [16] which is defined by the following formula, where RED is the red color channel and NIR is the Near Infra Red channel:

$$NDVI = \frac{NIR - RED}{NIR + RED} \tag{1}$$

3.3   Segmentation with U-Net Architecture

Convolutional neural networks are biologically inspired models that can learn features in a hierarchical fashion, specially designed to deal with variability in two-dimensional data, such as images in matrix format [13]. Convolutional neural networks consist of 3 layers: 1) convolution layer, which performs image filtering operations, and filters are formed by weights that are adjusted by the network during the training process, 2) subsampling layer, which reduces the image resolution at each step and 3) fully connected layer that is composed of neurons that perform the classification at the output of the [13] network.

Convolutional neural networks establish the state of the art for the image classification problem. However, for image segmentation problems, both the input to the network and the output to the network must be images. For this purpose, Totally Convolutional Networks were proposed, where the network produces an output in the same dimensions as the input image, performing a pixel-by-pixel segmentation of the input image, as is the case of U-net [19] shown in Fig. 4.

The U-net gets its name from its U-shaped architecture. The left side of the U-net is known as the encoder and is where the image enters and goes through convolution, ReLU activation and sub-sampling operations. After the input image goes through these operations, we call the result activation maps. These operations increase the number of activation maps and reduce their resolution as they approach the center of the network, which is why it is also known as the contraction path. In contrast, the right side of the U-net is known as expansion path or decoder, where activation maps are increased resolutions with the

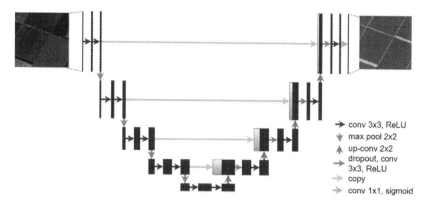

conv 3x3, ReLU
max pool 2x2
up-conv 2x2
dropout, conv 3x3, ReLU
copy
conv 1x1, sigmoid

Fig. 4. U-net architecture

up-convolution operation and activation maps are reduced with dropout operations. There is also an operation of copying the corresponding layer activation maps from the encoder to the decoder. In the end, after going through a 1×1 convolution and a sigmoid or softmax activation (the most common), the network output is a segmentation mask that has a resolution equal to or very close to the resolution of the input image.

3.4 Hyperparameter Optimization

Hyperparameters are parameters used to configure a Machine Learning model that cannot be estimated directly from network learning and must be configured before training a Machine Learning model, as they define the model architecture [26].

In the Hyperparameters optimization step, the fully convolutional network is trained with a combination of hyperparameters that are adjusted to optimize the results. In the experiments of this work, the best combination of hyperparameters that optimize the network performance is tested. The following are adjusted (Table 1):

3.5 Performance Evaluation

Image segmentation performance is measured from the Intersection over Union assessment metric, known as IoU. The metric mIoU (mean IoU) is defined below with its mathematical formulation in Eq. 2, considering that GT is the real region of the object, that $Pred$ is the region predicted by the network and c is number of components.

$$mIoU = \frac{1}{c} \sum_{i=1}^{c} \frac{Area(GT_i \cap Pred_i)}{Area(GT_i \cup Pred_i)} \qquad (2)$$

We also use metrics Precision (PRE), Recall and F-score, whose formulations are described as a function of the True Positive (TP), False Negative (FN), False

Table 1. Set of hyperparameters that will be tested

Hyperparameters	Test set
Backbone	VGG, ResNet, SeResNet, ResNext, SeResNext, SeNet, DenseNet, Inception, InceptionResNet, MobileNet and EfficientNet
Loss function	Jaccard, Dice, Categorical Focal, Categorical Cross Entropy and combinations
Batche size	2, 4, 6, 8, 10
Optimizer	Adam, Ftrl, Adagrad, Adamax, RMSprop, SGD, Nadam

Positives (FP) and True Negatives (TN) [29].

$$PRE = \frac{TP}{TP + FP} \tag{3}$$

$$Recall = \frac{TP}{TP + FN} \tag{4}$$

$$Fscore = \frac{2 \times PRE \times SEN}{PRE + SEN} \tag{5}$$

4   Experiments and Results

A *dataset* was created to segment plantation areas, where images were acquired from the *Sentinel-2* satellite and obtained through the *Google Earth* platform with the selection of the necessary bands and fragmentation of the region of interest in 9860 256 × 256 resolution image blocks. So far, 250 images have been tagged that have gone through the review and correction stages.

4.1   Data Description

The *dataset* built contains 8 classes that can be used for a variety of types of applications. In the experiments of this article, the 8 classes are not used separately, but groupings of them, as the objective is to segment planting regions. In Table 2 are presented the classes of each one of these steps and their correspondence with the original classes of the dataset.

4.2   Hyperparameter Test

One hundred random combinations of hyperparameters were tested and the combination with the best result is Backbone: EfficientNetB7, Batch Size: 8, Loss Function: *Binary Focal Loss* and Optimizer: Adam.

Table 2. Definition of study classes.

Step 1 classes	Original dataset classes
Plantation	Mature Plantation
	Young Plantation
	Soil Prepared for Planting
Non-plantation	Path/Road in the Plantation
	Grass or Forest
	Sand or Rock
	Water
	Building

4.3   Segmentation of Plantation Areas

The network input is composed of four bands of satellite images which were the RGB and NIR bands. Visual results are shown in Fig. 5, with the segmentation of Plantation areas represented in dark green color and Non-Plantation areas represented in gold color. We can see in the example images that the planting areas are well delimited and visually close to the ground truth (GT) segmentation but contain apparent segmentation error noises that can be improved with a post-processing step.

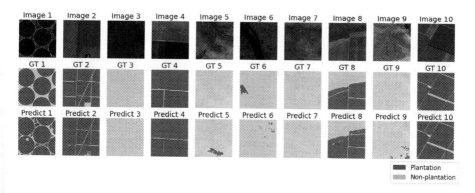

Fig. 5. In the first line some images in RGB, in the central line the true segmentation mask for the Planting and Non-Planting classes and in the last line the result of the network segmentation. Images 1, 2, 4, 8 and 10 are of farms, images 3 and 6 are of urban areas with a river/lake and images 5, 7 and 9 are of rocky areas. (Color figure online)

The numerical results of the segmentation are presented in Table 4 and are consistent with the observations of the visual results. The mean IoU had a result of 84.04%, which can be considered a median result for medical applications due to the critically of the application, but is a reasonably consistent result for an agricultural and satellite imagery application. Precision, Recall and F-score results had results above 90% (Table 3).

Table 3. Numerical result of the metrics of U-net architecture.

Class	IoU	Precision	Recall	F-score
Plantation	88.26%	94.83%	92.57%	93.67%
No Plantation	79.81%	86.92%	90.41%	88.57%
Mean	84.04%	90.87%	91.49%	91.12%

It was not possible to make a direct comparison (planting/non-planting segmentation area) with other works, but for a general comparison, the works cited in the Related Works section had the following results:

Table 4. Related works results

Author	Model	Dataset	Task	Result
[2]	AgriSegNet [2]	Agriculture-Vision [8]	Segmentation 6 plantation classes	47.96% mIoU
[7]	U-net based architecture [19]	Agriculture-Vision [8]	Segmentation 6 plantation classes	63.9% mIoU
[3]	DeepLabV3+ [6]	Slovenia Dataset	Segmentation trees, shrubs and grass	78.0% accuracy
[23]	U-net based architecture [19]	BigEarthNet Dataset [21] + CORINE Dataset [5]	Segmentation plantation areas	77% accuracy

5   Conclusion

In this work, a method for plantation area segmentation was presented and as a contribution the work also included the creation of a plantation area segmentation dataset. The network hyperparameters were adjusted considering the U-net backbone, the optimizer, loss function and batch size. The best combination of hyperparameters was obtained to U-net returned mean IoU results above 80%. The main contributions achieved are the construction of a satellite image dataset that can help other researchers in similar studies; and the creation of a method for the segmentation of plantation areas that can be used as one of the initial steps of an automated process of inspection of rural establishments for tax purposes.

As future work, the next step for creating an automated inspection process for rural establishments for tax purposes is to use the predicted segmentation area to estimate production in weight measurement units and compare with official data declared by rural producers for the tax administration. Various optimizations can be made to the network architecture such as using another base architecture in place of U-net, such as the DeepLab architecture, or creating a new architecture. Finally, it is still recommended to increase the number of images in the dataset and test other pre-processing possibilities.

Acknowledgements. The authors thank the National Council for Scientific and Technological Development (CNPq), the Coordination for the Improvement of Higher Education Personnel (CAPES) and the Foundation for Research and Scientific and Technological Development of the State of Maranhão (FAPEMA) for the financial support for the development of this work.

References

1. Alemohammad, H., Booth, K.: LandCoverNet: a global benchmark land cover classification training dataset (2020)
2. Anand, T., Sinha, S., Mandal, M., Chamola, V., Yu, F.R.: AgriSegNet: deep aerial semantic segmentation framework for IoT-assisted precision agriculture. IEEE Sens. J. **21**, 17581–17590(2021)
3. Ayhan, B., Kwan, C.: Tree, shrub, and grass classification using only RGB images. Remote Sensing **12**(8) (2020). https://doi.org/10.3390/rs12081333. https://www.mdpi.com/2072-4292/12/8/1333
4. Brugnaro, R., Del Bel Filho, E., Bacha, C.J.C.: Avaliação da sonegação de impostos na agropecuária brasileira. Agric. São Paulo, SP (50), 15–27 (2003)
5. Büttner, G., Feranec, J., Jaffrain, G., Mari, L., Maucha, G., Soukup, T.: The CORINE land cover 2000 project. EARSeL eProceedings **3**(3), 331–346 (2004)
6. Chen, L.C., Papandreou, G., Kokkinos, I., Murphy, K., Yuille, A.L.: DeepLab: semantic image segmentation with deep convolutional nets, atrous convolution, and fully connected CRFs. IEEE Trans. Pattern Anal. Mach. Intell. **40**(4), 834–848 (2017)
7. Chiu, M.T., et al.: The 1st agriculture-vision challenge: methods and results. arXiv preprint arXiv:2004.09754 (2020)
8. Chiu, M.T., et al.: Agriculture-vision: a large aerial image database for agricultural pattern analysis. In: Proceedings of the IEEE/CVF Conference on Computer Vision and Pattern Recognition, pp. 2828–2838 (2020)
9. Cristóvam, J.S.d.S., Saikali, L.B., Sousa, T.P.d.: Governo digital na implementação de serviços públicos para a concretização de direitos sociais no brasil. Sequência (Florianópolis) (84), 209–242 (2020)
10. Demir, I., et al.: DeepGlobe 2018: a challenge to parse the earth through satellite images. In: The IEEE Conference on Computer Vision and Pattern Recognition (CVPR) Workshops, June 2018
11. He, K., Zhang, X., Ren, S., Sun, J.: Deep residual learning for image recognition. In: Proceedings of the IEEE Conference on Computer Vision and Pattern Recognition, pp. 770–778 (2016)
12. Kamilaris, A., Prenafeta-Boldú, F.X.: Deep learning in agriculture: a survey. Comput. Electron. Agric. **147**, 70–90 (2018)

13. LeCun, Y., Bengio, Y., Hinton, G.: Deep learning. Nature **521**(7553), 436–444 (2015)
14. Rustowicz, R., Cheong, R., Wang, L., Ermon, S., Burke, M., Lobell, D.: Semantic segmentation of crop type in Africa: a novel dataset and analysis of deep learning methods. In: Proceedings of the IEEE/CVF Conference on Computer Vision and Pattern Recognition (CVPR) Workshops, June 2019
15. Mutanga, O., Kumar, L.: Google earth engine applications (2019)
16. Perez, A., Lopez, F., Benlloch, J., Christensen, S.: Colour and shape analysis techniques for weed detection in cereal fields. Comput. Electron. Agric. **25**(3), 197–212 (2000)
17. Rakhlin, A., Davydow, A., Nikolenko, S.: Land cover classification from satellite imagery with U-net and Lovasz-Softmax loss. In: Proceedings of the IEEE Conference on Computer Vision and Pattern Recognition (CVPR) Workshops, June 2018
18. Ribeiro, C.M.N.: Classificação do uso e cobertura do solo do estado de goiás empregando redes neurais artificiais (2019)
19. Ronneberger, O., Fischer, P., Brox, T.: U-net: convolutional networks for biomedical image segmentation. In: Navab, N., Hornegger, J., Wells, W.M., Frangi, A.F. (eds.) MICCAI 2015. LNCS, vol. 9351, pp. 234–241. Springer, Cham (2015). https://doi.org/10.1007/978-3-319-24574-4_28
20. da Silva, M., Cesario, A.V., Cavalcanti, I.R.: Relevância do agronegócio para a economia brasileira atual. Apresentado em X ENCONTRO DE INICIAÇÃO À DOCÊNCIA, UNIVERSIDADE FEDERAL DA PARAÍBA (2013). http://www.prac.ufpb.br/anais/IXEnex/iniciacao/documentos/anais/8.TRABALHO/8CCSADAMT01.pdf
21. Sumbul, G., Charfuelan, M., Demir, B., Markl, V.: BigEarthNet: a large-scale benchmark archive for remote sensing image understanding. In: IGARSS 2019–2019 IEEE International Geoscience and Remote Sensing Symposium, pp. 5901–5904. IEEE (2019)
22. Tohá, C., Solari, R.: A modernização do estado e a gerência pública. Revista do Serviço Público **48**(3), 84–103 (1997)
23. Ulmas, P., Liiv, I.: Segmentation of satellite imagery using U-Net models for land cover classification. arXiv preprint arXiv:2003.02899 (2020)
24. Wada, K.: labelme: Image Polygonal Annotation with Python (2016). https://github.com/wkentaro/labelme
25. Woebbecke, D.M., Meyer, G.E., Von Bargen, K., Mortensen, D.A.: Color indices for weed identification under various soil, residue, and lighting conditions. Trans. ASAE **38**(1), 259–269 (1995)
26. Yang, L., Shami, A.: On hyperparameter optimization of machine learning algorithms: theory and practice. Neurocomputing **415**, 295–316 (2020)
27. Yang, M.D., Tseng, H.H., Hsu, Y.C., Tsai, H.P.: Semantic segmentation using deep learning with vegetation indices for rice lodging identification in multi-date UAV visible images. Remote Sens. **12**(4), 633 (2020)
28. Zhu, N., et al.: Deep learning for smart agriculture: concepts, tools, applications, and opportunities. Int. J. Agricult. Biolog. Eng. **11**(4), 32–44 (2018)
29. Zhu, W., Zeng, N., Wang, N., et al.: Sensitivity, specificity, accuracy, associated confidence interval and roc analysis with practical SAS implementations. NESUG Proc. Health Care Life Sci. Baltimore Maryland **19**, 67 (2010)

Use and Interpretation of Item Response Theory Applied to Machine Learning

Jade Dias[1], Caio Maia Rodrigues[2], and Abner Cardoso Rodrigues[1]($\boxtimes$)

[1] Graduate Program in Neuroengineering, Edmond and Lily Safra International Institute of Neuroscience, Santos Dumont Institute, Av. Alberto Santos Dumont, 1560 - Zona Rural., Macaiba, RN 59280-000, Brazil
abner.neto@isd.org.br

[2] XP Investimentos, Rio de Janeiro, Brazil

Abstract. Machine Learning (ML) has been gaining prominence in health, research and engineering, but despite the wide use of its predictive results, users of ML systems often have a poor understanding of its operation. In general, many algorithms have a so-called "black box" structure, whose logic is not interpretable. Therefore, there is a line of research dedicated to clarifying how models make their decisions. In this context, Item Response Theory (IRT), widely applied in educational tests, can be an alternative for understanding and interpreting ML models. IRT consists in logistic models that relate given responses given to the items with skills of their respondents and to the items parameters, such as: difficulty, discrimination and guessing. In this work, we are interested in characterizing the ML instances according to the IRT parameters, and establishing criteria for instance augmentation, as a way to make them easier for the model, without modifying its performance. To this end, we divided the study into two experiments: the first one consists in increasing the items of greater difficulty, discrimination and guessing, adding noise to them; and the second one consists of reducing a class and increasing it progressively observing the change in the item's parameters. The results show that the increase in fact causes a reduction in the values of the IRT parameters, and that there is a proportional relationship between them, without affecting the accuracy of the models. In this sense, it is possible to observe a relationship between the IRT parameters and its decision power in the model, and therefore, unfolding it as a promising tool for understanding ML models.

Keywords: Machine learning · Interpretability · Item response theory

1 Introduction

Machine Learning (ML) is a set of mathematical techniques that use example data to approximate a function, which creates a mapping between input and desired output data. ML has been used for pattern recognition, classification and

Supported by CAPES Higher Education Improvement Coordination.

P. R. d. A. Ribeiro et al. (Eds.): LAWCN 2021, CCIS 1519, pp. 15–24, 2022.
https://doi.org/10.1007/978-3-031-08443-0_2

prediction [1], but despite the wide applicability of ML algorithms in solving real problems, one of the difficulties of its usage is the low interpretability. Many of the ML models are black boxes that don't explain their options in a way that humans understand. This lack of transparency and accountability of predictive models can have serious consequences in criminal justice, medicine and other domains [2]. A missing step in the construction of a ML model is precisely an explanation of its logic, expressed in an understandable and readable format, which highlights the videos seized by the model, allowing to understand and validate its decision reasoning [7].

Even without a mathematical definition for interpretability, it can be understood as the degree to which a human being can understand the cause of a decision on a model [3]. Interpretability in ML refers to methods and models that make behavior and predictions in ML systems understandable to human language [4].

Understanding how models make their decisions is important because: i) in many cases, researchers are related to the biological significance of the predictive model rather than the predictive accuracy of the model [5], that is, for certain problems obtaining the prediction alone (what) is not enough, the model should also explain how to reach at the prediction (why) [6] ii) possible biases and artifacts hidden in the data can lead to unfair or unethical decisions [4] and knowing more about how the decision process is made can help to understand more about the data and flaws of the model [6] iii) an explanation of the decision mechanisms in an understandable and readable format to comprehend and validate the decision [7]. This validation can be useful to detect bias in ML models [6].

There are some methods that aim to interpret ML models, such as: (1) Permutation Feature Importance [8]; (2) Partial Dependence Plot [9]; (3) Individual Conditional Expectation Plot [10]; (4) Accumulated Local Effects [11]. However, these methods have some disadvantages, such as: computational cost, leading to processing slowness; dependence on human interpretability, in cases of graphic visualization; dimensional limitation, since the graphic visualization is limited to three dimensions; they are based only on the analysis of model attributes.

Item Response Theory (IRT), widely applied mainly in educational testing and psychometric assessment [12], is an alternative that is already being used for understanding and interpreting ML models [13]. The application of IRT as an adaptive tool is suggested as a new perspective for a better understanding of the results of machine learning experiments and, by extension, other artificial intelligence experiments [13]. The IRT considers a set of models that associate the predictions given to the item with the latent abilities of the respondents [14]. In this model, the probability of a correct answer is a function of the student's skill and the difficulty of the item [15]. In order to derive the respondent's skill score, Item Characteristic Curves (ICC) are used to represent the probability of choosing the correct item given the subject's skill [12].

One way to use the idea of IRT with ML is to consider each sample data in the training set as an item in a questionnaire and each ML model as a respondent. This approach can bring advantages over classical interpretation methods, such as: better assessment of model skills; identification of the most difficult instances; measurement of the classifier's proficiency level; and the probability that a classifier can correctly classify the situation without actually learning the features of the training data, called a guessing parameter.

In this article, we will present the IRT approach as an alternative for interpreting ML models, as well as a way to evaluate classifiers by their level of proficiency, and classify instances by their level of difficulty. The purpose is to use IRT to obtain instance-level characteristics, such as discrimination and difficulty, and use them as a guide for instance augmentation, that is, as a method to identify which examples need data augmentation. The hypothesis of this work is that we can, with IRT, characterize the problematic items for learning the algorithm, interpret these items and improve learning by collecting more examples of training, similar to the problematic items. The increase in examples aims to make difficult instances easier, as classifiers start to classify more variations of that same instance until they perform well.

In [13], Martinez et al. uses IRT parameters to provide important information about the proficiency level of the classifiers, using their coefficients as metrics to evaluate the models and verify how these models are improving over time. They sought to interpret IRT parameters for application in machine learning, detailing what each coefficient can say about its dataset or about the model. Unlike Martinez, here we are performing an application of IRT results to guide data augmentation and improve prediction results. Despite the different approach, we used a lot of the theory provided by Martinez et al. to interpret our results.

The rest of the article is organized as follows. Section 2 provides an overview of the IRT. Section 3 details the dataset, packages and experiments performed. Finally, Sect. 4 presents the results and discussion.

2   Item Response Theory

IRT is a set of mathematical models that seek to represent the probability of an individual giving a certain answer to an item [16]. It is a logistic mathematical function that depends on the item parameters and the respondent's ability (or abilities). The models presented in this work are formulations valid only for the analysis of items of a dichotomous nature, that is, subject to only two answers (true or false; right or wrong; 1 or 0). Dichotomous logistic models can have 1, 2, 3 and 4 parameters, which consider, respectively: (1) only the difficulty of the item; (2) difficulty and discrimination; (3) difficulty, discrimination and guessing; (4) the first three parameters, in addition to the upper and lower limits, which represent the maximum or minimum probability of getting a certain item right.

Of the models proposed by IRT, the 3-parameter logistic model is given by:

$$P(U_{ij} = 1|\theta_j) = c_i + (1 - c_i)\frac{1}{1 + e^{-Da_i(\theta_j - b_i)}}$$

with i = 1, 2, $\cdots$, I, e j = 1, 2, $\cdots$, n, where:

θ_i represents the skill (latent trait) of the j-th individual.

$P(U_{ij} = 1|\theta_j)$ is the probability that an individual j with skill θ_j will correctly answer the item i and is called an Item Response Function (IRF).

b_i is the difficulty (or position) parameter of the i item, measured on the same scale as the skill.

a_i is the discrimination (or slope) parameter of item i, with a value proportional to the slope of the Item Characteristic Curve (ICC) at point b_i.

c_i is the item parameter that represents the probability of individuals with low ability to correctly answer the item i (often referred to as the chance of hitting, or guessing).

D is a scaling factor, constant is equal to 1. The value 1.7 is used when you want the logistic function to provide similar results to the normal ogive.

3   Methodology

The method consists of applying the IRT model to a controlled experiment using an image database well known in the AI/ML/Data Science community, commonly used as a reference to validate their algorithms, the Fashion MNIST.

3.1   Data

Fashion MNIST is a clothing image dataset. The database has a training set of 60.000 examples and a test set of 10.000 examples. Each example consists of a grayscale image of 28×28 pixels, associated with a label of 10 classes, including: 0 - shirt; 1 - pants; 2 - sweater; 3 - dress; 4 - coat; 5 - sandals; 6 - shirt; 7 - tennis; 8 - bag; 9 - boots. The Fashion MNIST set is very similar to the popular MNIST set, sharing the same image size and division structure between training and testing, however, the Fashion MNIST proves to be a more robust set, due to the greater complexity of its images.

3.2   Experiment Design

In order to verify the initial hypothesis, we divided the work into two experiments. The first experiment seeks to answer the first question of the work: "Does increasing the training examples really reduce the item's difficulty?"; and the second experiment aims to determine the effect on the IRT indices from the proportional increase, with the goal finding out if the difficulty, discrimination and guessing exhibit a behavior proportional to the increase of examples.

To answer this questions, we will resample the most difficult, discriminating and guessing items, and we will verify the item parameters behavior, as well as the model accuracy with the resampling.

In [13], there is a suggestion to remove items with low discrimination as a way to improve the assessment of classifiers, leaving only those instances that better discriminate good models from bad models. However, doing this can mean removing a noise or only instances that are well labeled, hence, unlike Martinez et al. proposes, we do not remove instances with bad coefficients, but rather increase the instances that are favorable to our results.

Experiment 1. The experiment consists of loading the entire dataset of images, and performing classification training with six ML models: Decision Trees; Random Forests; Neural networks; AdaBoost; Naive Bayes; and Quadratic Discriminant Analysis (QDA). In the second stage of the experiment, 100 examples of each class of the test set are selected. With the dichotomous prediction results for the 100 items (zero for a wrong prediction, and 1 for a correct prediction), the IRT model is used to identify item characteristics such as difficulty, discrimination, and guesswork.

Obtaining the most difficult item, it is increased by 1.000 times and its coefficient of difficulty is checked. The same is true for the most discriminating and highest guessing item. Enhancement the items is performed by replicating the item and using common strategies in data augmentation such as adding noise, rotation, magnification and sharpening of the image to it, like [17].

Experiment 2. The experiment consists of loading the image dataset, reducing the number of training examples of the first class of the dataset (class: shirt) and then performing classification training with the same six AM models. Training set reduction happens gradually with each iteration by: 90%, 75%, 50%, 25%, and 10%.

The purpose of this experiment is to see if the increased rate of training examples for a class affects the parameters of each item. It includes both the items the class that underwent augmentation, as well as the other classes.

4   Results and Discussion

4.1   Experiment 1

When applying IRT to the test set predictions, we took the indices whose coefficients were the highest. We perform the 1.000-fold augmentation from these items and look at the new coefficients. This experiment was performed 10 times and the mean of the coefficients was obtained. Table 1 shows the average of the original item coefficients (no augmentation) and the coefficients after augmentation. Table 2 shows the average of the original accuracies (no augmentation) for each classifier, and accuracies after augmentation by discrimination, by difficulty and by guessing.

Table 1. IRT coefficients for classifications with and without augmentation.

Coefficients	Original	Augmented
Discrimination (a)	4.978	3.971
Difficulty (b)	7.111	4.072
Guessing(c)	0.393	0.250

Table 2. Model accuracies for classification of the original dataset, and the dataset augmented by discrimination, by difficulty, and by guessing.

Classifiers	Original	Augmented by discrimination	Augmented by difficulty	Augmented by guessing
Decision tree	0.6938	0.6929	0.6935	0.6944
Random forest	0.678	0.6742	0.6802	0.6985
Neural net	0.8526	0.8534	0.8557	0.8514
Ada boost	0.5425	0.5396	0.5505	0.5676
Naive bayes	0.5856	0.5786	0.5687	0.5639
QDA	0.5715	0.5584	0.5597	0.5677

It can be noted that three coefficients were, in fact, reduced (Table 1) (Reductions: a: 20.23%; b: 42.74%; c: 36.39%), while the classifiers accuracy remained, i.e., the augmentation promoted a reduction in the IRT parameters, without changing classifiers efficiency (Table 2).

4.2   Experiment 2

The relationship between difficulty and augmentation is represented by the Fig. 1. The boxplot represents the distribution of the difficulty coefficients for all items analyzed by the IRT, including items from the non-augmented class. It is possible to observe that there was a decrease in item difficulty when increasing the number of examples by 75% of the original size. Increases below that did not cause a significant change in the difficulty parameter.

With the box plot, we were able to analyze the behavior of the difficulty in general, but the confidence interval presented is large, so we cannot infer much about the graphs. This fact occurs because the increase in a class does not change the difficulty behavior of the entire system, but rather specifically for the augmented class. In order to verify the variation of the difficulty parameter by class, the calculation of the average difficulty of the items in the same class for each increase was performed. To verify the effect of individual augmentation, we plot the difficulty curve for each class (Fig. 2), and each color indicates a garment in the dataset. Figure 2, it is possible to observe that the "T-shirt" class, which has been increased, is a curve that exhibits a greater variation in difficulty, decreasing as the number of examples increases.

The relationship between discrimination and augmentation is represented by Fig. 3. From the 75% rate of increase, the discrimination of the dataset increases considerably. This means that the data is now more easily differentiating between good and bad classifiers.

As a way to verify the classes that most contribute to this behavior, we performed an individual analysis of the class considering the average of discrimination for each increase rate (Fig. 4).

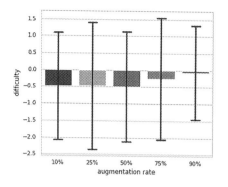

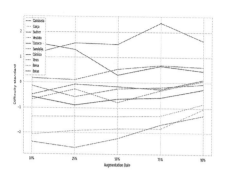

Fig. 1. Discrimination versus augmentation rate

Fig. 2. Average discrimination per class versus augmentation rate

The Fig. 4 shows that all classes exhibit the same behavior, remaining constant up to 50% and increasing from that rate. Despite the similar behavior, the T-shirt and boot weight classes had the greatest discriminating power.

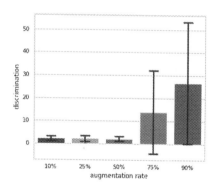

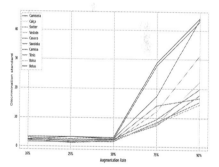

Fig. 3. Difficulty versus augmentation rate

Fig. 4. Average difficulty per class versus augmentation rate

The same analysis was performed for the guessing parameter of the IRT model. Figure shows that there is a drop in guessing for training models from the 75% rate of increase for one class (Figs. 5 and 6).

Analysing individual classes, it is possible to observe that there is a tendency of decreasing guesswork as the examples increase. However, by increasing the rate to 95%, the guessing increases. In addition, it is possible to identify that the T-shirt class is the class with the lowest guessing coefficient, decreasing from the rate of 75%.

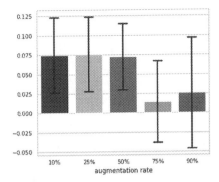

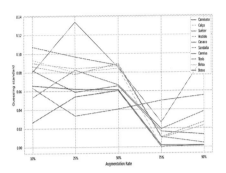

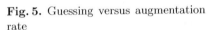

Fig. 5. Guessing versus augmentation rate

Fig. 6. Average guessing per class versus augmentation rate

The accuracy measure characterizes the hit rate per classification model. To evaluate the accuracy by item class we divided the instances into 6 bins ordered by the difficulty parameter, like [12]. For each bin, we calculate the average difficulty of the instances in the bin, and calculate the frequency of right responses of the classifier. With the sum of hits, we calculate the accuracy through the sum of correct predictions for each class, divided by the number of examples in that class. The result of the accuracy by class is presented as the average of all accuracies at each increase rate. On the x-axis we have the rate of increase divided into 6 bins, and on the y-axis we have the average accuracy for each bin.

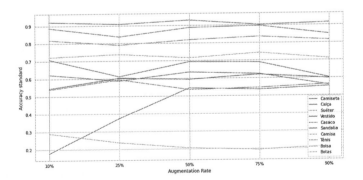

Fig. 7. Accuracy per class versus augmentation rate

Figure 7 demonstrates that the accuracy remains practically constant for all classes, with the exception of the t-shirt class, whose accuracy increases linearly up to 50% enhancement. This suggests that the augmentation contributes positively to increasing the accuracy of the predictive model, however this increase occurs up to 50%, an iteration in which most classification models saturate, reaching their maximum limit and therefore the accuracy value remains constant for higher rise rates. Furthermore, it is possible to observe that there is no change in the accuracy of the other classes, therefore, for this dataset, the enhancement is beneficial and specific, i.e., it does not influence the accuracy of the model for non-augmented classes.

In [13], Martinez et al. performs the analysis of proficiency through the Characteristic Curve of the Classifier (CCC) that shows the relationship between difficulty and accuracy for each classifier. The result is similar to ours, however we evaluated the relationship between accuracy and augmentation rate for each class. But, knowing through experiment 1 and 2 that the rate of increase is directly proportional to the difficulty coefficient, and knowing that the result per class is an average of the six classifiers, it is possible to draw a parallel between the results obtained by Martinez et al. and this one. For example, at Martinez, the accuracy is lower for higher difficulty values, as can be seen from the blue curve in 7.

5   Conclusion

The work found a reliable relation between the increase of data points for training and change in the IRT parameters, showing that it is possible to increase the instances without modifying the accuracy of the models. This strategy can be useful in data augmentation and small data scenarios where difficult parameter from IRT can be employed to identify problematic items. However, IRT alone does not help us to interpret ML models in a broad way. For this, it would be necessary to combine IRT with some tools for visualizing the items and the decision boundaries. With these visualizations we can determine if an item labeled as difficult is in a noisy or in a misclassified region. In future works, we intend to apply IRT in conjunction with a decision boundary map to visualize where the most difficult, more discriminating and highest guessing items are located on the boundary and find out if it is possible to change the boundary by increasing examples.

References

1. Tarca, A., Carey, V., Chen, X., Romero, R.: Machine learning and its applications to biology. PLoS Comput. Biol. **3**(6), e116 (2007)
2. Rudin, C.: Stop explaining black box machine learning models for high stakes decisions and use interpretable models instead. Nat. Mach. Intell. **1**, 206–215 (2019)
3. Miller, T.: Explanation in artificial intelligence: insights from the social sciences. Artif. Intell. **267**, 1–38 (2019)
4. Pedreschi, D., Giannotti, F., Guidotti, R., Monreale, A., Ruggieri, S., Turini, F.: Meaningful explanations of Black Box AI decision systems. In: Proceedings of the AAAI Conference on Artificial Intelligence, pp. 9780–9784 (2019)
5. Xu, C., Jackson, S.: Machine learning and complex biological data. Genome. Biol. **20**, 76 (2019). https://doi.org/10.1186/s13059-019-1689-0

6. Molnar, C.: Interpretable Machine Learning. Lulu.com, Leanpub, Victoria (2020)
7. Kroll, J., Huey, J., Barocas, S., Felten, E., Reidenberg, J., Robinson, D., Yu, H.: Accountable algorithms. Univ. Pennsylvania Law Rev. (2017)
8. Breiman, L.: Random forests. Mach. Learn. **45**, 5–32 (2001). https://doi.org/10.1023/A:1010933404324
9. Friedman, J.: Greedy function approximation: a gradient boosting machine. Ann. Stat JSTOR. 1189–1232 (2001)
10. Goldstein, A., Kapelner, A., Bleich, J., Kapelner, A.: Package 'ICEbox' (2017)
11. Apley, D., Zhu, J.: Visualizing the effects of predictor variables in black box supervised learning models. J. Royal Stat. Soc. Ser. B (Stat. Methodol.). **82**(4), 1059–1086 (2020)
12. Prudêncio, R., Hernández-Orallo, J., Martınez-Usó, A.: Analysis of instance hardness in machine learning using item response theory. In: Second International Workshop on Learning over Multiple Contexts in ECML (2015)
13. Martínez-Plumed, F., Prudêncio, R., Martínez-Usó, A., Hernández-Orallo, J.: Making sense of item response theory in machine learning. In: Proceedings of the Twenty-second European Conference on Artificial Intelligence, pp. 1140–1148 (2016)
14. Embretson, S., Reise, S.: Item Response Theory. Psychology Press, London (2013)
15. Chen, Z., Ahn, H.: Item response theory based ensemble in machine learning. Int. J. Autom. Comput. **17**(5), 621–636 (2020). https://doi.org/10.1007/s11633-020-1239-y
16. de Andrade, D., Tavares, H., da Cunha, R.: Teoria da Resposta ao Item: conceitos e aplicações. ABE, Sao Paulo (2000)
17. Zhong, Z., Zheng, L., Kang, G., Li, S., Yang, Y.: Random erasing data augmentation. Proceedings of the AAAI Conference on Artificial Intelligence, pp. 13001–13008 (2020)

AI and ML Applied to Robotics

Towards Loop Closure Detection for SLAM Applications Using Bag of Visual Features: Experiments and Simulation

Alexandra Miguel Raibolt da Silva[1](✉) ⓘ, Gustavo Alves Casqueiro[1] ⓘ,
Alberto Torres Angonese[2] ⓘ, and Paulo Fernando Ferreira Rosa[1](✉) ⓘ

[1] Instituto Militar de Engenharia (IME), Praça Gen. Tibúrcio, 80 - Urca,
Rio de Janeiro, RJ, Brazil
{raibolt,gustavo.casqueiro,rpaulo}@ime.eb.br
[2] Faculdade de Ed.Tec.do Estado do Rio de Janeiro (FAETERJ/Petrópolis),
Av. Getúlio Vargas, 335 - Quitandinha, Petrópolis, RJ, Brazil
aangonese@faeterj-petropolis.edu.br
http://www.ime.eb.mil.br, http://www.faeterj-petropolis.edu.br

Abstract. This paper presents a new approach to exploring sparse and binary convolutional filters in traditional Convolutional Neural Networks (CNN). Recent advances in the integration of Deep Learning architectures, particularly in mobile autonomous robotics applications, have motivated several researches to overcome the challenges related to the limitations of computational resources. One of the biggest challenges in the area, is the development of applications to address the Loop Closure Detection problem in Simultaneous Localization and Mapping (SLAM) systems. For such application, it is necessary to use exhaustive computational power. Nevertheless, resource optimization of Convolutional Neural Network models enhances the capability of integration. Therefore, we propose the reformulation of convolutional layers through Local Binary Descriptors (LBD) to achieve this kind of optimization of CNN's resources. This paper discusses the evaluation of a Bag of Visual Features (BoVF) approach, extracting features through local descriptors (e.g., SIFT, SURF, KAZE), and local binary descriptors (e.g., BRIEF, ORB, BRISK, AKAZE, FREAK). The descriptors were evaluated in the recognition and classification steps using six visual datasets (i.e., MNIST, JAFFE, Extended CK+, FEI, CIFAR-10, and FER-2013) through a Multilayer Perceptron (MLP) classifier. Experimentally, we demonstrated the feasibility of producing promising results by combining BoVF with MLP classifier. Additionally, we can assume that the computed descriptors generated by a Local Binary Descriptor alongside the proposed hybrid DNN (Deep Neural Network) architecture can satisfactorily accomplish the results for the optimization of a CNN's resources applied to the Loop Closure Detection problem.

Keywords: Embedded vision · SLAM · Feature descriptors · Bag of visual features · Multilayer perceptron

© Springer Nature Switzerland AG 2022
P. R. d. A. Ribeiro et al. (Eds.): LAWCN 2021, CCIS 1519, pp. 27–47, 2022.
https://doi.org/10.1007/978-3-031-08443-0_3

1   Introduction

An important issue addressed by mobile robots is the Simultaneous Localization and Mapping (SLAM) problem [18], where consists in solving complex tasks, such as mapping and localization. Unfortunately, these two tasks cannot perform independently; that is, they act in a complementary way. A growing interest in using cameras as a cheap alternative to inertial sensors and lasers for SLAM mapping and localization tasks emerged [5], proving that it is possible to combine Computer Vision (CV) techniques with the SLAM problem, acknowledged in the literature as vision-based SLAM—VSLAM. Dynamic environments, lightning changes, low frame rate with high-speed performance, and Loop Closure Detection (LCD) are in the area of VSLAM topics of relevance that becomes challenging tasks, as society's need for autonomous robots increasingly cheaper, more robust, and efficient arises, which CV can provide us with those techniques. In the last two decades, the growing research in Pattern Recognition (PR) and Machine Learning (ML) based on Deep Learning (DL) has leveraged the emergence of several techniques to address the problem of VSLAM. Techniques like Convolutional Neural Network (CNN) [45] and Recurrent Neural Network (RNN) [38] provide excellent results in the Feature Extraction process and classification patterns in visual data and in VSLAM tasks [14,43]. From this point of view, we are strongly motivated to develop a system capable of solving the LCD problem with cheap and efficient computational performance, discarding the use of resources such as distance sensors and lasers, which commonly are expensive and demand a high computational complexity.

In this paper, we propose the development of an adaptation of a hybrid Deep Neural Network (DNN) architecture: the Long-term Recurrent Convolutional Network (LRCN) [17] (known by its more generic name and widespread in the literature: CNN LSTM), for integration with a VSLAM system with the Robotic Operating System (ROS) and simulator Gazebo for NVIDIA JetBot with Jetson Nano. Figure 1 shows a flowchart of the proposed system, where consists of the following steps:

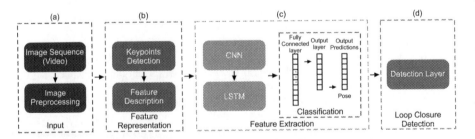

Fig. 1. Flowchart of the proposed system. (a) represents the Input step; (b) represents the Feature Representation step; (c) represents the Feature Extraction step; and (d) represents the Loop Closure Detection step.

- (a) Input: The purpose of this step consists in the configuration and calibration of the monocular camera to obtain sequential images (video). This step consists of preprocessing the sequential images obtained, such as changing the RGB color mode pattern (most typical) to grayscale (Local Feature Descriptors and Local Binary Descriptors only work with input images in the grayscale color mode pattern), and it also consists in the application of resizing sequential images obtained in different sizes;
- (b) Feature Representation: The purpose of this step is to produce a Feature Detection process and then compute the descriptors through the Local Binary Descriptors that will be chosen at the end of the experiments presented in this paper;
- (c) Feature Extraction: The purpose of this step is to reformulate the same computed descriptors obtained in the previous step through the Local Binary Descriptors into convolutional filters. We expect that the adaptation of the proposed CNN architecture achieves the same goals as standard CNN architecture. This step's ultimate purpose is to adapt a hybrid Deep Neural Network architecture—the CNN LSTM. Its challenge is to investigate the best methods to achieve the reformulation and implementation of descriptors through convolutional filters to produce a sparse and binary model as an efficient alternative to standard CNNs, which will be integrated into a hybrid DNN architecture;
- (d) Loop Closure Detection: The purpose of this step is to implement LCD in a VSLAM system itself. Therefore, the LCD will be based on the hybrid DNN architecture developed in the previous step.

To achieve the development of the proposed system, this paper aims primarily to cover experimental and preliminary simulation work. Where comprises the evaluation of a Bag of Visual Features (BoVF) [39] approach, extracting features through Local Feature Descriptors and Local Binary Descriptors for the tasks of recognition and classification on six visual datasets (MNIST [24], JAFFE [29], Extended CK+ [22,28], FEI [41], CIFAR-10 [23], and FER-2013 [19]) through the Multilayer Perceptron (MLP) [31] classifier. By evaluating good results and efficiency of each descriptor alongside the MLP classifier, empirically, it can be assumed that the computed descriptors can accomplish satisfactory results alongside the CNN architecture, that is, as a convolutional filter. For choosing the best Local Binary Descriptors was determined to evaluate the efficiency of five Local Binary Descriptors renowned in the literature and SLAM applications: Binary Robust Independent Elementary Features (BRIEF) [10,11], Oriented FAST and Rotated BRIEF (ORB) [37], Binary Robust Invariant Scalable Keypoints (BRISK) [25], Accelerated KAZE (AKAZE) [2], and Fast Retina Keypoint (FREAK) [1]. Additionally, three Local Feature Descriptors renowned in the literature and SLAM applications were evaluated too: Scale Invariant Feature Transform (SIFT) [26,27], Speeded-up Robust Features (SURF) [7], and KAZE [3]. We expect that the experiment and preliminary simulations lead us to the right choice of a Local Binary Descriptor (see Sect. 2) that will be addressed in this work's next steps. Then, we present another partial experiment that consists of performing Feature Detection and Description in step (b) using the Local Binary Descriptor chosen in the previous experiment and preliminary simulations and reformulated in step (c) into convolutional filters of the proposed system's CNN architecture, shown in Fig. 1.

In addition to the Introduction, this paper is organized as follows: in Sect. 2 a brief literature review is presented, covering other works related to this paper. Section 3 presents the methodologies adopted for the development of this work. In Sect. 4, the experimental configuration and the results of the experiments and simulations carried out during the development of this work so far. Furthermore, in Sect. 5, a brief discussion of this work is presented, as well as this work's next steps to be carried out in the upcoming months.

2   Related Works

One of the significant steps in the proposed methodology in this work is to detect keypoints and compute descriptors in sequential images, as shown in Fig. 1. We intend to perform Feature Detection and Description in step (b) of the proposed system—an essential method for VSLAM systems. There are many algorithms for this purpose. The efficiency between these algorithms can be seen in several works performed by the scientific community, in which the analyses and evaluations were applied [12,33]. In highlight, [20] presents the performance evaluation between different Local Binary Descriptors and different pairs of detectors and descriptors. The authors evaluate the performance among three descriptors: BRIEF, ORB, and BRISK, while using the SIFT and SURF descriptors as a baseline. In [8], the authors present an evaluation of Local Binary Descriptors such as BRIEF, ORB, BRISK, and FREAK. The results show that BRISK is the descriptor with the highest number of best matches and the highest percentage of accuracy compared to each Local Binary Descriptors. After the literature review and comparative analysis, it is possible to see in Table 1 a summary of each descriptor's invariance.

Table 1. Invariance of Descriptors.

Detector	Descriptor	Rotation	Scale	Brightness	Viewpoint
SIFT	**SIFT**	✓	✓	✓	✓
SURF	**SURF**	✓	✓	✓	✓
KAZE	**KAZE**	✓	✓	x	x
-	**BRIEF**	x	x	✓	x
ORB	**ORB**	✓	x	✓	x
BRISK	**BRISK**	✓	✓	✓	✓
-	**FREAK**	✓	✓	✓	x
AKAZE	**AKAZE**	✓	✓	x	x

However, recent research indicates that based on CNN architecture techniques outperforms the handcrafted resources for representing images in a meaningful way explored in robotics. In [16], the authors provide a comparative study of three distinct classes of Local Feature Descriptors in which handcrafted resources, trained CNN, and pre-trained CNN were used. The work aimed to evaluate its efficiency for combining keypoints in robotics applications, taking into account descriptors' ability to deal with conditional changes (e.g., lighting and viewpoint). The final results of the comparative study carried out show that: (a) the handcrafted descriptors compared with any CNN-based descriptor method are not competitive; (b) regarding changes of viewpoint, the trained CNN-based descriptor methods perform better than the pre-trained CNN-based descriptor methods; (c) in contrast, regarding changes of lighting, the pre-trained CNN-based descriptor methods perform better than the trained CNN-based descriptor methods; nonetheless, they consume much memory.

In the proposed methodology, another significant step is to perform a Feature Extraction in sequential images that cross step (b) to step (c) of the proposed system, as shown in Fig. 1. We intend to perform Feature Extraction with a trained CNN-based descriptor method due to the good results already presented. The idea of combining these two techniques is not new [4,6], however, to generate a hybrid DNN architecture with efficient computational performance, reducing computational complexity compared to other hybrid DNN architectures, it was decided to reformulate the computed descriptors into convolutional filters with sparse and binary nature of convolutional layers of the proposed CNN architecture. This type of reformulation is feasible, as shown in [21], in which the authors propose the Local Binary Convolution (LBC), a compelling alternative to the convolutional layer in standard CNN architectures, which to reduce the computational complexity in standard CNN architecture, the authors present Local Binary Convolutional Neural Networks (LBCNN), a novel architecture based on the principles of Local Binary Patters (LBP). Additionally, the LBC layer reduces the model's complexity due to its sparse and binary nature, consequently, reducing the computational and memory requirements, becoming an applicable model in real-world environments with scarce and limited resources.

As already commented, this paper discusses the evaluation of the BoVF approach, a classic technique for image classification, widely disseminated by the scientific community. This is one of the essential methods used in the CV field, also known as Bag of Visual Words (BoVW) and inspired by a Bag of Words (BoW) [9] approach, a technique widely used in document classification) through MLP classifier. BoVF is a simple and low computational cost approach in which the general idea is to represent each image sample presented into a visual dataset as a frequency histogram of visual features of each feature present in the dictionary of visual features. Some other works that use the principle of the BoVF approach can be shown in [15,32].

Another significant step in the methodology proposed in this work is integrating the system shown in Fig. 1 with a VSLAM system of a mobile robotic platform. There has been a growing interest in the scientific community in the evaluation and use of NVIDIA's Jetson Nano for VSLAM systems [34,36].

3 Proposed Approach

To better understand the BoVF approach with the MLP classifier, we will present in detail the techniques used in each step of the BoVF approach, followed by the behavior of the MLP model used in this experiment and preliminary simulation.

3.1 Bag of Visual Features

Briefly, the BoVF approach can be divided into three steps: (a) Feature Representation step; (b) Visual Vocabulary Generation step; and (c) Image Representation step. We can see these steps in more detail below:

Feature Representation. Finding interesting features in images is the function of a Local Feature Descriptor or a Local Binary Descriptor. This task becomes essential in applications of topics related to CV and PR, as in the case of a Structure from Motion (SfM), Object Detection, and Content-based Image Retrieval (CBIR). In this work, we use the term keypoint to discriminate an interesting feature. To recognize those keypoints, it uses the Feature Detection step. Through the Feature Description step, it is possible to obtain information about each interesting feature.

It is possible to perform Feature Matching (FM) because, ideally, it is expected that such information obtained is invariant concerning the transformation of some form (e.g., rotation, scale, brightness, or viewpoint) of an image. In this way, it is possible to find that feature again. It was determined the evaluation of the efficiency of five Local Binary Descriptors: BRIEF, ORB, BRISK, AKAZE, and FREAK. Additionally, three Local Feature Descriptors were evaluated too: SIFT, SURF, and KAZE. Through the descriptors already presented, the keypoints will be detected from an input image (presented in both training and test samples on each visual dataset), and then the interesting features (descriptors) will be computed. At the end of this operation, it was obtained a feature vector with dimensions number of keypoints × number of descriptors.

Visual Vocabulary Generation. Now, it is needed to generate the dictionary of possible visual vocabulary over the collection of feature vectors. To learn the visual vocabulary, generally, a clustering algorithm is performed. For this experiment, we decided to use the unsupervised learning K-Means clustering algorithm. K-Means clustering is a standard algorithm used to partition samples into k distinct clusters, grouping samples with relevant features. Therefore, considering a visual dataset T, where each n keypoints is represented by a d-dimensional real vector:

$$T = \{x_i\}_{i=1}^{n} \tag{1}$$

The K-Means clustering algorithm aims to partition the n keypoints into $k(\leq n)$ distinct clusters $C = \{c_1, c_2, ..., c_k\}$. Therefore, for each, C_i a μ_i centroid is associated with it. In this way, we can establish μ_i as the average of every element of the cluster, where n_i is the number of elements in each cluster C_i, that is:

$$\mu_i = \frac{1}{n_i} \sum_{x_j \in C_i} x_j \tag{2}$$

As mentioned above, the K-means clustering algorithm aims to partition the n keypoints into $k(\leq n)$ distinct clusters, in which the resulting distribution is the one that each keypoint is close to the others within the same cluster. Thus, it is assumed that the closer, the more similar they are. In other words, the K-means clustering algorithm aims to minimize an objective function, in this case, the Sum of Squared Errors (SSE) of the distance of each keypoint concerning its distance to centroids:

$$J = \sum_{j=1}^{k} \sum_{i=1}^{n} \left\| x_i^{(j)} - \mu_i \right\|^2 \tag{3}$$

In the Eq. 3, J represents the objective function, k the number of clusters, n the number of cases, and $\left\| x_i^{(j)} - \mu_i \right\|$ the Euclidean distance between a keypoint x_i and a centroid μ_i. Thus, the K-means clustering algorithm returns the center (centroid) of each group (cluster), and each cluster center will be treated as the vocabulary of the visual dictionary (acting as a visual feature).

Image Representation. Finally, each cluster's frequencies are calculated (computed for both the training-set and test-set), resulting in a Histogram of Visual Features, none other than the BoVF. Finally, the Histogram of Visual Features can be used later with a classifier (e.g., K-Nearest Neighbors (K-NN), Support Vector Machine (SVM), or MLP). In this work, it was chosen the MLP to be used as a classifier. In Fig. 2, it is possible to observe what happens in the BoVF approach illustratively.

3.2 Multilayer Perceptron

With the MLP model used in this work, each input node x_i $(x_1, x_2, ..., x_n)$ is associated with a synaptic weight w_i $(w_1, w_2, ..., w_n)$, where the value of synaptic weights are randomly initialized. The entry also has an activation threshold b (bias), representing a fixed value other than 0. In this sense, the linear combination process occurs, producing the activation potential s, in which the input nodes are weighted by their respective associated synaptic weights $(x_1 \cdot w_1 + x_2 \cdot w_2 + ... + x_n \cdot w_n)$, and by the activation threshold b, where n represents the size of the input vector, as seen in the Eq. 4.

$$s = \sum_{i=1}^{n} w_i x_i + b \tag{4}$$

After this process, the sum of the inputs weighted by their associated synaptic weights plus the activation threshold, that is, the activation potential s, is

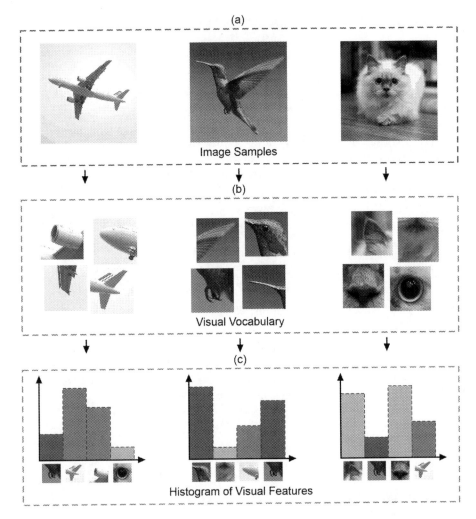

Fig. 2. Representation of BoVF approach. (a) represents the image samples presented in a visual dataset; (b) represents the Visual Vocabulary generated by the K-means clustering algorithm; (c) represents each cluster's frequencies calculated, resulting in a Histogram of Visual Features.

submitted to an activation function f, as seen in the Eq. 5 below:

$$f(s) = max(0, s) \tag{5}$$

The activation function used in this model was the Rectified Linear Unit (ReLU) function. Therefore, if the activation potential s is greater than the activation threshold, the MLP model will be considered to be activated (output y will be equal to 1), or deactivated otherwise.

Finally, the experiments and preliminary simulation consist of comparing the accuracy, computational efficiency, and performance of each of the Local Feature Descriptors and Local Binary Descriptors algorithm (presented in Sect. 1) through the recognition and classification task by the MLP classifier. It will also compare the processing time on generating the BoVF index in both training and test steps. By analyzing each algorithm's results, we expect to be able to choose an efficient Local Binary Descriptors that will be addressed in this work's next steps. For a better understanding, Fig. 3 shows a flowchart of the BoVF approach with MLP classifier for the training step. In comparison, Fig. 4 shows a flowchart of the BoVF approach with MLP classifier for the test step.

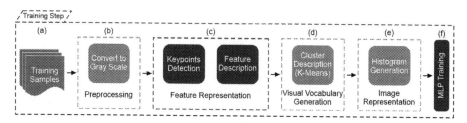

Fig. 3. BoVF approach with MLP classifier for training step. (a) represents the training samples presented in a visual dataset; (b) represents the preprocessing step; (c) represents the Feature Representation step; (d) represents the Visual Vocabulary Generation step; (e) represents the Image Representation step; and (f) represents the MLP Training step.

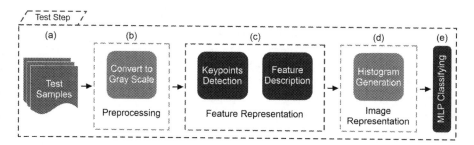

Fig. 4. BoVF approach with MLP classifier for test step. (a) represents the test samples presented in a visual dataset; (b) represents the preprocessing step; (c) represents the Feature Representation step; (d) represents the Image Representation step; and (f) represents the MLP Classifying step.

4   Experimental Setup and Results

In this Section, details about the experimental setup applied in the experiment and preliminary simulations of this work are presented, followed by the results.

4.1 Experimental Setup

It was decided to use the NVIDIA® Jetson™ family as an embedded GPU system: NVIDIA's Jetson Nano. We intend to integrate NVIDIA's Jetson Nano with a mobile robotics platform in this work's next steps. All experiments and preliminary simulations performed in this paper were carried out through NVIDIA's Jetson Nano. Python 3.6 language, OpenCV 4.1, and Scikit-learn 0.19 packages are used to perform the experiments presented in this paper. The source code and future updates are available at the GitHub repository[1]. BRIEF and FREAK algorithms are only descriptors. For these two scenarios, the ORB and SURF detectors were used, respectively, while for the other algorithms, the same descriptors were used as detectors. Regarding the classifier, we evaluated the efficiency of this experiment with six MLP classifiers. However, the best performing of the MLP classifiers will be more detailed in Subsect. 4.2.

4.2 Results

Some algorithms, like SIFT and SURF, performed very well working on smaller patches, but the majority of them, like ORB, achieved excellent results on 32×32 patches, to find keypoints and compute descriptors. Since MNIST, JAFFE, Extended CK+, CIFAR-10, and FER-2013 have such tiny images, it was impossible to achieve results in these visual datasets using BRIEF, AKAZE, and FREAK descriptors. That happened because these descriptors do not fit appropriately in the images present in these visual datasets. To avoid the return of keypoints without descriptors, the BRIEF, AKAZE, and FREAK remove them. However, with those three descriptors, it was possible to achieve results on FEI visual dataset, since it's image's size is 120×120 pixels, being somewhat more significant (bigger) for BRIEF, AKAZE, and FREAK. When descriptors operate on JAFFE and FEI visual datasets, the results in steps (c), (d), and (e) regarding the training step, shown in Fig. 3, and the results in steps (c) and (d) regarding the test step, shown in Fig. 4, are achieved almost instantly (with a tiny variance between zero and seven seconds). That occurs for both visual datasets because they have very few samples, in case 150 and 280 images for the training-set, respectively, and 63 and 120 images for the test-set.

Regarding the BoVF approach on the training step, the Local Feature Descriptor SURF took the least time to extract features. In contrast, the Local Binary Descriptor, ORB, exceeds other descriptors in this step for each visual dataset. Since MNIST has tiny images, the same case that occurs with BRIEF, AKAZE, and FREAK descriptors happen with BRISK. In this case, it was not possible to achieve any results. Still regarding the BoVF approach of training step shown in Fig. 3. The next step (d) consists of using the K-Means clustering algorithm to generate the dictionary of possible visual vocabulary over the collection of feature vectors extracted in the previous step. Considering the processing time in step (d) for SIFT, SURF, KAZE, ORB, and BRISK descriptors on MNIST, Extended CK+, CIFAR-10, and FER-2013 visual datasets the

---

[1] https://github.com/whoisraibolt/BoVF-with-MLP-classifier.

Local Features Descriptors, SURF took the least time to generate the dictionary of possible visual vocabulary. In contrast, regarding the Local Binary Descriptors, BRISK was the fastest to do that. As already commented, since MNIST has tiny images, the same case that occurs with BRIEF, AKAZE, and FREAK descriptors also happen with BRISK, and, in this case, it was not possible to achieve any results. Nevertheless, considering the BoVF approach of training step shown in Fig. 3, the next step (e) consists of calculating each cluster's frequencies returns to the previous step, resulting in a Histogram of Visual Features. The Histogram of Visual Features for descriptors, when performed over JAFFE and FEI visual datasets, was achieved instantly. When it comes to the processing time to obtain the Histogram of Visual Features for SIFT, SURF, KAZE, ORB, and BRISK descriptors on MNIST, Extended CK+, CIFAR-10, and FER-2013 visual datasets, SURF takes less time to obtain the Histogram of Visual Features than the other Local Features Descriptors, while BRISK achieved the bests results compared to most of the Local Binary Descriptors. After generating a Histogram of Visual Features, it is passed to step (f) to train the MLP model.

Regarding the BoVF approach of test step shown in Fig. 4, we can see the processing time in steps (c) and (d) for SIFT, SURF, KAZE, ORB, and BRISK descriptors on MNIST, Extended CK+, CIFAR-10, and FER-2013 visual datasets presented in this work. SURF takes less time to extract features and obtain the Histogram of Visual Features than the other Local Features Descriptors and Local Binary Descriptors. After generating a Histogram of Visual Features, the inference is performed, in step (e). In Table 2 and Table 3, it is possible to see the results achieved through the MLP classifier, in which the performance and efficiency of six different sets of parameters were evaluated: BRIEF, AKAZE, and FREAK descriptors on FEI visual dataset and SIFT, SURF, KAZE, ORB, and BRISK descriptors on each visual dataset. It is possible to observe that the best results achieved with each descriptor over the MLP classifiers were over FEI visual dataset, and the highest score achieved was with the MLP classifier named "ML6" with AKAZE.

Table 2. Accuracy rate (%) at the test steps for BRIEF, AKAZE, and FREAK on FEI.

Algorithms	Visual dataset	Multilayer percepton models					
		MLP1	MLP2	MLP3	MLP4	MLP5	MLP6
BRIEF	**FEI**	0.78	0.74	0.77	0.76	0.82	0.85
AKAZE		0.85	0.87	0.83	0.84	0.83	0.86
FREAK		0.47	0.47	0.47	0.51	0.51	0.54

In many cases, using other MLP classifiers, it is possible to observe that the models with each visual dataset did not produce satisfactory outcomes for recognition and classification tasks. In general, they performed a low accuracy rate, except with the JAFFE visual dataset, where they performed a high overfitting

Table 3. Accuracy rate (%) at the test steps for SIFT, SURF, KAZE, ORB, and BRISK on each visual dataset.

Algorithms	Visual dataset	Multilayer percepton models					
		MLP1	MLP2	MLP3	MLP4	MLP5	MLP6
SIFT	MNIST	0.67	0.67	0.67	0.68	0.67	0.68
	JAFFE	0.10	0.10	0.10	0.21	0.21	0.25
	Extended CK+	0.38	0.38	0.40	0.41	0.44	0.39
	FEI	0.69	0.67	0.63	0.75	0.76	0.72
	CIFAR-10	0.25	0.25	0.25	0.25	0.25	0.24
	FER-2013	0.26	0.27	0.27	0.26	0.26	0.26
SURF	MNIST	0.68	0.68	0.67	0.69	0.68	0.68
	JAFFE	0.10	0.10	0.10	0.21	0.22	0.21
	Extended CK+	0.40	0.37	0.40	0.43	0.49	0.44
	FEI	0.72	0.74	0.61	0.74	0.72	0.74
	CIFAR-10	0.11	0.11	0.11	0.18	0.19	0.18
	FER-2013	0.26	0.26	0.26	0.25	0.24	0.24
KAZE	MNIST	0.65	0.65	0.66	0.67	0.68	0.66
	JAFFE	0.08	0.19	0.24	0.22	0.21	0.22
	Extended CK+	0.36	0.36	0.41	0.44	0.42	0.43
	FEI	0.62	0.62	0.63	0.58	0.67	0.68
	CIFAR-10	0.25	0.25	0.25	0.25	0.24	0.24
	FER-2013	0.26	0.25	0.26	0.26	0.25	0.25
ORB	MNIST	0.53	0.52	0.53	0.52	0.53	0.52
	JAFFE	0.14	0.13	0.10	0.11	0.19	0.14
	Extended CK+	0.31	0.31	0.30	0.30	0.27	0.29
	FEI	0.50	0.57	0.58	0.65	0.64	0.70
	CIFAR-10	0.23	0.23	0.23	0.22	0.22	0.21
	FER-2013	0.26	0.25	0.25	0.26	0.25	0.26
BRISK	MNIST	-	-	-	-	-	-
	JAFFE	0.11	0.11	0.11	0.19	0.19	0.21
	Extended CK+	0.26	0.29	0.31	0.27	0.30	0.34
	FEI	0.82	0.82	0.82	0.85	0.84	0.82
	CIFAR-10	0.13	0.13	0.13	0.13	0.13	0.20
	FER-2013	0.25	0.25	0.25	0.24	0.24	0.25

rate. The MLP classifiers named "MLP3", "MLP4", "MLP5", and "MLP6" over FEI visual dataset with ORB presented a high underfitting rate. Other Local Binary Descriptors that stood out with FEI visual dataset are BRIEF and BRISK.

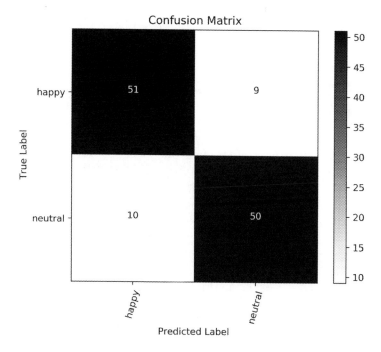

Fig. 5. Confusion matrix by BRISK on FEI with the "ML5" model.

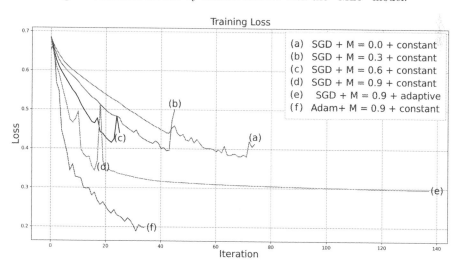

Fig. 6. Training loss by BRISK on FEI with the "ML5" model.

However, the descriptor that has achieved prominence and that provided out-standing results regarding the invariance to rotation, scale, lighting, and viewpoint in many other works is BRISK. Because of that, we chose to use BRISK as the primary descriptor to be used in this work's next steps.

In Fig. 5, it is possible to see the Confusion Matrix by BRISK on FEI visual dataset with the "MLP5" model. The "MLP5" model over FEI visual dataset with BRISK predicted correctly the basic emotion happy 51 times (true positive), and neutral 50 times (true negative). In contrast, it predicted incorrectly happy 9 times (false positive) and neutral 10 times (false negative). In this context, "MLP5" model over FEI visual dataset with BRISK had an accuracy of 84%, as it got 101 out of 120 predictions correct. Furthermore, it is possible to see the Training Loss of the six MLP classifiers' graph over FEI visual dataset with BRISK in Fig. 6. Note, that in Fig. 6, it is not possible to view the curve (d) referent to the "ML4" model, this occurs because curve (d) follows the same path of the curve (e) referent to the "ML5" model until more or less iteration 20, as both models' configuration parameters are more or less similar.

It was found that many algorithms had results below expectations. We believe this happens because most of the visual datasets that were used have tiny images. However, as described in [15], for the BoVF approach to distinguish relevant changes in parts of the image, the dictionary's size must be large enough; however, not so large as to distinguish irrelevant variations such as noise. With the chosen grouping method (K-means clustering algorithm), it is common to define empirically the value to k. By modifying this parameter, we believe that the results achieved can be enhanced. We also believe that modifying some parameters of the descriptors can also enhance it. Regarding the MLP model, other techniques (e.g., dropout) can be explored to improve accuracy.

We emphasize that the purpose of this work is not to achieve the best accuracy rate by MLP classifier, but only to comprehend NVIDIA's Jetson Nano operation and obtain an overview of its procedure, besides knowing and evaluating the performance of the descriptors alongside the MLP classifier discussed here.

4.3   Other Results

To better understand a novel approach to exploit sparse and binary convolutional filters in standard CNN, we present in detail the techniques used in each step of the proposed reformulation, followed by the behavior of the convolutional layer in this experiment and preliminary simulation. Also we present the experiment and preliminary simulation carried out of the CBIR approach based on Auto-Encoders, in which we believe it can help us as a baseline when evaluating the construction of the proposed adaptation of the hybrid DNN architecture shown in Fig. 1.

Reformulation of Convolutional Filters Through a Local Binary Descriptor. A convolutional layer is the main operation in images inserted in a CNN, and its main objective is to extract features from input images. An g image is generated by converting a f convolutional filter (commonly known as kernel) with the input image I, and q is the size of the convolution mask, defined by the Eq. 6:

$$g(m, n) = \sum_{i=1}^{q} \sum_{j=1}^{q} f(i, j) I(m - i, n - j) \tag{6}$$

A filter can highlight a certain feature present in an image, such as shadows, borders, among others, and the convolution result is commonly known as a feature map. One of the most significant steps in that operation is the selection of convolutional filters to be used. There are many ways to do that, most commonly being determined empirically. The ability to universalize the selection of convolutional filters is one of the motivations and inspirations behind the proposed reformulation design. Figure 7 shows a flowchart of the proposed reformulation.

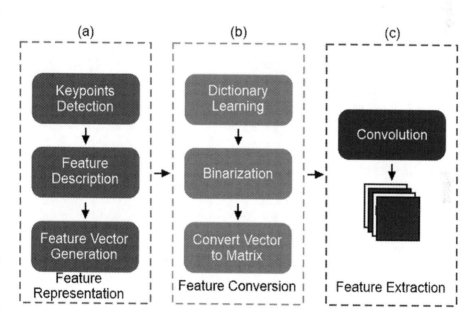

Fig. 7. Flowchart of the proposed reformulation. (a) represents the Feature Representation step; (b) represents the Feature Conversion step; and (c) represents the Feature Extraction step.

As can be seen in Fig. 7, the proposed reformulation involves: (a) Feature Representation step, as primarily block, responsible for executing keypoints detection in the training-set, and then the descriptors are computed; with this, a feature vector is generated; next, (b) Feature Conversion step, with consists in reduce to dimensionality through the Dictionary Learning (DL) algorithm applied to the feature vector generated by the previous step, reducing the feature vector while making it sparse, followed by a binarization process, in this case, signal function, become the nature of the feature vector into sparse and binary, followed by transformation of the feature vector into a square matrix, resulting in what is known in the literature as filter-weights; and finally, set all center square matrix with a negative value (-1). At this moment, the filter-weights are ready to be used as a kernel in the convolution operation. Figure 8 shows the convolution behavior through the 64 filter-weights of size 7×7, generated in the same way. We can comprehend that 64 convolutional filters f of size 7×7 were applied to the input image I, resulting in 64 feature maps g. The black filters indicate that the filter will positively respond to the black pixels in the input images (1), while the white filters indicate that the filter will negatively respond to the black pixels in the input images (-1). The grayscale filters represent 0.

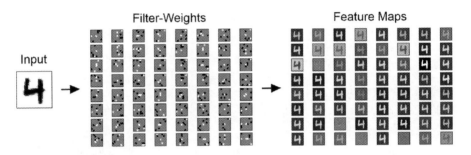

Fig. 8. Convolution behavior through the 64 convolutional filters of size 7×7 generated through the BRISK descriptor's reformulation.

The proposed reformulation was successfully developed, and the generated convolutional filters presented good feature maps. The source code and future updates is available at the GitHub repository[2]. Furthermore, to effectively evaluate the proposed reformulation's efficiency, it is necessary to implement the proposed system's CNN architecture shown in Fig. 1. Later, an extensive work of validation and analysis of the results obtained (e.g., classification accuracy, computational consumption, among others) on the efficiency and accuracy of the proposed system's CNN architecture adaptation will be provided in this work's next steps.

Denoising Auto-Encoder for Content-Based Image Retrieval. Another experiment carried out in corresponding to the experiment described above was the study and evaluation of the CBIR approach (being a classic technique for image retrieval problem, widely disseminated by the scientific community) based on Auto-Encoders. This study and evaluation will lead us to future works on image retrieval using DL and Semantic-Based SLAM [13,40] approaches, where CBIR come showing very effectiveness in SLAM and VSLAM domain, as it can handle a large amount of data in real-world environments. In addition, we believe

---

[2] https://github.com/whoisraibolt/Reformulation-of-Convolutional-Filters-through-Descriptors.

it can help us as a baseline when evaluating the construction of the proposed adaptation of the hybrid DNN architecture shown in Fig. 1.

Initially, the denoising Auto-Encoder was built and was trained with the MNIST visual dataset (which will be available to be retrieved through CBIR queries). Then, using the first half of the Auto-Encoder, the encoding part, we built the CBIR system, which retrieves and displays on-screen the images retrieved from an input, and displays the computed scores related to these images. An arbitrary image was used to make the query, as can be seen in Fig. 9, and it is possible to observe the retrieved images. In Fig. 9, the retrieved images by the CBIR system are extremely similar to the query image filled in, as the same time that they correspond to the same digit. This demonstrates the ability of the Auto-Encoder in encoding similar images even where the corresponding image labels are not presented. However, in this experiment, we are working with a linear search with $O(N)$ complexity, so we must attend to the scalability of the CBIR system. Considering this, we intend in future works to better explore the CBIR system using denoising Auto-Encoder, focus on working with datasets for SLAM and LCD problem, such as New College and the City Center datasets originally used by FAB-MA [35], LipIndoor and LipOutdoor datasets [30], Bovisa dataset [42], and KITTI dataset [44].

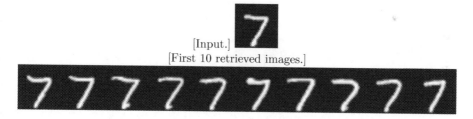

[Input.]
[First 10 retrieved images.]

Fig. 9. CBIR system: images retrieved from an input.

5   Discussion and Future Works

An extensive literature review was performed in this work, going through the theoretical bases that support the proposed adaptation. Furthermore, the methodology to be applied will allow us to choose the approach to build a low computational cost and robust system, with efficient computational performance and reduced computational complexity for the task of LCD for a VSLAM system.

The descriptor to be addressed in future work in step (b), and reformulated in step (c) into convolutional filters of the proposed system's CNN architecture shown in Fig. 1 has been defined, and now we can advance to the next steps in future work. Regarding this, new activities will occur in the development of this work, consisting of:

- A comparative evaluation of CBIR approach based on Hand-Crafted Features and based on Auto-Encoders;
- Implementation of the adaptation of CNN: The purpose of this step consists of implementing the proposed adaptation of the CNN, presenting the new layer design for the proposed architecture;
- Construction of the proposed system: The purpose of this step consists of implementing the proposed adaptation of the hybrid DNN architecture, at the same time, a model with efficient computational performance, as well as reducing the computational complexity, to solve the LCD problem;
- Integration with a VSLAM system: The purpose of this step consists of the integration of the proposed system with a VSLAM system with the ROS and Gazebo simulator for NVIDIA JetBot with Jetson Nano.

Our approach is promising; in the next steps of this work, we expect to demonstrate that the proposed methods reduce the computational complexity of the model, and it is potentially able to perform the task of LCD for a VSLAM system.

Acknowledgments. – This work was financed in part by the CoordenaçÃo de Aperfeiçoamento de Pessoal de Nível Superior—Brasil (CAPES)—Finance Code 001.
– This work was carried out with the support of the Programa de CooperaçÃo Acadêmica em Defesa Nacional (PROCAD-DEFESA).

References

1. Alahi, A., Ortiz, R., Vandergheynst, P.: FREAK: fast retina keypoint. In: 2012 IEEE Conference on Computer Vision and Pattern Recognition, pp. 510–517. IEEE (2012)
2. Alcantarilla, P.F., Solutions, T.: Fast explicit diffusion for accelerated features in nonlinear scale spaces. IEEE Trans. Patt. Anal. Mach. Intell **34**(7), 1281–1298 (2011)
3. Alcantarilla, P.F., Bartoli, A., Davison, A.J.: KAZE features. In: Fitzgibbon, A., Lazebnik, S., Perona, P., Sato, Y., Schmid, C. (eds.) ECCV 2012. LNCS, vol. 7577, pp. 214–227. Springer, Heidelberg (2012). https://doi.org/10.1007/978-3-642-33783-3_16
4. Anwer, R.M., Khan, F.S., van de Weijer, J., Molinier, M., Laaksonen, J.: Binary patterns encoded convolutional neural networks for texture recognition and remote sensing scene classification. ISPRS J. Photogramm. Remote. Sens. **138**, 74–85 (2018)
5. Aqel, M.O.A., Marhaban, M.H., Saripan, M.I., Ismail, N.B.: Review of visual odometry: types, approaches, challenges, and applications. Springerplus **5**(1), 1–26 (2016). https://doi.org/10.1186/s40064-016-3573-7
6. Barroso-Laguna, A., Riba, E., Ponsa, D., Mikolajczyk, K.: Key .net: keypoint detection by handcrafted and learned CNN filters. In: Proceedings of the IEEE/CVF International Conference on Computer Vision, pp. 5836–5844 (2019)
7. Bay, H., Tuytelaars, T., Van Gool, L.: SURF: speeded up robust features. In: Leonardis, A., Bischof, H., Pinz, A. (eds.) ECCV 2006. LNCS, vol. 3951, pp. 404–417. Springer, Heidelberg (2006). https://doi.org/10.1007/11744023_32

8. Bekele, D., Teutsch, M., Schuchert, T.: Evaluation of binary keypoint descriptors. In: 2013 IEEE International Conference on Image Processing, pp. 3652–3656. IEEE (2013)

9. Blei, D.M., Ng, A.Y., Jordan, M.I.: Latent dirichlet allocation. J. Mach. Learn. Res. **3**, 993–1022 (2003)

10. Calonder, M., Lepetit, V., Ozuysal, M., Trzcinski, T., Strecha, C., Fua, P.: Brief: computing a local binary descriptor very fast. IEEE Trans. Pattern Anal. Mach. Intell. **34**(7), 1281–1298 (2011)

11. Calonder, M., Lepetit, V., Strecha, C., Fua, P.: BRIEF: binary robust independent elementary features. In: Daniilidis, K., Maragos, P., Paragios, N. (eds.) ECCV 2010. LNCS, vol. 6314, pp. 778–792. Springer, Heidelberg (2010). https://doi.org/10.1007/978-3-642-15561-1_56

12. Chatoux, H., Lecellier, F., Fernandez-Maloigne, C.: Comparative study of descriptors with dense key points. In: 2016 23rd International Conference on Pattern Recognition (ICPR), pp. 1988–1993. IEEE (2016)

13. Chen, B., Yuan, D., Liu, C., Wu, Q.: Loop closure detection based on multi-scale deep feature fusion. Appl. Sci. **9**(6), 1120 (2019)

14. CS Kumar, A., Bhandarkar, S.M., Prasad, M.: DepthNet: a recurrent neural network architecture for monocular depth prediction. In: Proceedings of the IEEE Conference on Computer Vision and Pattern Recognition Workshops, pp. 283–291 (2018)

15. Csurka, G., Dance, C., Fan, L., Willamowski, J., Bray, C.: Visual categorization with bags of keypoints. In: Workshop on Statistical Learning in Computer Vision, ECCV, vol. 1, pp. 1–2. Prague (2004)

16. Dai, Z., Huang, X., Chen, W., He, L., Zhang, H.: A comparison of CNN-based and hand-crafted keypoint descriptors. In: 2019 International Conference on Robotics and Automation (ICRA), pp. 2399–2404. IEEE (2019)

17. Donahue, J., et al.: Long-term recurrent convolutional networks for visual recognition and description. In: Proceedings of the IEEE Conference on Computer Vision and Pattern Recognition, pp. 2625–2634 (2015)

18. Durrant-Whyte, H., Bailey, T.: Simultaneous localization and mapping: part I. IEEE Rob. Autom. Mag. **13**(2), 99–110 (2006)

19. Goodfellow, I.J., et al.: Challenges in representation learning: a report on three machine learning contests. In: Lee, M., Hirose, A., Hou, Z.-G., Kil, R.M. (eds.) ICONIP 2013. LNCS, vol. 8228, pp. 117–124. Springer, Heidelberg (2013). https://doi.org/10.1007/978-3-642-42051-1_16

20. Heinly, J., Dunn, E., Frahm, J.-M.: Comparative evaluation of binary features. In: Fitzgibbon, A., Lazebnik, S., Perona, P., Sato, Y., Schmid, C. (eds.) ECCV 2012. LNCS, vol. 7573, pp. 759–773. Springer, Heidelberg (2012). https://doi.org/10.1007/978-3-642-33709-3_54

21. Juefei-Xu, F., Naresh Boddeti, V., Savvides, M.: Local binary convolutional neural networks. In: Proceedings of the IEEE Conference on Computer Vision and Pattern Recognition, pp. 19–28 (2017)

22. Kanade, T., Cohn, J.F., Tian, Y.: Comprehensive database for facial expression analysis. In: Fourth IEEE International Conference on Automatic Face and Gesture Recognition, Proceedings, pp. 46–53. IEEE (2000)

23. Krizhevsky, A., Hinton, G., et al.: Learning multiple layers of features from tiny images (2009)

24. LeCun, Y., Bottou, L., Bengio, Y., Haffner, P.: Gradient-based learning applied to document recognition. Proc. IEEE **86**(11), 2278–2324 (1998)

25. Leutenegger, S., Chli, M., Siegwart, R.: BRISK: binary robust invariant scalable keypoints. In: 2011 IEEE International Conference on Computer Vision (ICCV), pp. 2548–2555. IEEE (2011)
26. Lowe, D.G.: Distinctive image features from scale-invariant keypoints. Int. J. Comput. Vision **60**(2), 91–110 (2004)
27. Lowe, D.G., et al.: Object recognition from local scale-invariant features. In: ICCV, vol. 99, pp. 1150–1157 (1999)
28. Lucey, P., Cohn, J.F., Kanade, T., Saragih, J., Ambadar, Z., Matthews, I.: The extended Cohn-Kanade dataset (CK+): a complete dataset for action unit and emotion-specified expression. In: 2010 IEEE Computer Society Conference on Computer Vision and Pattern Recognition Workshops (CVPRW), pp. 94–101. IEEE (2010)
29. Lyons, M., Akamatsu, S., Kamachi, M., Gyoba, J.: Coding facial expressions with Gabor wavelets. In: Third IEEE International Conference on Automatic Face and Gesture Recognition, Proceedings, pp. 200–205. IEEE (1998)
30. Mascharka, D., Manley, E.: Lips: learning based indoor positioning system using mobile phone-based sensors. In: 2016 13th IEEE Annual Consumer Communications Networking Conference (CCNC), pp. 968–971 (2016). https://doi.org/10.1109/CCNC.2016.7444919
31. Minsky, M., Papert, S.: Perceptrons. 1969. Cited on p. 1 (1990)
32. Morioka, N., Satoh, S.: Building compact local pairwise codebook with joint feature space clustering. In: Daniilidis, K., Maragos, P., Paragios, N. (eds.) ECCV 2010. LNCS, vol. 6311, pp. 692–705. Springer, Heidelberg (2010). https://doi.org/10.1007/978-3-642-15549-9_50
33. Patel, A., Kasat, D., Jain, S., Thakare, V.: Performance analysis of various feature detector and descriptor for real-time video based face tracking. Int. J. Comput. Appl. **93**(1) (2014)
34. Peng, T., Zhang, D., Liu, R., Asari, V.K., Loomis, J.S.: Evaluating the power efficiency of visual slam on embedded GPU systems. In: 2019 IEEE National Aerospace and Electronics Conference (NAECON), pp. 117–121. IEEE (2019)
35. Ramezani, M., Wang, Y., Camurri, M., Wisth, D., Mattamala, M., Fallon, M.: The newer college dataset: Handheld lidar, inertial and vision with ground truth. In: 2020 IEEE/RSJ International Conference on Intelligent Robots and Systems (IROS) (2020)
36. Rosa, P., Silveira, O., de Melo, J., Moreira, L., Rodrigues, L.: Development of embedded algorithm for visual simultaneous localization and mapping. In: Anais Estendidos da XXXII Conference on Graphics, Patterns and Images, pp. 160–163. SBC (2019)
37. Rublee, E., Rabaud, V., Konolige, K., Bradski, G.R.: ORB: an efficient alternative to sift or surf. In: ICCV, vol. 11, p. 2. Citeseer (2011)
38. Rumelhart, D.E., Hinton, G.E., Williams, R.J.: Learning internal representations by error propagation. Technical report, California Univ San Diego La Jolla Inst for Cognitive Science (1985)
39. Sivic, J., Zisserman, A.: Video google: a text retrieval approach to object matching in videos. In: NULL, p. 1470. IEEE (2003)
40. Tan, C.L., Egerton, S., Ganapathy, V.: Semantic slam model for autonomous mobile robots using content based image retrieval techniques: a performance analysis. Aust. J. Intell. Inf. Process. Syst. **12**(4), 32 (2010)
41. Thomaz, C.E., Giraldi, G.A.: A new ranking method for principal components analysis and its application to face image analysis. Image Vis. Comput. **28**(6), 902–913 (2010)

42. Valiente, D., Gil, A., Payá, L., Sebastián, J., Reinoso, Ó.: Robust visual localization with dynamic uncertainty management in omnidirectional slam. Appl. Sci. **7**, 1294 (12 2017). https://doi.org/10.3390/app7121294
43. Wang, S., Clark, R., Wen, H., Trigoni, N.: DeepVO: towards end-to-end visual odometry with deep recurrent convolutional neural networks. In: 2017 IEEE International Conference on Robotics and Automation (ICRA), pp. 2043–2050. IEEE (2017)
44. Xie, J., Kiefel, M., Sun, M.T., Geiger, A.: Semantic instance annotation of street scenes by 3D to 2D label transfer. In: Conference on Computer Vision and Pattern Recognition (CVPR) (2016)
45. Zhang, Z., Lyons, M., Schuster, M., Akamatsu, S.: Comparison between geometry-based and Gabor-wavelets-based facial expression recognition using multi-layer perceptron. In: Third IEEE International Conference on Automatic Face and Gesture Recognition, Proceedings. pp. 454–459. IEEE (1998)

Loss Function Regularization
on the Iterated Racing Procedure
for Automatic Tuning of RatSLAM
Parameters

Paulo Gabriel Borralho Gomes[1], Cicero Joe Rafael Lima de Oliveira[1],
Matheus Chaves Menezes[1]([✉]) [iD], Paulo Rogério de Almeida Ribeiro[2] [iD],
and Alexandre César Muniz de Oliveira[3] [iD]

[1] Universidade Federal do Maranhão, Vila Bacanga, São Luís 65080-805, Brazil
{gabriel.borralho,cicero.oliveira,matheus.menezes}@discente.ufma.br
[2] Curso de Engenharia da Computação, Universidade Federal Do Maranhão,
Vila Bacanga, São Luís 65080-805, Brazil
paulo.ribeiro@ecp.ufma.br
[3] Departamento de Informática, Universidade Federal do Maranhão, Vila Bacanga,
São Luís 65080-805, Brazil
alexandre.cesar@ufma.br

Abstract. Simultaneous localization and mapping (SLAM) is a fundamental problem in mobile robotics. Among the solutions to solve this problem, the RatSLAM is a SLAM algorithm inspired by the spatial navigation system of rodents. The RatSLAM has a set of parameters that must be adjusted for each new environment to generate a reasonable map. A proposed solution to tune these parameters has been presented in the form of a manual trial-and-error algorithm. This algorithm guides the tuning only in part of the environment, despite the adjustment being suitable for the entire environment. In addition, recent work has proposed an automatic parameter tuning solution using the Iterated Race (*irace*) and Iterative Closest Points (ICP). However, this automatic solution provides parameters values that might be suitable only for the environment places in which they were adjusted, i.e.the adjustment might not be adequate for the entire environment. This work proposes a regularisation of the automatic algorithm objective function to incorporate the advantages of the manual solution into it. The proposed process uses only part of a virtual environment to find the parameters for the Rat-SLAM. Then, these parameters are tested in new places and the entire environment. The results have shown that the parameters found by the approach can generalize for new areas, as well as be suitable to map the entire environment.

Keywords: SLAM · RatSLAM · Parameter tuning

FAPEMA Coopi-05109/18.

P. R. d. A. Ribeiro et al. (Eds.): LAWCN 2021, CCIS 1519, pp. 48–63, 2022.
https://doi.org/10.1007/978-3-031-08443-0_4

1   Introduction

A fundamental issue in autonomous mobile robots is their ability to navigate in unknown environments with little human intervention or without it. To perform this task, the robot should be able to map an unknown environment while simultaneously localizing itself in it. This problem is named Simultaneous Localisation and Mapping (SLAM) [15] and has been addressed by several approaches, such as the traditional ones [3,12,13] as well as bio-inspired solutions [17].

Among the bio-inspired solutions to solve the SLAM problem, the RatSLAM algorithm is inspired by how the hippocampus in the rodents' brain performs spatial navigation [9,11]. RatSLAM has been improved and applied on several works over the years [1,6,14]. However, the algorithm requires 31 parameters to work [1]. Additionally, these parameters must be set for each new environment.

To appropriately adjust RatSLAM for new environments, Ball and collaborators proposed a tuning algorithm that focuses only on two important parameters and uses only part of the environment (an environment segment with the robot in motion and a segment with a loop closure) [1]. On the other hand, the tuning of these two parameters assumes that the other ones are correct or close to the same ones used in similar environments tested in their work. Therefore, their proposed solution lacks instructions for setting parameters in environments that are significantly different from those previously tested.

Recently, Menezes and collaborators [5] have proposed an automatic parameter tuning method to solve the manual parameters adjustment in RatSLAM. Their approach applies the *irace* (Iterated Racing for Automatic Algorithm Configuration) [4] algorithm to systematically generate combinations of parameters values. Then, the created maps with RatSLAM and *irace* parameters are evaluated by the Iterative Closest Point (ICP) [2] algorithm, which computes the error between the created and the ground truth map of the environment.

The overall automatic process of this method is formulated as an optimization problem, where the objective function is designed to find a set of parameters that minimizes the errors (computed by ICP) between the created and the ground truth maps.

Although their tuning solution correctly finds the parameters that generate the environment map, it uses the entire environment, unlike the proposal presented in [1]. Using the complete environment could lead their method to a computationally expensive process, mainly in large environments. Furthermore, if the method uses only part of the environment, it also could generate over-adjusted parameters for these parts, but not suitable for new places from the same environment.

Therefore, this work aims to include the guidelines proposed by [1] in the automatic tuning method proposed by [5] through objective function regularisation. In this sense, regularisation refers to adding a penalty term to the objective function. Specifically, the objective function of the automatic algorithm receives the rules of the manual algorithm that find parameters for a given environment using only part of it in the tuning process.

In Sect. 2, a general vision of the RatSLAM algorithm and its parameters is presented. The parameter tuning approach is explained in Sect. 3. In Sect. 4, the experiments are designed. Section 5 shows the results, and Sect. 6 discusses them. Finally, Sect. 7 presents the conclusions of this work, as well as guides for future works.

2   The RatSLAM Algorithm

The RatSLAM algorithm was first introduced in 2004 [11] and since then it has been used to solve the SLAM problem for indoor and outdoor environments [7,8]. The algorithm is inspired by the hippocampus of rodents and how they perform mapping and localization tasks. Moreover, RatSLAM can accomplish such tasks using a low-cost sensor such as a monocular camera. The RatSLAM algorithm is described in the following subsection.

2.1   RatSLAM Structure

Figure 1 shows the structure of the RatSLAM that consists of four main parts: i) Speed Sensor; ii) Local View Cells; iii) Pose Cells Network, and iv) Experience Map.

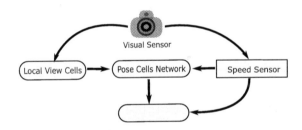

Fig. 1. The RatSLAM architecture.

Speed Sensor provides linear and angular speed information from the robot. Moreover, velocities can also be computed from the images, i.e. visual odometry, which can reduce the necessary sensor for RatSLAM to a single low-cost monocular camera.

The local view cells (LVC) is a 1-D array of local views (or templates) that processes and stores the environment information sent by the Visual Sensor. If the environment information is new (e.g. image from a new location), a new template is created. Otherwise, the correspondent template of the view information is activated.

The pose cell network (PCN) is a 3-D continuous attractor network analogous to the grid cells and head direction cells of the rodent's entorhinal cortex and hippocampus [10]. The activity on the PCN represents the robot's pose on the environment. Each cell on the X and Y network axis corresponds to the x and y coordinates of the 2-D environment, whereas the Z-axis corresponds to the robot's orientation on the ground. Path integration over the velocities sent by the Speed Sensor is performed on the PCN. Therefore, changes in the robot's speeds also modify the activity into the PCN. Moreover, the PCN links the current template from Local View Cells with its current activity location. Furthermore, when the robot performs a loop closure, that is, when the robot revisits an already mapped area, the network coordinates associated with the local view are activated, and this process corrects the robot's belief of its pose in the environment.

The Experience map is a 2-D topological-metric graph that represents the map of the environment. Each node in the graph is called an experience. In addition, each experience has information of the activity of the LVC and PCN at the moment the experience is created, as well as its pose information. When the activities in the LVC and PCN do not correspond to any previous experience, a new one is created. Furthermore, the link built between two experiences stores the euclidean distance and angular displacement between these experiences.

2.2   RatSLAM Parameters

The RatSLAM parameters (31 in total) are depicted on Table 1, where each one has a type-associated value. In addition, some parameters are highly sensitive, i.e. small changes may cause a huge variation in the mapping.

The Visual Odometry parameters are impacted by camera specification and they are related to the robot's translational and rotational speeds. The Local View parameters are responsible for the creation and comparison of templates. Thus, if they are misfitted they can cause over or under template sampling. The Pose Cells parameters influence the amount of energy inserted into the PCN when a scene is revisited. The Experience Map parameter *exp_loop* concerns the relocation of nodes and edges due to odometric errors throughout the experience map. For further details about these parameters refer to [1].

3   Improved Tuning Process

In this section, an improved tuning method is presented. It regulates the objective function of the automatic tuning [5] by inserting the tuning conditions presented on the manual adjustment algorithm [1].

In the tuning algorithm proposed by Ball *et al.* [1], only the *vt_match_threshold* and *pc_vt_inject_energy* parameter should be adjusted. The remaining parameters should be set similarly to one of the examples shown in their work. These examples support parameters for large real-world, 360°, and controlled small environments. However, if a different environment, e.g. a virtual

Table 1. RatSLAM parameters [1,5]

Module	Parameter's name	Type
Visual odometry	[vtrans_image_x_min, vtrans_image_x_max, vtrans_image_y_min, vtrans_image_y_max];	Integer
	[vrot_image_x_min, vrot_image_x_max, vrot_image_y_min, vrot_image_y_max];	Integer
	camera_fov_deg;	Integer
	camera_hz;	Integer
	vtrans_scaling;	Real
	vtrans_max	Real
Local view	vt_panoramic	Binary
	vt_shift_match;	Integer
	vt_step_match	Integer
	[image_crop_x_min image_crop_x_max image_crop_y_min image_crop_y_max]	Integer
	[template_x_size, template_y_size]	Integer
	vt_match_threshold;	Real
	vt_normalization;	Real
	vt_patch_normalization	Integer
Pose cells	pc_dim_xy	Integer
	exp_delta_pc_threshold	Real
	pc_cell_x_size	Real
	pc_vt_inject_energy	Real
	vt_active_decay	Real
	pc_vt_restore	Integer
Experience map	exp_loops	Integer

environment, is introduced, it is not guaranteed that the default values for the remaining parameters will work properly in this new environment. In addition, the manual tuning algorithm assumes that the velocities parameters are correctly adjusted before the tuning of the *vt_match_threshold* and *pc_vt_inject_energy*. In order to check the correct values for the Visual Odometry parameters, the rate $R = \dot{T}/\dot{E}$ should be closer to 0.5 or 1.0, where $\dot{T}$ is the number of visual templates and $\dot{E}$ is the number of experiences. After the tune of the Visual Odometry parameters, the *vt_match_threshold* is tune inside a loop function to keep the R rate between 0.5 and 1.0. Finally, the *pc_vt_inject_energy* is tune (inside another loop) to make RatSLAM closes a loop correctly in the environment.

The tuning process of RatSLAM by [5] is formulated as an optimization problem that takes into account the values of the parameters, the generated and the truth map. First, the irace package automatically generates a candidate parameter set for the RatSLAM. For each parameters file, a resulting map is obtained (generated map). Then, the deviations between the generated map and the ground truth map (obtained from robots odometry) are evaluated with the ICP algorithm. These evaluations are taken into account by irace to generate new combinations of parameters until this deviation reaches a stopping criterion. The objective function is described as follows [5]:

$$
p^* = \arg\min_{p \in \mathbf{P}} \sum_{k=1}^{N_V} er^{(p, v_k)}
\tag{1}
$$

that minimizes the residual error, $er^{(p, v_k)}$, between the generated map and the ground truth, computed by ICP over the 2D coordinates points. Each mapping is generated by the RatSLAM using a parameter set, p, and the input video stream v_k taken from N_V input files.

Since the ICP computes the mean squared error of the distances between the ground truth and generated map, the closest match between them leads to an error closer to 0, and the higher error variation will depend on the maximum distortion of the generated map. Therefore, the ICP can fairly represent the perfect match of the maps when the error between them is 0, but it cannot precisely inform their similarities if the error is higher than 0.

Improved Objective Function. It is assumed that the tuning method in [5] already corrects the *pc_vt_inject_energy* parameter if the ground truth map has a loop closure. This is due to the fact that the *irace* will positively consider parameters that generate maps similar to the ground truth one.

However, as the *irace* only considers the similarity between the two maps, it does not into account the R rate as proposed in [1], which recommends a generated map with a R rate $\in [\alpha, \beta]$: commonly $\alpha = 0.5$ and $\beta = 0.9$. To overcome these issues, the new proposed objection function is given as following:

$$
p^* = \arg\min_{p \in \mathbf{P}} \sum_{k=1}^{N_V} er^{(p, v_k)} \times (1 + \max\left(R^{(p, v_k)} - \alpha, \beta - R^{(p, v_k)}, 0\right)) \times
$$
$$
\log_{10}(N_x + 10)
\tag{2}
$$

where $(1 + \max{(R^{(p,v_k)} - \alpha, \beta - R^{(p,v_k)}, 0)})$ increases the error only if R rate is out of the recommended interval $[\alpha, \beta]$. The $\log_{10}(N_x + 10)$ penalises generated maps with higher number of nodes N_x.

Hence it is assumed that the *irace* gives priority to those parameters that maintain the R rate in the desired value, leading to configurations that generate maps with a minor number of points but are better distributed over the map.

4   Experimental Setup

In this section, the experimental setup is covered. First, information about the environment adopted is presented. Then, information regarding the *irace* tuning process is described. In this work, the xRatSLAM [14] is used for the RatSLAM implementation.

4.1   Environment Setup

To validate the improved objective function for the tuning algorithm, a 3D virtual environment of a research laboratory has been modeled in a framework developed to study biomimetic models of rodent behavior in spatial navigation learning tasks [16], as shown in Fig. 2a and similar to a real research laboratory [5].

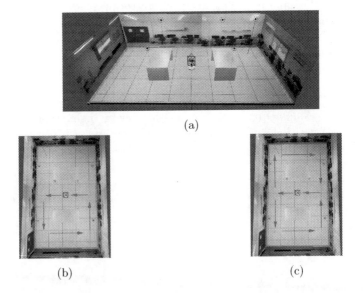

(a)

(b)   (c)

Fig. 2. Laboratory virtual environment. a) shows a view of the environment. b) displays the counterclockwise lap performed by the agent. c) depicts the *eight* shaped lap that has counterclockwise and clockwise laps.

Three videos have been generated from the virtual environment, where they are: i) a counterclockwise lap starting from the environment's middle, as shown in Fig. 2b; ii) a clockwise lap starting from the environment's middle; and iii) a *eight* shaped lap starting from the environment's middle (Fig. 2c). In addition, the *eight* lap is composed of both counterclockwise and clockwise laps.

The experiment consists in finding the parameters returned by the *irace* in one of the small laps, i.e. videos i) and ii), and testing these parameters in the other remaining videos, e.g. use the parameters previously found (on video i) on video ii) and iii). Note that video iii) is not included in the parameters acquisition step, it is only used for test. This experiment aims to test the parameters generalization, that is, acquiring them in one part of the environment and testing them in another, as suggested by Ball and colleagues [1].

Therefore, it is expected a generalization feature of the proposed tuning method if it successfully finds the parameters that are suitable for any part of the environment. In addition, the *eight* lap contains important features to be evaluated such as changing of directions (e.g. from clockwise to counterclockwise) and it covers the complete environment.

4.2   *irace* Setup

As previously mentioned, the *irace* is used to find the best parameters for the RatSLAM algorithm. However, a large number of parameters (see Table 1) can lead this approach to be a large time-consuming process. Moreover, there is no previous detailed information about range search for some parameters (unless they are attached to hardware specification, e.g. camera image size), which can result in a large number of parameter settings that generate similar map results. Therefore, to make the adjustment process feasible, the parameter space required by the irace has been empirically defined in this work and is described in Table 2.

In addition, few parameters related to the *Visual Template* and *Visual Odometry* had their values fixed to avoid non-relevant features of the images, such as floors and ceiling. These areas' features usually do not change over the environment and, therefore, can be removed from the RatSLAM mapping process.

The *irace* has been conducted in 10 iterations with 50 configuration per iteration. Moreover, it ran in parallel with 19 threads on a high-performance computing environment that employs Portable Batch System - (PBS)[1] for scheduling processes at nodes.

---

[1] https://www.openpbs.org/.

Table 2. Parameter spaces of RatSLAM for irace.

Name	Type	Range
# Local view		
vt_match_threshold	r	(0.0, 0.2)
vt_shift_match	i	(0, 10)
vt_step_match	i	(1, 3)
vt_normalisation	r	(0.1, 1.0)
image_crop_x_min	c	(40)
image_crop_x_max	c	(600)
image_crop_y_min	c	(150)
image_crop_y_max	c	(300)
vt_active_decay	r	(0.1, 1.0)
# Pose cells		
pc_vt_restore	r	(0.01, 0.1)
pc_dim_xy	i	(20, 40)
pc_vt_inject_energy	r	(0.1, 0.8)
pc_dim_th	c	(36)
exp_delta_pc_threshold	r	(0.7, 1.3)
pc_cell_x_size	r	(1)
# Experience map		
exp_loops	i	(1, 20)
# Visual odometry + Template size		
vtrans_image_x_min	c	(80)
vtrans_image_x_max	c	(560)
vtrans_image_y_min	c	(240)
vtrans_image_y_max	c	(360)
vtrans_scaling	i	(200,1000)
vtrans_max	r	(1.0, 20.0)
vrot_image_x_min	c	(80)
vrot_image_x_max	c	(560)
vrot_image_y_min	c	(240)
vrot_image_y_max	c	(360)
camera_fov_deg	i	(30, 150)
camera_hz	c	(1, 80)
template_x_size	i	(40,120)
template_y_size	c	(20,100)

5   Results

Table 3 presents the ICP errors, R rate, and the best-returned parameters by irace for the counterclockwise and clockwise instances. Since ICP errors higher than 0 cannot inform if the generated map is similar to the ground truth map, for these cases visual analyses are used to compare the paths between the maps. Moreover, the R rate for all scenarios were kept in the previously defined range $R \in [\alpha, \beta]$: $\alpha = 0.5$ and $\beta = 0.9$.

Figure 3 shows the Experience Map of the counterclockwise lap experiment. The map generated by the best configuration is displayed on the top-left. The

Table 3. Residuals, R rate and RatSLAM parameters' values for the best configurations.

Lap	Counterclockwise	Clockwise
Residual of ICP		
Counterclockwise	**0.052**	**0.199**
Clockwise	**0.162**	**0.122**
Eight	**0.081**	**0.379**
R rate		
Counterclockwise	**0.552**	**0.506**
Clockwise	**0.585**	**0.602**
Eight	**0.816**	**0.595**
Parameters	*Values*	
# Local view		
vt_match_threshold	0.064	0.196
vt_shift_match	2	1
vt_step_match	2	2
vt_normalisation	0.843	0.5793
vt_active_decay	0.442	0.438
# Pose cells		
pc_vt_restore	0.072	0.090
pc_dim_xy	35	26
pc_vt_inject_energy	0.333	0.278
pc_dim_th	36	36
exp_delta_pc_threshold	0.732	1.054
pc_cell_x_size	1	1
# Experience map		
exp_loops	12	13
exp_initial_em_deg	−25	38

top-right is the ground truth robot's movement. On the bottom-left, it exhibits the same counterclockwise map after the translation and rotation operations performed by the ICP. Lastly, the overlapping between the transformed map and the ground truth is displayed for visual comparison purposes.

Figure 4 and 5 show the Experience Maps of the clockwise and *eight* laps created by the counterclockwise parameters. These parameters built similar maps of both the eight (which is the entire environment) and the clockwise laps, even when these laps are not used in the tuning process.

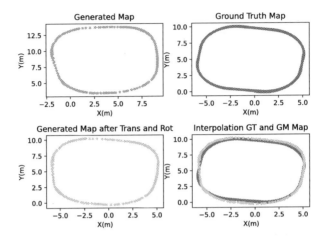

Fig. 3. Parameters of the counterclockwise experiment on counterclockwise lap. Top-left shows the experience map generated by the tuned parameters. Bottom-left displays the same map after ICP rotation and translation operations. Bottom-right depicts the best matching between the resulting map and the ground truth.

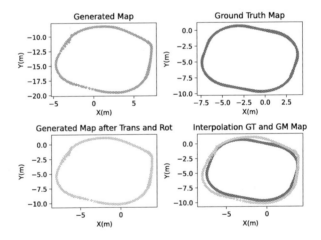

Fig. 4. Parameters of the counterclockwise experiment on clockwise lap.

Figure 6 shows the Experience Map of the clockwise lap experiment. Similar to the counterclockwise experiment, the map generated by the best irace configuration for this instance is displayed on Table 3.

Figures 7 and 8 depicts the clockwise parameters on the counterclockwise and *eight* laps. In the same way as the results of the counterclockwise lap, the clockwise lap parameters have been able to generate representative maps of the new environment places.

In order to exemplify the effect of the R in the improved objective function in this work, Fig. 9 shows a counterclockwise lap example using only the objective

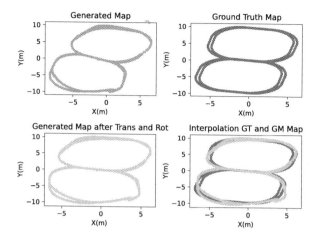

Fig. 5. Parameters of the counterclockwise experiment on *eight* lap.

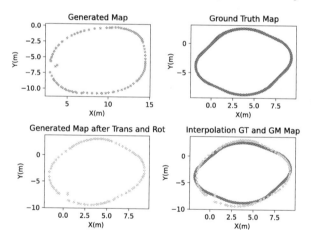

Fig. 6. Parameters of the clockwise experiment on the clockwise lap. Top-left shows the experience map generated by the tuned parameters. Bottom-left displays the same map after ICP rotation and translation operations. Bottom-right depicts the best matching between the resulting map and the ground truth.

function in 1 [5]. In this example, the ICP error and the R rate are equal to 0.141896 and 1 (one experience per template created), respectively.

In Fig. 10, it is depicted the same parameters of Fig. 9 when applied to the *eight* instance, where is visually notable the non-similarity between the generated map and the ground truth. The ICP error and the R rate are equal to 3.596 and 1, respectively.

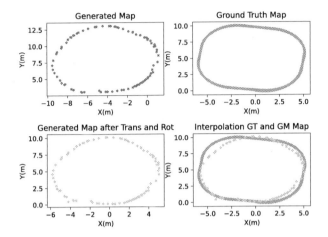

Fig. 7. Parameters of the clockwise experiment on the counterclockwise lap.

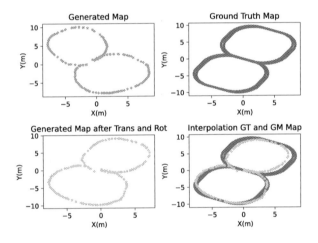

Fig. 8. Parameters of the clockwise experiment on the *eight* lap.

6   Discussion

Proposed by Ball and collaborators [1], the manual tuning solution for RatSLAM parameters could lead to a large time-consuming process to find parameters for new environments. This might occur due to the number of parameters needed for the RatSLAM. Their tuning algorithm focuses on two main parameters if the environment is similar to the ones previously tested in their work. On the other hand, for different environments, parameters such as visual odomentry should be tuned before their tuning algorithm is used. An advantage of their tuning algorithm is that found parameters by this process are suitable for the entire environment, even if they are tuned only in part of the environment.

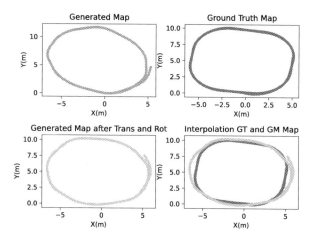

Fig. 9. Parameters of the counterclockwise experiment without the R rate on the counterclockwise lap. ICP error $= 0.141896$. R rate $= 1$ (not considered).

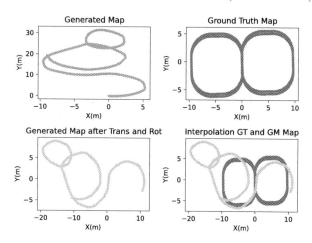

Fig. 10. Parameters of the counterclockwise experiment without the R rate on the *eight* lap. ICP error $= 3.596$. R rate $= 1$ (not considered).

Part of this problem has been addressed by Menezes and colleagues [5] when they proposed an automatic method to find the parameters. In their solution, a range of possible values could be given to each parameter, and the *irace* returns the best combination of values it had found for one or more environments. However, their solution might return parameters that work only for the trained environment, as shown in Fig. 9 and 10. Note that the ICP error for the trained instance in this example is comparable with the ones for the main experiments shown on Table 3, especially the ones for the clockwise column. In contrast, when these parameters were used on the *eight* lap, the results showed a distorted map with both high ICP error and R rate. Therefore, their algorithm lacks parameters generalization for new places from the same environment (i.e. tuned parameters only work in the familiar area), since they did not completely cover the solution proposed by Ball and collaborators [1].

As presented in Figure from 3 to 8, the regulated objective function proposed in this work was able to solve the generalization of the parameters for the counterclockwise and clockwise laps of the lab environment. This has been done by adding the R rate condition as part of the decision of the best configurations returned by *irace*. In addition, for all environments, the R rates had their values inside the desired range.

7   Conclusion

Simultaneous localization and mapping (SLAM) inspired on the spatial navigation system of rodents' brains (named RatSLAM) has a set of performance parameters that must be tuned for each new environment to generate a consistent map of the environment.

Tuning RatSLAM parameters could lead to a long-time consuming process. This process can be avoided using small chunks of the environment under mapping. In such cases, the tuning method needs to have good generalization power since the complete environment is not included in the training.

This work proposes regularisation on the objective function that guides the automatic adjustment procedure based on *irace*. The new tuning process can find the parameters for RatSLAM using only part of a virtual environment

For validation, parameters acquired were tested in parts of the environment that had not been trained before and the full environment. The results have shown that the parameters found can be generalized to untrained areas of the environment.

As future works, the solution proposed in this paper must be validated in more trajectories, including large real-world datasets.

Acknowledgements. This study was financed in part by the Coordenação de Aperfeiçoamento de Pessoal de Nível Superior - Brasil (CAPES) - Finance Code 001, and from FAPEMA/COOPI COOPI- 05109/18.

References

1. Ball, D., Heath, S., Wiles, J., Wyeth, G., Corke, P., Milford, M.: Openratslam: an open source brain-based slam system. Autonom. Robot. **34**(3), 149–176 (2013)
2. Cho, H., Kim, E.K., Kim, S.: Indoor slam application using geometric and ICP matching methods based on line features. Robot. Autonom. Syst. **100**, 206–224 (2018)
3. Le Corff, S., Fort, G., Moulines, E.: Online expectation maximization algorithm to solve the slam problem. In: 2011 IEEE Statistical Signal Processing Workshop (SSP), pp. 225–228, June 2011

4. López-Ibáñez, M., Dubois-Lacoste, J., Pérez Cáceres, L., Birattari, M., Stützle, T.: The irace package: Iterated racing for automatic algorithm configuration. Oper. Res. Perspect. **3**, 43–58 (2016). https://doi.org/10.1016/j.orp.2016.09.002

5. Menezes, M.C., et al.: Automatic tuning of RatSLAM's parameters by Irace and iterative closest point. In: IECON 2020 The 46th Annual Conference of the IEEE Industrial Electronics Society, pp. 562–568 (2020). https://doi.org/10.1109/IECON43393.2020.9254718

6. Menezes, M.C., de Freitas, E.P., Cheng, S., de Oliveira, A.C.M., de Almeida Ribeiro, P.R.: A neuro-inspired approach to solve a simultaneous location and mapping task using shared information in multiple robots systems. In: 2018 15th International Conference on Control, Automation, Robotics and Vision (ICARCV), pp. 1753–1758. IEEE (2018)

7. Milford, M.J., Wyeth, G.F.: Mapping a suburb with a single camera using a biologically inspired slam system. IEEE Trans. Robot. **24**(5), 1038–1053 (2008). https://doi.org/10.1109/TRO.2008.2004520

8. Milford, M., Wyeth, G.: Persistent navigation and mapping using a biologically inspired slam system. Int. J. Robot. Res. **29**(9), 1131–1153 (2010)

9. Milford, M., Wyeth, G., Prasser, D.: Ratslam on the edge: revealing a coherent representation from an overloaded rat brain. In: Intelligent Robots and Systems, 2006 IEEE/RSJ International Conference on, pp. 4060–4065. IEEE (2006)

10. Milford, M.J., Wiles, J., Wyeth, G.F.: Solving navigational uncertainty using grid cells on robots. PLoS Comput. Biol. **6**(11), e1000995 (2010)

11. Milford, M.J., Wyeth, G.F., Prasser, D.: Ratslam: a hippocampal model for simultaneous localization and mapping. In: Robotics and Automation, 2004. Proceedings. ICRA 2004. 2004 IEEE International Conference on, vol. 1, pp. 403–408. IEEE (2004)

12. Saman, A.B.S.H.M., Lotfy, A.H.: An implementation of slam with extended kalman filter. In: 2016 6th International Conference on Intelligent and Advanced Systems (ICIAS), pp. 1–4, August 2016

13. Sim, R., Elinas, P., Griffin, M., Little, J.J., et al.: Vision-based slam using the rao-blackwellised particle filter. In: IJCAI Workshop on Reasoning with Uncertainty in Robotics, vol. 14, pp. 9–16 (2005)

14. de Souza Muñoz, M.E., et al.: A parallel RatSlam C++ library implementation. In: Cota, V.R., Barone, D.A.C., Dias, D.R.C., Damázio, L.C.M. (eds.) LAWCN 2019. CCIS, vol. 1068, pp. 173–183. Springer, Cham (2019). https://doi.org/10.1007/978-3-030-36636-0_13

15. Taheri, H., Xia, Z.C.: Slam; definition and evolution. Eng. Appl. Artif. Intell **97**, 104032 (2021). https://doi.org/10.1016/j.engappai.2020.104032, https://www.sciencedirect.com/science/article/pii/S0952197620303092

16. Walther, T., et al.: Context-dependent extinction learning emerging from raw sensory inputs: a reinforcement learning approach. Sci. Rep. **11**(1) (2021). https://doi.org/10.1038/s41598-021-81157-z

17. Zeno, P.J., Patel, S., Sobh, T.M.: Review of neurobiologically based mobile robot navigation system research performed since 2000. J. Robot. **2016** (2016)

Controlling the UR3 Robotic Arm Using a Leap Motion: A Comparative Study

Diego A. Lopez[1], Manuel A. Lopez[1], Dario S. Muñoz[1], Jesús A. Santa[1], David F. Gomez[1], Dante Barone[3], Jim Torresen[4], and Jaime A. Riascos Salas[2(✉)]

[1] Mariana University, Pasto, Colombia
[2] University Institution of Envigado, Envigado, Colombia
`jarsalas@inf.ufrgs.br`
[3] Federal University Rio Grande do Sul, Porto Alegre, Brazil
[4] University of Oslo, Oslo, Norway

Abstract. Each day, robotic systems are becoming more familiar and common in different contexts such as factories, hospitals, houses, and restaurants, creating a necessity of seeking for affordable and intuitive interface for effective and engaging communication with humans. Likewise, innovative devices that offer alternative methods of interacting with machines allow us to create new interfaces, improving the learning training and motion application. Thus, this paper compares two interaction modes using leap motion to control a robotic manipulator (UR3) simulator. Users can control the robot through numerical gestures to set up the angle joints (coded mode) or counter/clockwise gestures to increase or decrease the angle values (open mode). We evaluate these modes objectively, capturing from 30 subjects the number of gestures and employed time to reach three specific poses. Likewise, we collected subjective questionnaires to compare the control methods and preferences. Our findings suggest that both methods employ similar gestures, but coded control takes less time with higher variations among ages. Moreover, subjects' preferences indicate a slight inclination towards the open mode. Finally, it is mandatory to explore different difficulties in the tasks and increase the population to have a more general understanding of the preferences and performance.

Keywords: Leap-motion · UR3 · Robotic arm · Human-computer interaction · Machine learning

1 Introduction

Nowadays, robots play an essential role in our daily lives and increasingly are being an active part of our societies, primarily in economics, social and developing domains such as manufacturing, agriculture, medical and healthcare, defense, land exploration, among others [4]. Human-Machine interaction (HMI) aims for new alternatives to improve communication and interaction with machines. These developments are continually applied in robotics, seeking to include new

© Springer Nature Switzerland AG 2022
P. R. d. A. Ribeiro et al. (Eds.): LAWCN 2021, CCIS 1519, pp. 64–77, 2022.
https://doi.org/10.1007/978-3-031-08443-0_5

devices in the control and interaction with robots. Currently, there are important developments on gesture-based interfaces to control robots; these explorations aim to create non-conventional and multi-modal modes such as using the head [10], gaze [8], arm [12], and hand [2] (among others) for interacting with either mobile and fixed robots. Therefore, current innovative devices, such as Leap Motion [16] that use a hand-gesture recognition system, have an essential role in the development of new interactive robotic interfaces, offering a more natural and familiar setup where hand gestures can be part of control commands.

Robotic manipulators are one of the most common robotic systems, consisting of a mechanical-articulated arm composed of a series of links joined each other, and to a fixed base [1]. The independent adjustment gives the movement of the robotic arms in each of their joints, so one form of interaction with the interfaces can be to associate the performance of hand gestures with the adjustment of joints, in which it may have different control modes based on the different use of gestures [13]. However, understanding such functionality requires the use of learning tools based on simulations. Indeed, the future advance of robotic manipulators will rely on simulated models to perform extensive physical and motion analysis before the actual implementation [7]. Thus, the creation of real-time simulators for either in-place or remote manipulator systems brings extreme value during the training of robot operators.

Hence, the focus of this article is to provide a new gestural interaction using a leap motion that allows the control of a robotic manipulator in a virtual simulator. We compare and propose two potential modes to create the interactive scenario: coded and open. The first one deals with the setup of joint angle values with numerical hand gestures, while the second one only uses clockwise and counterclockwise circle gestures to set up these values. We simulated the UR3 robotic platform from Universal Robotics [15] under Unity 3D. We captured the number of gestures and time employed to perform three basic motion activities, where users had to place the robot in a specific pose. Also, we included usability questionnaires and preferences questions to assess each interface mode subjectively.

The remainder of this paper is structured as follows: Sect. 2 presents related works that employed leap motion for controlling robotic platforms. Then, Sect. 3 shows the experimental procedure's materials and methods. Later, Sect. 4 provides the main findings and a discussion of them; and finally, Sect. 5 presents the conclusions and future directions.

2   Related Works

This section focuses on related works on hand gesture-based control of robots, mainly using Leap Motion. Different works incorporate the Leap Motion sensor for the movement of the robotic arm; initially, [14] designed and built from servomotors a prototype robotic arm to be controlled by Leap Motion, the data processing is done with the Arduino Uno micro-controller. They reported a high precision in the control of approximately 0.01 mm per second. We also found a

Leap Motion application [6], where a simulator similar to ours is created using hand gestures to control the UR10 robotic arm. This report differs from the current proposal in terms of the interaction, where they employ the gesture data to control the whole robot instead of individual joints. Likewise, different robotic platforms have been used for interaction with Leap Motion. Chen and colleagues [5], controlled a real robotic arm SCARA LS3-401 using Leap Motion. They reported satisfactory results for complete robot control. Similarly, Bassily et al. [3] controlled the robotic arm, Jaco of 6-DOF, with Leap Motion. They propose implementing a novel intuitive and adaptive manipulation scheme by developing a human-machine communication interface based on the optimal mapping of the user's hand movement. These works demonstrate several successful implementations of Leap Motion for robotics, allowing a more natural and comfortable interaction between humans and machines.

3   Materials and Methods

3.1   Overview

We created a UR3 robotic simulator to evaluate a leap motion interface that uses two modes of interaction: coded and open. We aim to compare them subjectively with questionnaires and objectively capture the number of gestures and time taken to complete a specific task. After the experiment, the participants had to complete the following questionnaires: a demographics information, simulator perception and comparative survey for each control mode presented, and Edinburgh Handedness. 30 healthy subjects (nine women) between 18 and 52 years old (u = 25.3, SD = 10.1) voluntary participated in this study where, following the COVID-19 restrictions, we carried out the tests with an inner circle of relatives and friends in an isolated house with all of the bio-security protocols.

3.2   Leap Motion

The Leap Motion is an optical tracking device that captures hand movements with high precision (an error of about 200 μm) [18]. Due to its high performance and relative low-average price, it has opened up new opportunities for gesture recognition [11] and interactive software application [9], allowing the development of effortless and natural interfaces. Leap Motion offers two data capturing configurations: "Desktop" and "VR." The main difference lies in operation, wherein "Desktop" captures data on a surface with a fixed position while "VR" refers to the active motion capture in virtual reality applications. To our approach, the "Desktop" mode is the most suitable. Following the previous analysis of the Leap Motion working area [17], we set up the interaction box with a minimum distance of 82.5mm and a maximum of 317.5 mm along the Y-axis. While Z-axis, the one perpendicular to the longest side of the sensor, is in the range of −73.5 mm to 73.5 mm. Finally, the range along the X-axis is −117.5 mm until 117.5 mm. Figure 1 shows the working area created to capture the data.

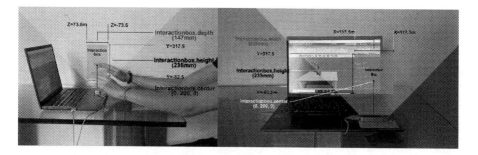

Fig. 1. Calibrating the interaction zone of the Leap Motion

3.3   Experimental Scenarios

Once the UR3 model has been fully functional in Unity, we created a Graphic User Interface to manipulate the robotic platform. To avoid visual preferences, this interface gives the same information independently of the control mode, namely, the objective measures (number of gestures and time) and the current pose of each angle and the control mode. Figure 2 shows the interfaces for each control mode. Also, we incorporated visual elements to support the subject during the interaction tasks. Initially, a virtual arm appears to create an ownership sensation because it follows every user's hand movements. Later, the selected join and link will be highlighted with green color and the color text where the angle information appears. Finally, the objective task appears to remember the final pose to be reached by the robot. Figure 3 shows the interface during the interaction.

3.4   Experimental Procedure

The subjects sat comfortably in a chair, where before using the simulator, clear instructions were provided regarding robotics terminology, the interfaces, Leap Motion, the control modes, and the three different tasks they had to execute. Likewise, before the data capture, participants interacted with the simulator and each gesture per mode and were asked to run simple trials similar to the real ones. Thirty subjects participated voluntarily in the experiment. Nine of them were women, ranging from 18 to 52 years old (u = 25.3, SD = 10.1). Nine of them manifested have previous experience with Leap Motion or related technologies, while 13 know about robotics and virtual simulators.

After the training, the subjects were instructed to carry out the interaction experience. We asked to complete the tasks as quickly as possible but focus on performing the gestures naturally. We counterbalanced the modes, so each participant starts with one mode, and after five minutes of resting, they perform the next mode. After running both modes, they were asked to fill two questionnaires: the Simulator Perception Survey (SPS) and the Edinburgh Handedness Inventory (EHI). The first one was designed to capture personal information

Fig. 2. Graphic user interface (GUI) for both modes of control.

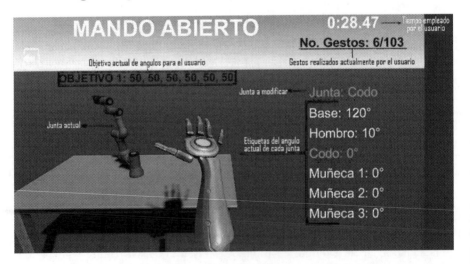

Fig. 3. Visual interface during the tasks execution. Selected join is highlighted with green. All the time the current and objective values are shown.

regarding the use of the simulator, difficulty, usability, and quality. Also, we asked about the mode preference in terms of efficiency, comfort, and movement precision. Since the Leap Motion is only developed for right-arm use, we ran the handedness survey to evaluate if laterality influenced the user's performance.

Two control modes were proposed and evaluated to manipulate the robot: "Open Control" and "Coded Control," presented individually in the following sections. However, both of them have three common interaction gestures: clockwise circle, counterclockwise circle, and swipe (a long linear movement of a finger, either left or right). They are used to change the join (swipe) and to increase the angle value (clockwise) or reduce the value (counterclockwise). Independently of the mode, they had to perform the same three tasks: to reach three specific poses, and each one is more difficult than the previous. The main difference lies in the number of gestures and how they have been used to set up the joint angles. The angle poses of each task corresponding to the base, shoulder, elbow, wrist1, wrist2, and wrist3 joints are the follows:

- 50° every joint;
- {50, 40, 30, –30, –40, –50°};
- {–10, 10, 30, –70, 10, 60°}.

The robot starts with its initial pose by default, that is, base equal to 90° and the other joints equal to 0° (Fig. 4).

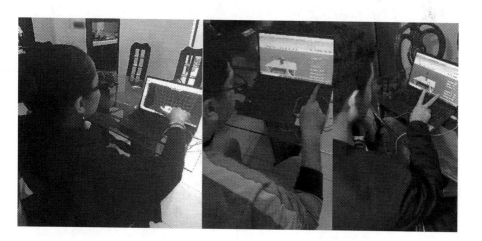

Fig. 4. Participants during the execution of the tasks

3.5   Coded Control

This mode allows using number gestures to set up the joint angles. It incorporates the representations of the hand gestures through the coordinates of different reference points of the hand. Thus, we obtained a database of 46 columns coming from different reference points for each spatial coordinate (X, Y, Z), namely, 15 for hand, three points per finger, and the corresponding digit label at the end digit and 900 rows coming from 100 captures per digit (from one up to nine). We used the Machine Learning Model Builder Toolbox in C# to train the model with the data. It compares several techniques and returns the best one based on cross-validation precision values. In this case, Multi-Layer Perceptron (MLP) obtained the higher result with an average of 99% precision. Thus, our system recognizes either of the digit gestures during the interaction task. The recognized digit is used as a multiplier by 10 for updating the angle; therefore, if a user would like to increase 40° a specific joint, namely the elbow from the base, (s)he should do twice the swipe movement towards the right to choose the elbow, later the gesture of the number four and finally the clockwise gesture to set up the angle. Thus, it should be four gestures in total. Figure 5 show the available gestures for this control mode, including the embodiment of the digits.

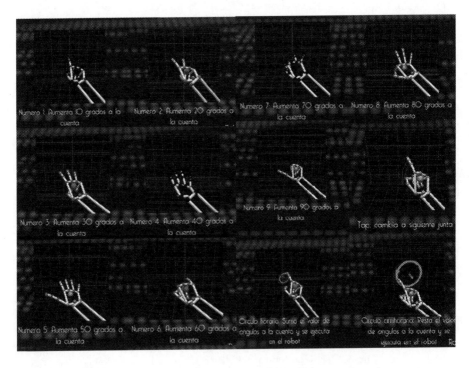

Fig. 5. Gestures employed during the coded control mode.

3.6 Open Control

Contrary to the coded control, the open mode uses only the three basic interaction gestures (clockwise, counterclockwise, and swipe) to set up a new pose angle. In other words, there are no digit gestures. The clockwise gesture means an increase of 10° while the counterclockwise a decrease of 10°. The swipe gesture is similar to the coded control, which means switching the selected joint. Thus, in this mode, for the previous example of increasing 40° the elbow angle from the base, the subject should do twice the swipe movement towards the right to choose the elbow, then four times the clockwise gesture to set up the new angle value. In total, there were five gestures. Figure 6 shows the interaction gestures used in this mode.

Fig. 6. Gestures employed during the open control mode.

4   Results

We initially compared the two modes using the number of gestures and time taken to accomplish the three tasks. As both of these variables are non-normal distribution (according to the Shapiro-Wilk normality test), we performed the paired Wilcoxon signed-rank test with continuity correction where neither of these variables reached a significant difference between control modes. Figures 7 and 8 show the gestures and time differences between the modes respectively. Firstly, we can see that the number of gesture are similar in both modes but with higher variance in the coded control. As the time is highly dependent on the number of gestures, a similar pattern is presented too; however, it takes less time for the coded control than the open one.

As we have a wide range of ages of our participants, from 18 up to 52, we decided to study the same variables among the different age ranges. Figures 9 and 10 present the variation obtained per age and control mode for number of gestures and time respectively. At first glance, the coded control took more gestures and time in participants from 40 to 47. Indeed, the time is the unique value where is higher for this control mode and age. The standard deviation is smaller in the open control for the number of gestures. Evidently, the younger participants obtained better results than the older ones. Presumably, it would be the technological appropriation typical of the 20 up 30 ages. Also, we study

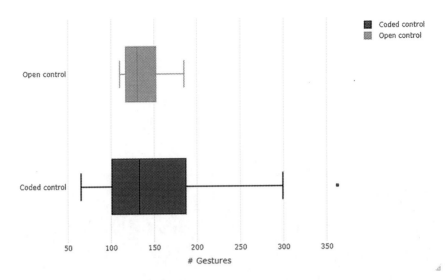

Fig. 7. Comparison of the number of gestures taken during the task execution per control modes. There is no a significant difference between them.

the relationship between age and the numerical results using Pearson's product-moment correlation. Thus, we found that age positively correlates with both the number of gestures ($r2 = 0.30$, p-value $= 0.01596$) and the time ($r2 = 0.35$, p-value $= 0.005384$), indicating that as older the participant as higher time and gestures employed for the tasks except for the last group (48–55 years old).

On the other hand, we analyze each control mode subjectively with the user's preferences survey, where the comparison question (CQ1) refers to with which one do you feel more comfortable; CQ2, which one represents a more efficient and natural interaction; and CQ3, which one do you feel harder to perform accurate movements. Figure 11 resumes these findings. We can see that subjects prefer the coded control over the open one in terms of comfort and natural interaction, while open control and coded one share the same preference in terms of easy-to-use. We also evaluated the influence of the user's previous experience with Leap Motion or related devices in the numerical results. Thus, we ran a 2-step Polychoric Correlation estimation reporting a high influence in the experience for the time ($x2 = 81.36$, p-value $= 0.02319$) and the number of gestures ($x2 = 65.69$, p-value $= 0.04567$), however, it is not conclusive since we need to run the experiment with an expert and a naive group.

Finally, the Simulator Perception Survey (SPS) offers a subjective view from the subjects about the simulator evaluated by ratings from zero (the worst) up to seven (the best). Figure 12 shows the summary of the answers for each question where the first one is related to how easy the simulator is; the second is how understandable the instructions are; how well the functionality is; and how visually well-looking the simulator is. We can see that participants found the simulator easy with a rating close to five, while the instructions were effectively

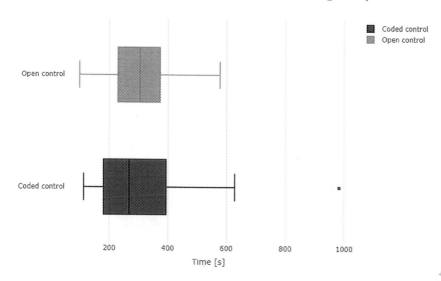

Fig. 8. Comparison of the time taken during the task execution per control modes. There is no a significant difference between them.

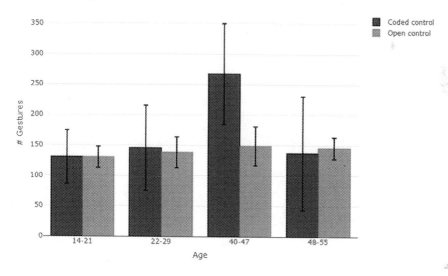

Fig. 9. Variations of the number of gestures among the age per control mode. This value is decreasing as younger the participant is.

presented with a rating superior to six. The visual aspect and functionality share a rating of almost six. These results demonstrate that, in general, there was a good acceptance of the simulator as a tool for controlling a virtual robot. Also, we studied the handedness influence on the numerical results. Thus, we ran a Pearson's product-moment correlation to find the relationship between the

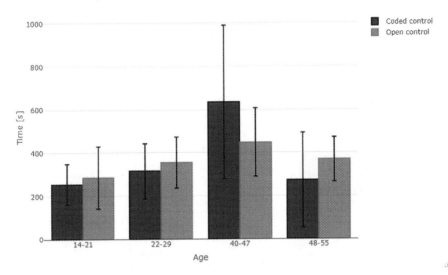

Fig. 10. Variations of the taken time among the age per control mode. This value is decreasing as younger the participant is.

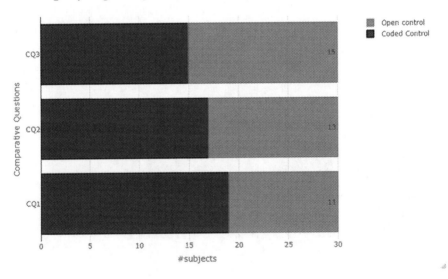

Fig. 11. Comparative question about the user's preferences between control modes. Q1: Which mode is the most comfortable for you to use?; Q2: Which mode presents a more efficient and fluid form of use?; Q3: Which mode gave you the most difficulty in making precise movements?

laterality index from the Edinburgh Handedness Inventory (EHI) and the time and number of gestures, where only for the time we found a significant value (r2 = 0.28, p-value = 0.02894). This finding indicates that, as was expected, the

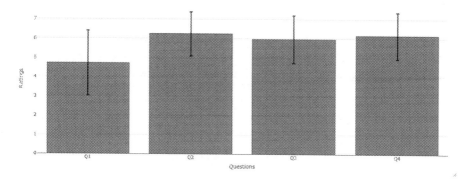

Fig. 12. Results from simulator perception survey (SPS). Q1: How easy is the use of the simulator?; Q2: How Understandable are the Instructions?; Q3: How is the Simulator working?; Q4: How aesthetically pleasing is the Simulator?. zero represents the worse value and seven the best.

Leap Motion is right-handedly dependent. However, extensive experiments with a balanced population between left and right-handed persons should be carried out to draw conclusive facts.

The above findings suggest that Leap Motion is a technology that could be used in different setups for robotic control. Moreover, it provides a natural way of interacting with machines since the hands are one of the most used modes to set up any device, and also it is very informative due to the large number of independent gestures created by the fingers and hand. Likewise, the possible implications of the control modes evaluated here range from the operator training for industrial manipulators, educational contexts, and social robot research that seeks to develop and study natural ways of interaction between humans and machines since the hand's gestures are one of the more intuitive modes of human communication, independently of the age. Indeed, that was one of the motivations for including an extensive range of ages in the experimentation; however, more studies should be carried out. Finally, new possible and complex control methods should be explored to improve the current findings in terms of precision and interaction. For example, including both hands could extend the number of control signals, expanding the control possibilities.

5   Conclusions

We created a simulator to compare two methods to control a robotic manipulator using a Leap Motion, a device to capturing and tracking hands movement. The open and coded modes use the hand's gesture to set up each joint angle to reach a specific pose. The coded mode recognizes number gestures to configure the angle value, while the open one only uses (counter)clockwise finger movement to increase or decrease the angle value. The difference between them lies in how these gestures are used. They shared the same interface and also the instructions to choose a specific joint.

Our findings suggest slight differences in the number of gestures and time, where coded control seems to have better results. However, no significance was reached. During the age evaluation, we found high variance for 40–47 years old in both modes, suggesting that older participants take more time to learn and execute while from 14 until 30 years, the performance is similar for both cases. Subjective analysis shows that the Coded control is the most preferred mode to reach work.

Our study is a step more towards the full inclusion of Leap Motion in robotic tasks since we use hands gestures to configure and control each joint individually instead of the complete robotic manipulator. While here we propose two alternatives to use such a device, several explorations and tasks should be done to evaluate Leap Motion's value in robotics deeply. Increasing the number of scenarios (tasks to be executed) and participants is mandatory to generalize the behavior presented here.

References

1. Robot Manipulators and Control Systems, pp. 35–107. Springer, US, Boston, MA (2007). https://doi.org/10.1007//978-0-387-23326-02
2. Ahmed, S., Popov, V., Topalov, A., Shakev, N.: Hand gesture based concept of human - mobile robot interaction with leap motion sensor. IFAC-PapersOnLine **52**(25), 321–326 (2019). https://doi.org/10.1016/j.ifacol.2019.12.543, https://www.sciencedirect.com/science/article/pii/S2405896319324620, 19th IFAC Conference on Technology, Culture and International Stability TECIS 2019
3. Bassily, D., Georgoulas, C., Guettler, J., Linner, T., Bock, T.: Intuitive and adaptive robotic arm manipulation using the leap motion controller. In: ISR/Robotik 2014; 41st International Symposium on Robotics, pp. 1–7 (2014)
4. Ben-Ari, M., Mondada, F.: Elements of Robotics. Springer, Cham (2018). https://doi.org/10.1007/978-3-319-62533-1
5. Chen, C., Chen, L., Zhou, X., Yan, W.: Controlling a robot using leap motion. In: 2017 2nd International Conference on Robotics and Automation Engineering (ICRAE), pp. 48–51 (2017). https://doi.org/10.1109/ICRAE.2017.8291351
6. Chen, S., Ma, H., Yang, C., Fu, M.: Hand gesture based robot control system using leap motion. In: Liu, H., Kubota, N., Zhu, X., Dillmann, R., Zhou, D. (eds.) ICIRA 2015. LNCS (LNAI), vol. 9244, pp. 581–591. Springer, Cham (2015). https://doi.org/10.1007/978-3-319-22879-2_53
7. Choi, H., et al.: On the use of simulation in robotics: opportunities, challenges, and suggestions for moving forward. In: Proceedings of the National Academy of Sciences, vol. 118, no. 1 (2021). https://doi.org/10.1073/pnas.1907856118, https://www.pnas.org/content/118/1/e1907856118
8. Fujii, K., Gras, G., Salerno, A., Yang, G.Z.: Gaze gesture based human robot interaction for laparoscopic surgery. Med. Image Anal. **44**, 196–214 (2018). https://doi.org/10.1016/j.media.2017.11.011, https://www.sciencedirect.com/science/article/pii/S1361841517301809
9. Galván-Ruiz, J., Travieso-González, C.M., Tejera-Fettmilch, A., Pinan-Roescher, A., Esteban-Hernández, L., Domínguez-Quintana, L.: Perspective and evolution of gesture recognition for sign language: a review. Sensors **20**(12) (2020). https://doi.org/10.3390/s20123571, https://www.mdpi.com/1424-8220/20/12/3571

10. Haseeb, M.A., Kyrarini, M., Jiang, S., Ristic-Durrant, D., Gräser, A.: Head gesture-based control for assistive robots. In: Proceedings of the 11th PErvasive Technologies Related to Assistive Environments Conference, pp. 379–383. PETRA 2018, Association for Computing Machinery, New York (2018). https://doi.org/10.1145/3197768.3201574, https://doi.org/10.1145/3197768.3201574

11. Marin, G., Dominio, F., Zanuttigh, P.: Hand gesture recognition with leap motion and kinect devices. In: 2014 IEEE International Conference on Image Processing (ICIP), pp. 1565–1569 (2014). https://doi.org/10.1109/ICIP.2014.7025313

12. Neto, P., Simão, M., Mendes, N., Safeea, M.: Gesture-based human-robot interaction for human assistance in manufacturing. Int. J. Adv. Manuf. Technol. **101**(1), 119–135 (2019). https://doi.org/10.1007/s00170-018-2788-x

13. Perumal, S.K.J., Ganesan, S.: Physical interaction and control of robotic systems using hardware-in-the-loop simulation. In: Basori, A.H., Shoushtari, A.L., Topalov, A.V. (eds.) Becoming Human with Humanoid, chap. 6. IntechOpen, Rijeka (2020). https://doi.org/10.5772/intechopen.85251

14. Pititeeraphab, Y., Choitkunnan, P., Thongpance, N., Kullathum, K., Pintavirooj, C.: Robot-arm control system using leap motion controller. In: 2016 International Conference on Biomedical Engineering (BME-HUST), pp. 109–112 (2016). https://doi.org/10.1109/BME-HUST.2016.7782091

15. Robots, U.: Universal robot ur3e. https://www.universal-robots.com/products/ur3-robot/ (2021). Accessed 11 Oct 2021

16. UltraLeap: Leap motion controller. https://www.ultraleap.com/product/leap-motion-controller/ (2021). Accessed 11 Oct 2021

17. Vysocký, A., et a;.: Analysis of precision and stability of hand tracking with leap motion sensor. Sensors **20**(15) (2020). https://doi.org/10.3390/s20154088, https://www.mdpi.com/1424-8220/20/15/4088

18. Weichert, F., Bachmann, D., Rudak, B., Fisseler, D.: Analysis of the accuracy and robustness of the leap motion controller. Sensors **13**(5), 6380–6393 (2013). https://doi.org/10.3390/s130506380, https://www.mdpi.com/1424-8220/13/5/6380

AI and ML Applied to Biomedical Sciences

Web Service Based Epileptic Seizure Detection by Applying Machine Learning Techniques

Pedro Augusto Araujo da Silva de Almeida Nava Alves[✉],
Alex Oliveira Barradas Filho, and Paulo Rogério de Almeida Ribeiro

Federal University of Maranhão, São Luís, MA 65080, Brazil
pedro.alves@darti.ufma.br

Abstract. Epilepsy is a neurological disorder characterized by the recurrence of epileptic seizures. Epileptic seizures are associated with abnormal electrical activity in the brain. Electroencephalogram (EEG) is a monitoring method that records the brain's electrical activity through electrodes placed on the scalp and is non-linear and dynamic in nature. Therefore, several studies were made to develop alternative approaches for the diagnosis of epileptic seizures. It is observed in the literature that the application of machine learning techniques yields satisfactory results for epileptic seizure detection. However, the researches obtained focused on the machine learning model developed rather than its applications on the real diagnosis. Therefore, in this study, we have proposed to train a machine learning model for epilepsy seizure detection and provide it as a web service through a Web API. We applied diverse machine learning methods such as Decision Trees, Logistic Regression, Support Vector Machines (SVM), and Multilayer Perceptron (MLP) and compared their results. We also applied different preprocessing methods such as Fourier Transform, Cosine Transform, Short-Term Fourier Transform, Wavelet Transform, and Wavelet Packet Decomposition, to find the best model to be used as a web service.

Keywords: Epileptic seizure detection · Frequency analysis · Machine learning · Web service

1 Introduction

Epilepsy is a neurological disorder caused by different etiologies and characterized by the occurrence of recurrent epileptic seizures [6]. Epileptic seizures have variable intensity and intervals, which can cause brief episodes or long periods of convulsion resulting in physical injuries [6]. This condition directly impairs the quality of life, as it has neurological, cognitive, psychological, and social consequences [6]

Epileptic seizures are associated with abnormal and excessive electrical activity in the brain [8]. The diagnosis of epileptic seizures involves consulting the

© Springer Nature Switzerland AG 2022
P. R. d. A. Ribeiro et al. (Eds.): LAWCN 2021, CCIS 1519, pp. 81–97, 2022.
https://doi.org/10.1007/978-3-031-08443-0_6

patient's medical history and identifying ictal or interictal discharges (IED) on the electroencephalogram (EEG) [14].

EEG is a non-invasive electrophysiological monitoring method that records brain electrical activity by placing electrodes in different positions on the scalp [10]. The EEG measures the voltage fluctuations over time that represent the brain activity in that region [10]. The EEG is considered a standard method to detect epilepsy due to its wide availability and low cost [6]. However, the EEG presents complex information of the patient, which provides long and error-prone analysis when performed manually [6].

This scenario has motivated the increase of alternative approaches for the diagnosis of epileptic seizures [1,14,17,23]. These methods extract linear and non-linear features in the frequency or time domain of the EEG signals. Then, these extracted features are used with machine learning techniques for automatic detection of epileptic seizures [2,10,19].

Even though there are several studies about the classification of epileptic seizures [8,10,14], it is necessary to share these models in order to make them more useful.

An approach that has been widely used to provide resources is a web service [3,11]. Web services can be an effective method to share developed classification models [22].

Thus, rather than provide another work on classification models for epileptic seizures, the present work aims to provide a classification system, through a Web API, that can be easily used for those who need to detect the seizures. Different preprocessed method were studied and applied in order to select the best approach. Diverse machine learning techniques were used to train several classification models, and the model with the best results was selected to be used in the web service. Then, with the classification model trained, this study provides a method to offer Epilepsy Seizure Classification as a web service. The goal of this work is to provide the web service as an instrument to be used by software engineers or any organization interested for real applications to be developed in this field.

This article is organized as follows: Sect. 2 describes the methodology used in this article, starting with the database obtained, the preprocessing methods used for the feature extraction, and the machine learning models trained to be used in the web service; Sect. 3 presents the results of the trained models, and the web service developed using the best model; and Sect. 4 covers the conclusion of this study.

2   Methodology

The method proposed in this work is represented in Fig. 1. It consists of: Acquire the database with the electroencephalograms; Preprocess the data based on a frequency domain analysis; Extract the features of the data; Develop the machine learning models; Select the best model and deploy it as a web service through a Rest API. Six Machine Learning methods were applied: K Nearest Neighbors,

Support Vector Machines, Decision Trees, Logistic Regression, Stochastic Gradient Descent Optimization, and Multilayer Perceptron Neural Network. Each method was optimized with hyperparameter tuning using grid search. Multiple models were trained with different hyperparameters combinations, and then evaluated using k-Fold cross-validation. Then, the model with the best hyperparameters was selected for each machine learning method. Also, five different preprocessing techniques were used resulting in five different datasets for each preprocessing method. So, each machine learning method was applied for each preprocessed dataset. The results are 25 models for each preprocessing and machine learning methods combination. The 25 models were further analyzed with classifications metrics and the best was selected for the web service. The dataset was divided in training dataset and test dataset before the grid search, to prevent bias of the hyperparameter tuning in the model selection. The training dataset was used in the grid search optimization, and the test dataset was used for the evaluation and model selection. The best model was then available trough a web-service Rest API.

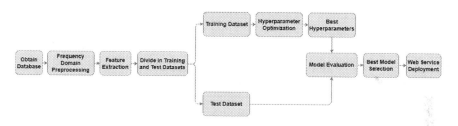

Fig. 1. Work flowchart

2.1   Database

The database was obtained from the electroencephalograms collected and made available by the *Temple University Hospital (TUH)* [12]. The available database contains 1947 recordings, with 571 classified with epileptic seizures and 1376 classified without epileptic seizures. Electroencephalogram signals were collected through electrodes placed on the scalp of patients at a sampling rate 250 Hz. The International System 10–20 was used, placing the 2 electrodes on the pre-frontal region(Fp); 5 electrodes on the frontal region (F); 4 electrodes on the temporal region (T); 3 electrodes on the parietal region (P); 3 electrodes on the central region (C); and 2 electrodes on the occipital region (O). The electroencephalogram signals are then available in EDF format (*European Data Format*) with the recordings of the 19 channels of the performed electroencephalogram.

2.2   Preprocessing

The database was preprocessed to extract the features used in the model training. The *delta, theta, alpha, beta* and *gamma* brain waves were extracted from each channel of the electroencephalogram [4,17]. A band-pass filter was applied at the intervals: 0.5 Hz to 4 Hz, 4 Hz to 8 Hz, 8 Hz to 12 Hz, 12 Hz to 35 Hz and 35 Hz to 100 Hz. Subsequently, five frequency domain analysis techniques were applied: Fourier transform, Cosine transform, Short Term Fourier Transform, Wavelet Transform, and Wavelet Packets Decomposition.

Fourier Transform
The Fourier transform is an operation that decomposes a temporal function $f(t)$ in the frequency spectrum using the following formula:

$$F(\xi) = \int_{-\infty}^{\infty} f(t) \cdot e^{-2\pi i \xi t} dt \tag{1}$$

The result of the operation is a complex function $F(\xi)$ whose absolute value represents the amount of frequency ξ present in the original function. For discrete signals such as the digital signals of the electroencephalogram, the discrete fourier transform is applied, represented by the following formula:

$$X_k = \sum_{n=0}^{N-1} x[n] \cdot e^{-\frac{2\pi i}{N} kn} \tag{2}$$

The result is a vector $\{X_k\} := X_0, X_1, ..., X_{N-1}$ with each position being a complex number that encodes both amplitude and phase of the sinusoidal component representing the frequency domain. As the electroencephalogram signal has a sampling rate of $250 Hz$, the absolute value of each position of the vector indicates the amount of frequency $N \cdot 0.004\ Hz$ present in the original signal.

Cossine Transform
In the Cosine transform, a variation of the Fourier transform is applied, in which only the cosine of the Euler formula is used, defined by the formula:

$$F(\nu) = \int_{-\infty}^{\infty} f(t) \cdot cos(-2\pi\nu t) dt \tag{3}$$

The discrete Cosine transform is defined equal to the discrete Fourier transform. It obtains only real components of the frequency domain, so is computationally more efficient.

Short-Term Fourier Transform
The Short-Term Fourier Transform (STF) is a non-stationary derivation of the Fourier Transform. The frequency spectrum obtained by this transform varies with time and is therefore non-stationary. This technique consists of applying the fourier transform at different times in the original signal, called short terms.

The Short Term Fourier Transform maps a real one-dimensional function, or signal, to a complex two-dimensional function in the frequency spectrum and its temporal location. The temporal localization is obtained using a windowing function $g(\tau)$, which extracts the short term of the signal in the time interval τ. Thus, the formula including the windowing function becomes:

$$F(\xi, \tau) = \int_{-\infty}^{\infty} f(t)g(t - \tau) \cdot e^{-2\pi i \xi t} dt \tag{4}$$

The result of the transform is the frequency spectrum obtained by the Fourier Transform, in a short time interval of the original function defined by the windowing function $g(\tau)$.

For digital signals, the discrete version of the Short Term Fourier Transform is also used. The Discrete Fourier Transform is also applied to the digital signal in different short terms of the signal using a discrete windowing function $h[t]$. The Short Term Discrete Fourier Transform formula becomes:

$$X_{k,m} = \sum_{n=0}^{N-1} x[n]h[n - m] \cdot e^{-\frac{2\pi i}{N} kn} \tag{5}$$

The result of the transform is a complex matrix with each line representing time interval component, and each column representing the frequency spectrum.

Wavelet Transform
The wavelet transform is defined by the inner product between the input function and the wavelet function after a scale factor a and shift factor b, denoted by the following formula:

$$F(a, b) = \frac{1}{\sqrt{|a|}} \int_{-\infty}^{\infty} \overline{\psi\left(\frac{x - b}{a}\right)} \cdot f(x) dx \tag{6}$$

The scaling and shift factors (a and b) allow to obtain information about the original signal at high and low frequencies, and at different moments of the signal. The wavelet function ψ is used as an impulse applied to the system represented by the original signal [15].

The discrete wavelet transform is used for digital signals. In the discrete wavelet transform, the scaling factor a is defined in discrete values of $a_j = 2^j$. The shift factor is also defined in discrete values of $b_j = 2^j k$. The discrete wavelet transform algorithm divides the process into $n = log_2(N)$ levels. At each level j, a low-pass and high-pass filter is applied at the $y_{j-1}[k]$ output signal from the previous level, according to the formulas 7 and 8

$$y_{low} = \sum_{k=-\infty}^{\infty} x[k] \cdot g[2n - k] \tag{7}$$

$$y_{high} = \sum_{k=-\infty}^{\infty} x[k] \cdot h[2n - k] \tag{8}$$

The $h[t]$ is the impulse function of the high-pass filter defined by the wavelet with discrete values, represented by formula 9, and g[t] its quadrature mirror filter. The discrete coefficients y_{high}, also called detailed components, have only half the frequencies for the level j and it is the output of the wavelet transform for the level j. The discrete coefficients y_{low}, also called approximate components, have the other half of the frequencies. The components are then recursively passed to the algorithm for the nexe level $j+1$. Thus, the transform calculates the detailed and approximate components at each level, and pass the approximate components to calculate the components of the next level. The final discrete Wavelet transform is formed by the set of all detailed components generated at each level with approximate component generated at the last level, resulting in $n + 1$ coefficients.

$$h[t] = \frac{1}{\sqrt{2^j}} \cdot \psi \left(\frac{-t}{2^j} \right), t = 1, 2^j, 2^{2j}, ..., 2^N \tag{9}$$

Wavelet Packet Decomposition

Wavelet Packet Decomposition is a variation of the Wavelet Discrete Transform where more filters are applied to the signal in the algorithm for calculating the coefficients. When calculating the Wavelet Transform, the detailed components are the final results of the transform, while the approximate components are used to calculate the coefficients for the next level. In Wavelet Packet Decomposition, both detailed and approximate components are passed to the next level, generating 2 branches in the recursion for each component as the input. So, the algorithm grows exponentially with 2^n coefficients while the Wavelet transform has $n + 1$ coefficients.

2.3   Feature Extraction

After extracting the five brainwaves intervals for each of the 19 channels, 95 waves were obtained for each electroencephalogram. Then, the preprocessing method was applied on the signals extracted for each of the five preprocessing methods. Thus, five different datasets were obtained for the frequency domain analysis of each method. The Features of the dataset were extracted by calculating five statistical characteristics: Average Value, Standard Deviation, Average Energy, Average Absolute Value, Skewness [20]. These features are respectively defined on the following formulas:

$$\mu = \frac{1}{N} \sum_{k=0}^{N-1} x[k] \tag{10}$$

$$\sigma = \sqrt{\frac{1}{N-1} \sum_{k=0}^{N-1} (x[k] - \mu)^2} \tag{11}$$

$$AE = \frac{1}{N} \sum_{k=0}^{N-1} (x[k])^2 \tag{12}$$

$$AAV = \frac{1}{N} \sum_{k=0}^{N-1} |x[k]| \tag{13}$$

$$S = \frac{\sum_{k=0}^{N-1}(x[k] - \mu)^3}{N * \sigma^3} \tag{14}$$

Each electroencephalogram is transformed into 95 signals by applying the frequency analysis preprocessing method. After extracting the five statistical features, each electroencephalogram is then encoded as 475 final features. So, five datasets are obtained with 1947 samples and 475 features, 1 for each preprocessing method.

2.4   Machine Learning

The database has a total of 1947 samples, with 571 classified with epileptic seizures and 1376 without. Since database is unbalanced, the total samples used were reduced to balance it [5]. 571 samples were randomly selected from the class without epileptic seizures, resulting in a total of 1142 samples used. Also, each dataset was divided in training and test dataset, to avoid a bias during the selection of the best optimized model. 80% of the dataset was used as the training dataset, and 20% as the test dataset. The training dataset was used in the hyperparameter optimization, and the test dataset used to evaluate the best model of the optimization.

Different models were developed and evaluated to obtain the most efficient model. Each machine learning method was optimized by tuning its hyperparameters to obtain the model with the best result. The method used for optimization was the grid search [7,21]. The method consists of selecting the possible values of each hyperparameter. Then, for each combination of the hyperparameters values, models are trained and evaluated to select the best hyperparameter combination. To select the best hyperparameter during the optimization, k-fold cross-validation [13,16,24] was used with $k = 10$. The k-Fold consists of further splitting the training dataset into k partitions, with $k - 1$ used for training, and 1 for testing. The partition used for testing is permuted so all k partitions are used at least 1 time for testing, and therefore, used $k - 1$ times for training. Finally, k models are trained and the evaluation metrics are calculated for each fold. The evaluation of the hyperparameter combination is the average of the folds metrics. For the best hyperparameter selection, the accuracy metric was used, defined by the formula 17.

After the optimization, the best hyperparameters values was selected for each machine learning method and preprocessing dataset. Then, a model was trained with the hyperparameters values on the whole training dataset. Finally, each model was evaluated on the test dataset, using the classification metrics: precision, sensitivity, accuracy, and F1-Score. The classification metrics are defined by the formulas 15, 16, 17, and 18.

$$precision = \frac{TP}{TP + FP} \tag{15}$$

$$sensitivity = \frac{TP}{TP + FN} \tag{16}$$

$$accuracy = \frac{TP + TN}{TP + FP + TN + FN} \tag{17}$$

$$F_1 = \frac{2TP}{2TP + FP + FN} \tag{18}$$

The metrics uses the confusion matrix [18] calculated. The TP, TN, FN and FP values used in the formula represents the true-positive, true-negative, false-negative and false-positive values respectively of the confusion matrix. With the metrics evaluation, the results were compared to select the best models between the techniques. To select the final model, the bayesian information criterion (BIC) was calculated for the best models, since it can be used for model selection[9]. The BIC is represented by the formula 19. In the formula, k represents the model parameters, n is the number of samples in the data, and $\hat{L}$ is the model likelihood, or in this case, its evaluation metric. Thus, the final model was selected to be used in the web service.

$$BIC = k \cdot ln(n) - 2ln(\hat{L}) \tag{19}$$

2.5   Web Service

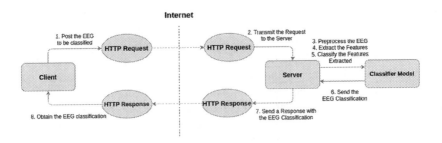

Fig. 2. Web service architecture

After the best model has been selected, it was deployed as a web service. The web service architecture used was REST (Representational State Transfer). Since the models developed were training and saved using the programming language Python, the service was also deployed in Python. The library used to handle the HTTP request was Flask. The library handles the GET, POST, PUT, and DELETE HTTP requests, which form the main REST operations. The web service was then developed to handle those HTTP requests contained the client electroencephalogram, as well as send a response to the client via HTTP with the model classification prediction. The process of EEG seizure classification prediction via the web service is represented by the Fig. 2

3 Results

3.1 Model Optimization

The machine learning techniques used were: Support Vector Machine (SVM), Logistic Regression, Decision Trees, K Nearest Neighbor (KNN), Multilayer Perceptron Neural Networks (MLP), and Stochastic Descending Gradient Optimization (SGD). Each machine learning method was applied in each preprocessing dataset. The hyperparameters were optimized with the accuracy metric used as best hyperparameter selection. The results of the optimization for each machine learning method per dataset are represented by Table 1, 2, 3, 4, 5 and 6. Each row presents the 5 best models for each preprocessing method column, with the best results in bold.

Table 1. KNN optimization

Fourier	Cosine	STF	Wavelet	Wavelet packet
77.0831%	77.4104%	76.4226%	**78.9465%**	**80.2628%**
73.9047%	77.1859%	74.3442%	78.1808%	79.6046%
73.5702%	76.9709%	73.9142%	78.1713%	79.0612%
73.458%	75.3249%	70.5112%	77.4128%	78.2895%
71.3784%	74.2379%	67.6469%	75.8696%	77.0855%

Table 2. SVM optimization

Fourier	Cosine	STF	Wavelet	Wavelet packet
51.4238%	**51.8645%**	**51.2076%**	**51.9709%**	**51.7559%**
51.4238%	51.757%	51.0977%	51.7547%	51.0977%
51.3151%	51.4262%	50.989%	51.5337%	51.0977%
51.3139%	51.3151%	50.989%	51.5337%	51.0965%
51.2052%	51.2076%	50.9878%	51.3151%	51.0965%

The results for the Support Vector Machine are close regardless of the preprocessed dataset used. The results of K Nearest Neighbors, Logistic Regression and

Table 3. MLP optimization

Fourier	Cosine	STF	Wavelet	Wavelet packet
74.6751%	76.4178%	75.7561%	**79.5975%**	**78.5069%**
74.447%	76.0882%	74.232%	79.2726%	77.9443%
74.3383%	75.7561%	74.0002%	78.397%	77.8488%
74.005%	75.3237%	69.6166%	77.3041%	76.9685%
72.4701%	74.0158%	69.0743%	76.8705%	76.8669%

Table 4. Logistic regression optimization

Fourier	Cosine	STF	Wavelet	Wavelet packet
68.0948%	66.9828%	67.8655%	**70.0669%**	**71.8156%**
68.0948%	66.8813%	67.7556%	69.0815%	71.1538%
67.7676%	66.8765%	67.3184%	69.0815%	70.8242%
58.4353%	62.9419%	63.1558%	64.478%	62.9443%
58.4353%	62.6099%	63.0471%	63.9298%	62.7222%

Multilayer Perceptron Neural Networks have an increase between 3% and 5% for the Wavelet Transform and Wavelet Packet Decomposition datasets. The results of Stochastic Gradient Descent Optimization were higher for the Fourier Transform and Short Term Fourier transform, while the results for Decision Tree were higher only for the Short Term Fourier Transform. The methods that obtained the best results were Decision Trees, Multilayer Perceptron Neural Networks and K Nearest Neighbors, with best values close to 80%. The Logistic Regression also obtained close results, with best values around 70%. Both Support Vector Machines and Stochastic Gradient Descendant Optimization obtained the worst results, with best values close 55%.

Table 5. SGD optimization

Fourier	Cosine	STF	Wavelet	Wavelet packet
59.9737%	52.629%	**58.7733%**	56.5815%	53.4245%
59.7611%	51.9709%	57.1249%	55.2699%	53.4161%
59.1042%	50.6605%	55.1517%	54.0576%	52.4283%
58.9623%	50.2263%	54.6141%	53.4136%	52.1691%
58.8429%	49.5215%	53.973%	52.6136%	52.0619%

Table 6. Decision Tree Optimization

Fourier	Cosine	STF	Wavelet	Wavelet packet
75.9974%	75%	**79.3968%**	73.5738%	74.4505%
75.6677%	74.8901%	78.7339%	73.2465%	74.2284%
75.6677%	74.6715%	78.5165%	73.1378%	74.1245%
75.4479%	74.5604%	78.4066%	73.1366%	73.9011%
75.0084%	74.4577%	78.2979%	73.0339%	73.5702%

3.2   Model Selection

The best model of each machine learning method and each preprocessing dataset were evaluated using the other classification metrics in the test dataset and their results are represented by Fig. 3, 4, 5 and 6. The K Nearest Neighbors had the best results for the precision metric, but had low results for the recall, and therefore low values for F1 score as well. The Support Vector Machine had the best values for recall with almost 100% for all preprocessing methods, but the worst values for the other metrics. The models with the best results for all the metrics were the Multilayer Perceptron Neural Network for the Cosine Transform and Wavelet Transform preprocessing methods with least 80% for all 4 metrics. Thus, the BIC was calculated for the both methods using the F1 and accuracy metric, since they both use all of the confusion matrix. Since the BIC for the MLP with the Wavelet Transform was higher than the MLP with the Cosine transform, it was selected to be used in the web service.

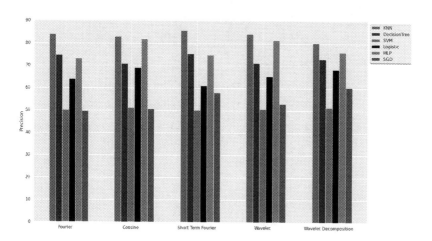

Fig. 3. Precision results

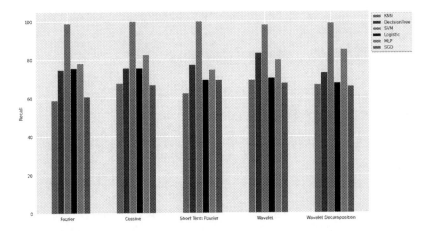

Fig. 4. Recall results

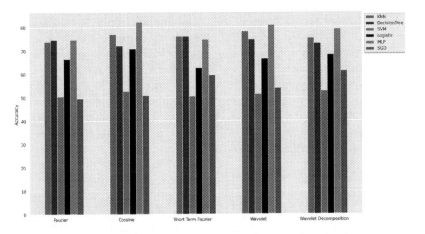

Fig. 5. Accuracy results

Even though the best model was evaluated with the classification metrics around 80%, it can be improved with other approaches. In [10] a model was developed with 94.2% of accuracy through features extracted with Principal Component Analysis applied to the time domain. In [23], the authors achieved 88.3% of accuracy in a multi-class classification using pre-trained convolutional networks for feature extraction. The work in [17] developed a model with 82.5% accuracy, using Filter Bank Common Spatial Pattern (FBCSP) for feature extraction in the Motor Imagery EEGs, with accuracy close to the present work. In [14], a new method for classification using fractional linear prediction was used achieving 95.33% of accuracy.

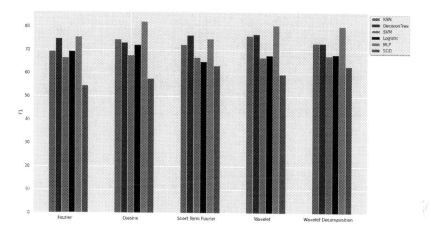

Fig. 6. F1 Score results

3.3 Web Service

After the best model was selected, it was deployed as web service via a REST API. The methods and urls handled by the API are described in Table 7. The API offers information about the service itself, and the model used trough GET operations. The API handles a POST operation for the prediction with the EEG data as an EDF file. Attached to the POST, the user sends the binary data of the EDF file to be processed by the service and passed to the model. When the web service receives a POST with the EEG, it preprocess and extract the features based on the selected model preprocessing method. The features are passed to the selected model for the classification. The service then sends a HTTP Response with the prediction of seizure detection.

Table 7. Web services URL descriptions

Method	URL	Description
GET	/	General description of the web service
GET	/Model	Contains the details of the model used for the prediction
GET	/Model/Metrics	Contains the evaluation metrics of the model
GET	/Model/Predict	Contains the details of the EEG to be sent as .edf file for seizure detection prediction
POST	/Predict	Predict epilepsy seizure on the EEG data posted

The web service API was developed in a local machine. To test the seizure detection prediction, cURL, a command line tool, was used to send the HTTP

Fig. 7. EEG prediction with seizure detected

request. The usage of the web service with the cURL is represented by Fig. 7 and 8.

Fig. 8. EEG prediction with no seizure detected

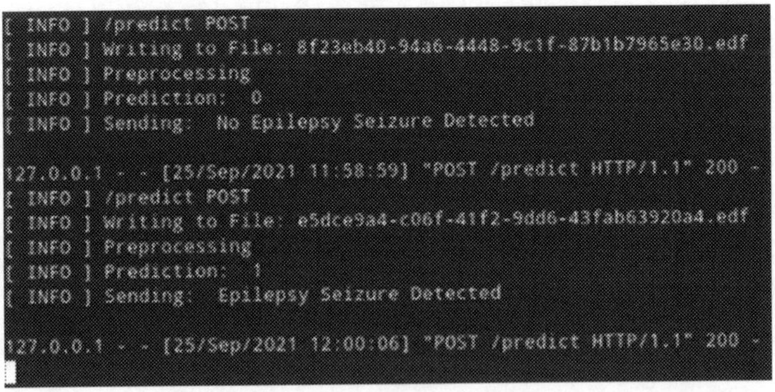

Fig. 9. Web service running

A POST HTTP request was sent to the server to detect epilepsy seizure on the EEG represented by the EDF files sent. The server showed by the Fig. 9 receives the EEG data, preprocess the data, and pass it to the machine learning model, as proposed on Fig. 2. The server send the prediction as a HTTP response, as previously demonstrated (Fig. 7 and 8).

Even though the web service offers a simple Rest API, it can be used as a middleware for the detection of epileptic seizure in EEG's. The simple architecture of the Rest API offers a straightforward communication for the classification of EEG's which can be used on different levels of abstraction and types of systems requiring the web service. However, the API is not scalable for more complex systems using the web service, which can be adjusted but modifying the API to be used in computer clusters depending of the type of the system.

4 Conclusion

This work applied some of the principal methods of machine learning techniques and frequency domain analysis to develop a classifier model of epileptic seizures in electroencephalogram. Five different preprocessing methods were used to compare the results: Fourier Transform, Cosine Transform, Short Term Fourier Transform, Wavelet Transform, and Wavelet Packet Decomposition. After their features extracted, six Machine Learning methods were applied: K Nearest Neighbors, Support Vector Machines, Decision Trees, Logistic Regression, Stochastic Gradient Descent Optimization, and Multilayer Perceptron Neural Network. The best model developed was then selected to be used as the classifier deployed as web service. The model was deployed trough a REST API, to handle HTTP Requests with electroencephalogram data. The web service developed can be used as a method to classify electroencephalogram with the developed model. Thus, it is a possible way to make available classification models for epilepsy seizures.

Even though the developed model achieved satisfactory results, as stated in the previous section, it can be improved by using the more complex preprocessing and feature extraction methods used in the previous cited works. However, the goal of this research was accomplished by successfully deploying a epilepsy seizure classification model as a web service. Thus, it suggests that a web service can be a valid method to deploy the classification models for possible systems interested in seizure detection via the web service as middleware.

References

1. Acharya, U.R., Subbhuraam, V.S., Ang, P., Yanti, R., Suri, J.: Application of non-linear and wavelet based features for the automated identification of epileptic EEG signals. Int. J. Neural Syst. **22**, 1250002 (2012). https://doi.org/10.1142/S0129065712500025
2. Adeli, H., Zhou, Z., Dadmehr, N.: Analysis of EEG records in an epileptic patient using wavelet transform. J. Neurosci. Methods **123**(1), 69–87 (2003)
3. AlShahwan, F., Moessner, K., Carrez, F.: Distribute provision strategies of restful-based mobile web services. In: 2011 IEEE Global Telecommunications Conference - GLOBECOM 2011, pp. 1–6 (2011). https://doi.org/10.1109/GLOCOM.2011.6133992

4. Amorim, E., et al.: Quantitative EEG reactivity and machine learning for prognostication in hypoxic-ischemic brain injury. Clin. Neurophysiol. **130**(10), 1908–1916 (2019)

5. Bao, L., Juan, C., Li, J., Zhang, Y.: Boosted near-miss under-sampling on SVM ensembles for concept detection in large-scale imbalanced datasets. Neurocomputing **172**, 198–206 (2016). https://doi.org/10.1016/j.neucom.2014.05.096, https://www.sciencedirect.com/science/article/pii/S0925231215006098

6. Chang, B.S., Lowenstein, D.H.: Mechanisms of disease. New Engl. J. Med. **349**, 1257–1266 (2003)

7. Chen, H., Liu, Z., Cai, K., Xu, L., Chen, A.: Grid search parametric optimization for FT-NIR quantitative analysis of solid soluble content in strawberry samples. Vib. Spectrosc. **94**, 7–15 (2018). https://doi.org/10.1016/j.vibspec.2017.10.006, https://www.sciencedirect.com/science/article/pii/S0924203117301030

8. Chisci, L.: Real-time epileptic seizure prediction using AR models and support vector machines. IEEE Trans. Biomed. Eng. **57**(5), 1124–1132 (2010). https://doi.org/10.1109/TBME.2009.2038990

9. Ding, J., Tarokh, V., Yang, Y.: Model selection techniques: an overview. IEEE Sig. Process. Mag. **35**(6), 16–34 (2018). https://doi.org/10.1109/MSP.2018.2867638

10. Duan, L., Bao, M., Miao, J., Xu, Y., Chen, J.: Classification based on multilayer extreme learning machine for motor imagery task from EEG signals. Procedia Comput. Sci. **88**, 176–184 (2016)

11. Fensel, D., Bussler, C.: The web service modeling framework WSMF. Electron. Commer. Res. Appl. **1**(2), 113–137 (2002). https://doi.org/10.1016/S1567-4223(02)00015-7, https://www.sciencedirect.com/science/article/pii/S1567422302000157

12. Harati, A., Choi, S., Tabrizi, M., Obeid, I., Picone, J., Jacobson, M.: The temple university hospital EEG corpus, pp. 29–32, December 2013. https://doi.org/10.1109/GlobalSIP.2013.6736803

13. Jiang, G., Wang, W.: Error estimation based on variance analysis of k-fold cross-validation. Pattern Recogn. **69**, 94–106 (2017). https://doi.org/10.1016/j.patcog.2017.03.025, https://www.sciencedirect.com/science/article/pii/S003132031730136X

14. Joshi, V., Pachori, R.B., Vijesh, A.: Classification of ictal and seizure-free EEG signals using fractional linear prediction. Biomed. Sig. Process. Control **9**, 1–5 (2014). https://doi.org/10.1016/j.bspc.2013.08.006, https://www.sciencedirect.com/science/article/pii/S1746809413001195

15. Junsheng, C., Dejie, Y., Yu, Y.: Application of an impulse response wavelet to fault diagnosis of rolling bearings. Mech. Syst. Sig. Process. **21** (2007). https://doi.org/10.1016/j.ymssp.2005.09.014

16. Ling, H., Qian, C., Kang, W., Liang, C., Chen, H.: Combination of support vector machine and k-fold cross validation to predict compressive strength of concrete in marine environment. Constr. Build. Mater. **206**, 355–363 (2019). https://doi.org/10.1016/j.conbuildmat.2019.02.071, https://www.sciencedirect.com/science/article/pii/S0950061819303666

17. Luo, J., Gao, X., Zhu, X., Wang, B., Lu, N., Wang, J.: Motor imagery EEG classification based on ensemble support vector learning. Comput. Methods Program. Biomed. **193**, 105464 (2020)

18. Luque, A., Carrasco, A., Martín, A., de las Heras, A.: The impact of class imbalance in classification performance metrics based on the binary confusion matrix. Pattern Recogn. **91**, 216–231 (2019). https://doi.org/10.1016/j.patcog.2019.02.023, https://www.sciencedirect.com/science/article/pii/S0031320319300950

19. Malmivuo, J., Plonsey, R.: Bioelectromagnetism. 13. Electroencephalography, pp. 247–264, January 1995
20. Patil, P.N., Patil, P.P., Bagkavos, D.: A measure of asymmetry. Stat. Pap. **53**(4), 971–985 (2012). https://doi.org/10.1007/s00362-011-0401-6
21. Pontes, F., Amorim, G., Balestrassi, P., Paiva, A., Ferreira, J.: Design of experiments and focused grid search for neural network parameter optimization. Neurocomputing **186**, 22–34 (2016). https://doi.org/10.1016/j.neucom.2015.12.061, https://www.sciencedirect.com/science/article/pii/S0925231215020184
22. Prusti, D., Rath, S.K.: Web service based credit card fraud detection by applying machine learning techniques. In: TENCON 2019–2019 IEEE Region 10 Conference (TENCON), pp. 492–497 (2019). https://doi.org/10.1109/TENCON.2019.8929372
23. Raghu, S., Sriraam, N., Temel, Y., Shyam Vasudeva Rao, P.L.K.: EEG based multi-class seizure type classification using convolutional neural network and transfer learning. Neural Netw. **124**, 202–212 (2020)
24. Xiong, Z., Cui, Y., Liu, Z., Zhao, Y., Hu, M., Hu, J.: Evaluating explorative prediction power of machine learning algorithms for materials discovery using k-fold forward cross-validation. Computational Mater. Sci. **171**, 109203 (2020). https://doi.org/10.1016/j.commatsci.2019.109203, https://www.sciencedirect.com/science/article/pii/S0927025619305026

Health Issues and Computational Neuroscience

Machine Learning Search of Novel Selective NaV1.2 and NaV1.6 Inhibitors as Potential Treatment Against Dravet Syndrome

Maximiliano Fallico[1,2] (ID), Lucas N. Alberca[1,2,3] (ID), Denis N. Prada Gori[1,2] (ID), Luciana Gavernet[1,2] (ID), and Alan Talevi[1,2(✉)] (ID)

[1] Laboratory of Bioactive Research and Development (LIDeB), Faculty of Exact Sciences, National University of La Plata (UNLP), 47 and 115, B1900AKN La Plata, Buenos Aires, Argentina
alantalevi@gmail.com
[2] Consejo Nacional de Investigaciones Científicas y Técnicas (CONICET), CCT La Plata, La Plata, Buenos Aires, Argentina
[3] Laboratorio de Señalización y Mecanismos Adaptativos en Tripanosomátidos, Instituto de Investigaciones en Ingeniería Genética y Biología Molecular (INGEBI), Buenos Aires, Argentina

Abstract. Dravet syndrome is a type of drug-resistant and devastating childhood epilepsy, which begins in the first year of life. Etiologically, it is most frequently associated with loss-of-function *de novo* mutations in the gene SCN1A, which encodes for the NaV1.1 channel, a voltage-operated sodium channel highly expressed in inhibitory GABAergic interneurons. Dysfunction of this channel causes global hyperexcitability. Whereas exacerbation of seizures in Dravet patients has been observed after the administration of voltage-operated sodium channel blockers with low or no selectivity towards specific channel subtypes, recent preclinical evidence suggests that highly selective blockade of sodium channels other than NaV1.1 or the selective activation of NaV1.1 could correct the Dravet phenotype.

Here, we report the development and validation of ligand-based computational models for the identification of selective NaV1.2 or NaV1.6 with no inhibitory effect on NaV1.1. The models have been jointly applied to screen the chemical library of the DrugBank 5.1.8 database, in order to select starting points for the development of specific drugs against Dravet syndrome. The ligand-based models were built using free software for molecular descriptor calculation (Mordred) in combination with in-house Python scripts. Training data was retrieved from ChemBL and specialized literature, and representatively sampled using an in-house clustering procedure (*RaPCA*). Linear classifiers were generated using a combination of the random subspace method (feature bagging) and forward stepwise. Later, ensemble learning was used to obtain meta-classifiers, which were validated in retrospective screening experiments before their use in the final, prospective screen.

Keywords: Dravet syndrome · Selective sodium channel blockers · NaV1.1 · NaV1.2 · NaV1.6 · Epilepsy · Virtual screening · In silico screening

P. R. d. A. Ribeiro et al. (Eds.): LAWCN 2021, CCIS 1519, pp. 101–118, 2022.
https://doi.org/10.1007/978-3-031-08443-0_7

1 Introduction

Dravet syndrome, previously known as severe myoclonic epilepsy of infancy, is a dev-astating and drug-resistant type of epilepsy that manifests in the first year of life; it is associated with ataxia, severe cognitive disability, deficit in social interaction, and altered circadian rhythm [1, 2]. The disease usually begins around 6 months of age, with seizures triggered by temperature (fever, hot weather, a hot bath), after which seizures become progressively more frequent and severe. Even with access to the most modern diagnostic and care techniques, 15% of Dravet patients die before reaching adolescence [1]. It is a rare disorder, with an incidence of about 1 in 16,000 to 40,000 children born in high-income countries [3, 4] and it has been included in the list of rare disorders of the Genetic and Rare Diseases Information Center of the United States (https://rarediseases.info.nih.gov/diseases). Such disorders, due to their low incidence and low investment return, usually require the intervention of public agencies and non-profit organizations to develop new diagnostic tools and specific therapeutic solutions, as reflected by the recent creation of international consortia and programs with these objectives, e.g., the Rare Diseases Program of the Food and Drug Administration (FDA) or the International Rare Diseases Research Consortium [5].

The etiology of Dravet syndrome is associated in most cases to heterozygous loss of function of the NaV1.1 channel, due to deletion or loss of functionality caused by de novo mutations of the SCN1A gene [6, 7]. Dysfunction of NaV1.1, which is highly expressed in inhibitory GABAergic interneurons, causes global hyperexcitability. This phenotype is predictably worsened by administration of voltage-operated sodium channel blockers with low or no selectivity towards specific channel subtypes such as phenytoin, oxcarbazepine or lamotrigine, which are contraindicated [8–10]. However, recent preclinical evidence in animal models of Dravet suggests that highly selective blockade of sodium channels other than NaV1.1 or, alternatively, the selective activation of NaV1.1 could correct the Dravet phenotype [11, 12].

Although challenging due to the similarity of the drug-binding sites of the different channel subtypes, achieving high selectivity in sodium channel blockers is feasible, as proven by the recent success in the development of small molecules capable of selectively inhibiting the NaV1.7 subtype, with great potential as analgesics and neuropathic pain treatments [13–15]. Clinical trials of several such selective NaV1.7 blockers are currently underway, including Pfizer's PF-05089771 (which successfully completed phase II studies), or GDC-276 and GDC-0310 (Xenon Pharmaceuticals). Based on this premise, here we have implemented in silico screening campaigns to identify selective NaV1.2 or NaV1.6 blockers, with no predicted inhibitory activity on NaV1.1. For such purposes, we have trained and validated ligand-based meta-classifiers capable of identifying blocking agents of NaV1.1, NaV1.2, and NaV1.6. NaV1.2 and NaV1.6 were then used as drug targets, whereas NaV1.1 was used as anti-target. All the models have been developed based on freely available software and in-house scripts, assuring their portability.

2 Methods

2.1 Dataset Collection, Curation, and Labeling

Three datasets consisting of compounds with blocking properties on NaV1.1, NaV1.2 and/or NaV1.6 were extracted from ChEMBL (https://www.ebi.ac.uk/chembl/). Only compounds with reported single point activity data or IC_{50} measured against the alpha subunit of human sodium channels were considered. In the case of NaV1.1 and NaV1.6, owing to the scarcity of data, this search was complemented with data from specialized literature (the list of papers from which compounds were extracted is presented as Supplementary Material). Literature search was performed in Scopus (https://www.scopus.com/) using the following keywords and Booleans: "Sodium channel" AND/OR "NaV1.1" AND/OR "Nav1.6" AND/OR "SCN1A" AND/OR "SCN8A" AND/OR "inhibition" AND/OR "inhibitor" AND/OR "patch clamp" AND/OR "epilepsy" AND/OR "anticonvulsive". Duplicated data were removed. ChEMBL data were further curated by removing compounds with anomalous/atypical activity data or with data which were not extracted from journals. Toxins and compounds with molecular weight above 1 kDa were also excluded, as the focus of the models would be small, drug-like molecules. Since only conformation-independent molecular descriptors would be included in the models, when data from optical isomers were reported, only one of them was kept whenever both isomers belonged to the same activity class, and the compounds were disregarded if the isomers belonged to different activity classes.

2D molecular representations were standardized using the standardization tool MolVS, written using the RDKit chemistry framework (https://molvs.readthedocs.io/en/latest/). Sets of 91, 167, and 91 compounds survived the curation steps for NaV1.1, NaV1.2 and NaV1.6, respectively. Compounds with $IC_{50} < 10\ \mu M$ or with percentage of inhibition above 50% at $10\ \mu M$ (or at lower concentrations) were labelled as ACTIVE compounds. Otherwise, they were labelled as INACTIVE compounds. The composition of the three datasets is shown in Table 1.

Table 1. Composition of the NaV1.1, NaV1.2 and NaV1.6 datasets.

	NaV1.1	NaV1.2	NaV1.6
Active	44	112	39
Inactive	47	55	52

The molecular diversity of the entire dataset, as well as within and between each category of compounds can be visually appreciated in the heatmap displayed in Fig. 1, which shows, for every channel and every compound pair, the Tanimoto distance computed using Morgan fingerprints. The three datasets are provided as Supplementary Material in.csv format.

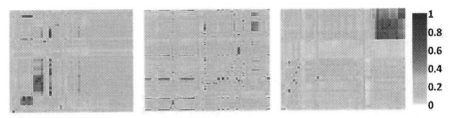

Fig. 1. The heatmaps illustrate the molecular diversity of the datasets, with blue bits corresponding to similar compounds pairs and pale-yellow bits corresponding to dissimilar compounds pairs. NaV1.1 (left), NaV1.2 (middle), NaV1.6 (right).

2.2 Dataset Partitioning into Training and Test Sets

It has been reiteratively observed that representative partitioning of datasets into training and test sets tends to yield better results in the validation stage(s) [16–18]. In the current study, thus, an in-house representative sampling procedure was used to split the datasets into a training set that was used to infer the models and a test set that was used to independently assess the models' performance (i.e., their predictive power). The approach, which we called RaPCA, is based on a combination of the random subspace approach (feature bagging, which stochastically explores random subsets of the features), and Principal Component Analysis (PCA) for feature reduction purposes: PCA extracts a sequence of p unit vectors, where the ith vector corresponds to the direction of a line that best fits the data in the correspondent feature subspace while being orthogonal to the first $i-1$ vectors.

The active and inactive compounds within each dataset are clustered separately, 1612 molecular descriptors were calculated with Mordred 1.2.0 [19]. Molecular descriptors with low information content (variance below 0.05) were removed. 1000 subsets of 200 descriptors each were randomly generated, and redundant molecular descriptors (Pearson correlation coefficient above 0.4) were removed. From the resulting feature subsets, only those consisting of 10–20 descriptors were kept, and the two principal components were computed. The k-means clustering procedure was then applied, systematically varying the number of k clusters between 2 and 20 and computing the silhouette coefficient [20] for every k value. The clustering scheme corresponding to the highest value of the silhouette coefficient was selected. A graphical summary of the clustering approach is provided in Fig. 2. The correspondent script (*RaPCA.py*) is provided as Supplementary Material; the tunable parameters (e.g., maximum Pearson correlation coefficient, maximum number of clusters to be considered, etc.) can be selected by the user in future applications of the method.

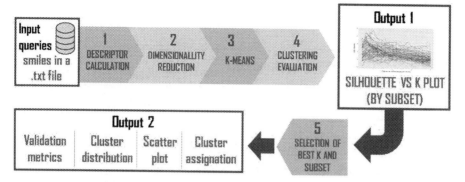

Fig. 2. A graphical summary of the RaPCA clustering method, combining feature bagging, principal component analysis and k-means optimization.

2.3 Molecular Descriptor Calculation and Modeling Procedure

1612 conformation-independent descriptors were computed with Mordred 1.2.0. A random subspace approach was again applied to obtain 1000 subsets of 200 descriptors each. In the random subspace approach, subsets of molecular descriptors are randomly sampled, and each model is trained from one subset of the features [21, 22]; consequently, the resulting models do not reiteratively focus on those features that display high explanatory power for the training examples. A dummy variable was used as the dependent variable (class label). It was assigned observed values of 1 for compounds within the ACTIVE class and observed values of 0 for compounds in the INACTIVE class. A Forward Stepwise procedure was used to obtain 1000 linear classifiers, one per feature subset. Only one molecular descriptor every 10 training examples was allowed into the model, to prevent overfitting. A maximum Pearson correlation coefficient of 0.85 was considered and no descriptor with regression coefficient with p-value above 0.05 was incorporated into the models. The predictive ability of each individual model was assessed through external validation, using the independent test set described in the preceding section, computing the global accuracy.

The predictive power and robustness of the models were initially assessed through Leave-Group-Out (LGO) cross-validation and Fisher's randomization tests. In the case of randomization, the class label was scrambled across the compounds in the training set. The training set with the randomized dependent variable was used to train new models from the descriptor selection step. Such a procedure was repeated 1000 times within each random subspace. It is expected that the randomized models will perform poorly compared to the real ones. Regarding LGO cross-validation, random stratified subsets of 10% of the total training set compounds were removed from the training set in each cross-validation round, and the model was generated again using the remaining compounds. The resulting model was used to predict the class label for the removed sample. The procedure was repeated 1000 times. The results were informed as the average accuracy across the folds; this was compared with the accuracy of the model inferred from the original, whole training set, and also, as advised by Gramatica [23], to the No-Model error rate or risk, i.e., the error provided in absence of model, which in our case corresponds to 0.5.

2.4 Ensemble Learning

Classifier ensembles (or meta-classifiers) often provide better generalization and accuracy than individual classifiers [24, 25]. As described in the next section, we have run two retrospective in silico screening experiments, the first of which is used to assess the enrichment power of the individual classifiers and train model ensembles, whereas the second retrospective screen is used to validate the performance of the ensembles. The libraries subjected to retrospective virtual screening are obtained by seeding the compounds that compose the test sets among a high number of putative inactive compounds termed decoys. Decoys have been obtained here by application of an in-house script that behaves similarly to the well-known Directory of Useful Decoys enhanced [26] (see next section for details).

The best individual classifiers are selected and combined according to their performance in the first retrospective screen, using the area under the Receiving Operating Characteristic (ROC) curve (AUCROC) as performance criterion. Systematic combinations of the 2 to N x 10/100 best performing classifiers were analyzed, N being the number of instances in the training set. Five combination schemes were applied to obtain a combined score: Average score (AVE), Average Ranking (RANK), Minimum operator (MIN), Product operator (PROD) and Average Voting (VOT) as computed by Zhang and Muegge [27].

For comparison purposes, the performance of our model ensembles was compared with those emerging from the combination of feature bagging on the descriptor pool (3000 random subspaces of 200 descriptor each) and three other machine learning algorithms: Random Forest (RF), Multi-layer Perceptron (MLP) and Support Vector Machine (SVM). These algorithms have been implemented through the sklearn package in Python using the default parameters.

2.5 Retrospective Screening

To estimate the enrichment performance of the individual models and model ensembles in a realistic virtual screening setting, two retrospective virtual screening experiments were implemented. For that purpose, the known active compounds in the test sets were seeded among a large number of decoys obtained with the help of an in-house decoy generation algorithm that we have termed LUDe (LIDeB Useful Decoys). Briefly, this algorithm is fed with molecular representations of known active compounds and retrieves from ChEMBL compounds paired through some general physicochemical properties but with distinctive molecular topology. For each active compound used as query, we extracted from ChEMBL compounds with similar molecular weight (±2 Dalton in comparison with the query), log P ((±0.5 log units in comparison with the query), number of rotatable bonds (±1), number of H-bond acceptors (±1), number of H-bond donors (±1). Three successive filters were then applied to select, among the retrieve compounds, those that are less similar, topologically speaking, to the query compound: 1) Tanimoto similarity coefficient between the query compound and each potential decoy was calculated, using

Morgan fingerprints, radius 2, and only decoys with similarity coefficient of at most 0.3 were kept; 2) the maximum common substructure between the query and the decoy is found using RDKit's rdFMCS module; the ratio between the number of atoms in the maximum common substructure and the query compound is calculated, and only decoys with ratio below 0.5 are kept; 3) only decoys with different scaffolds than the query compound are kept. For such a purpose, RDKits's MurckoScaffold tool is used. Finally, the resulting list of decoys are compared with all the remaining active compounds in the dataset and only those with Tanimoto similarity below 0.3 with every active compound are retained. Up to 100 decoys per query compound are used. The general workflow to obtain decoys is graphically displayed in Fig. 3. The composition of the libraries used to assess the performance of NaV1.1, NaV1.2 and NaV1.3 models through two retrospective screens is summarized in Table 2. Note that in any case the yielding of active compounds of the correspondent library is around 0.01. Also note that, due to data scarcity, in the cases of NaV1.1 and NaV1.6 the active compounds seeded in both the retrospective screening libraries (first and second retrospective screen for each channel subtype) are identical, whereas the decoys used in each case have varied. In the case of NaV1.2, the available data allowed the use of completely different libraries for the retrospective screens. The corresponding script is provided as Supplementary Material (LUDe.py).

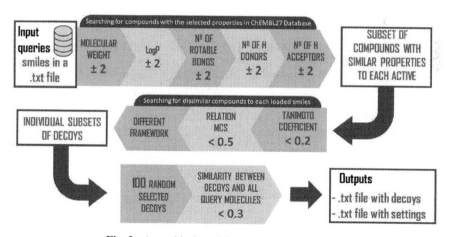

Fig. 3. A graphical workflow of the LUDe method.

The performance of the individual classifiers and the classifier ensembles in each library was assessed using different enrichment metrics were computed, namely: AUCROC, the Boltzmann-Enhanced Discrimination of the Receiver Operating Characteristic (BEDROC), the area under the Precision Recall curve (AUPR) and enrichment factor 1% ($EF_{0.01}$) [28, 29]. The DeLong method was used to compare the AUCROC values from a statistical viewpoint.

Table 2. Composition of the libraries used for retrospective screen experiments, for the three subtypes of sodium channels considered in this study. The true active and inactive compounds used for such purposes are the test set compounds for each channel subtype.

Screen	NaV1.1			NaV1.2			NaV1.6		
	Active	True inactive	Putative inactive	Active	True inactive	Putative inactive	Active	True inactive	Putative inactive
Retrospective screen 1	14	17	1210	29	0	1477	9	22	756
Retrospective screen 2	14	0	852	28	0	1463	9	0	475

2.6 Use of Positive Predictive Value Surfaces to Choose a Score Threshold for the Prospective Screen

The Positive Predictive Value (PPV) answers a very pragmatic question: how many in silico hits emerging from a virtual screening campaign should be submitted to experimental confirmation to obtain a true, confirmed hit. For instance, a PPV of 0.5 implies that about one every two hits will confirm the predicted activity experimentally. Estimation of PPV is however hampered by its dependency on the yielding of active compounds (*Ya*) in a chemical library, which is not known *a priori* in prospective virtual screens.

$$PPV = \frac{SeYa}{SeYa + (1 - Sp)(1 - Ya)} \tag{1}$$

where *Se* represents the sensitivity associated to a given score cutoff value and *Sp* represents the specificity.

Equation (1) was applied to build PPV surfaces: 3D plots showing the interplay between PPV, the *Se/Sp* ratio and *Ya* were built for each individual classifier and for each model ensemble. Using the first retrospective screening library for each subtype of sodium channel, *Se* and *Sp* were computed in all the range of possible cutoff score values and *Ya* was varied between 0.001 and 0.01, assuming that the *Se/Sp* ratio would remain invariant no matter the *Ya*. Visual inspection of the resulting PPV surfaces (see Fig. 4 for an example) was used to assist in the selection of a score threshold value with a desired range of PPVs.

2.7 Prospective Virtual Screen

The model ensembles that, for each channel subtype, showed the best performance in the retrospective virtual screening experiments were used to screen DrugBank 5.1.8, an online database focused on chemical substances that may be subject to drug repurposing, e.g., approved, investigational and withdrawn drugs [30]. The molecular representations of the compounds in this database were standardized as previously described for the dataset compounds and 1612 molecular descriptors were calculated with Mordred 1.2.0.

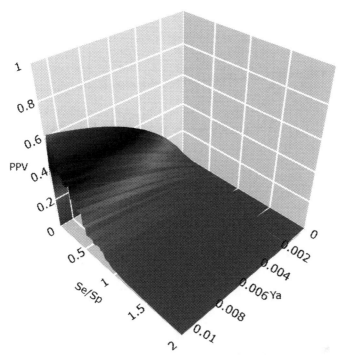

Fig. 4. PPV surface for the best model ensemble obtained for the NaV1.2 channel.

The extent of extrapolation approach [31] was used for applicability domain assessment, using a critical value of $3d/n$, n being the number of descriptors included in each model. For model ensembles, the proportion of models in the ensemble for which the screened compound falls within the applicability domain was calculated. A screened compound was regarded as an in silico hit when it was predicted as a blocker of NaV1.2 or NaV1.6 and a non-blocker of NaV1.1.

3 Results and Discussion

A ligand-based prospective virtual screening approach was used to discover selective NaV1.2 or NaV1.6 blockers, with no inhibitory effect on NaV1.1, as potential therapeutic agents for Dravet syndrome. Dataset compounds were retrieved from ChEMBL or from specialized literature, and representatively sampled into training and test sets by using an in-house clustering method, RaPCA, based on a combination of feature bagging, dimensionality reduction through PCA and k-means optimization. RaPCA showed an excellent performance in all cases, with observed silhouette coefficient values for the optimal clustering between 0.82 and 0.95 (see Fig. 5 for a representative example, corresponding to clustering of NaV1.1 active compounds).

1,000 individual linear classifiers were generated by applying a combination of random subspace and forward stepwise on a pool of 1,612 Mordred molecular descriptors. The individual models were validated both internally (through cross-validation and randomization tests) and externally. Equation 2 provides an example of linear model (corresponding to the best NaV1.2 model):

$$\text{Model } 225 = -0.369 + 0.052 * \text{SssNH} + 0.017 * \text{EState\_VSA5} + 0.44$$
$$* \text{GATS7are} + 0.027 * \text{ETA\_dBeta} + 0.087 * \text{AATSC7Z} + 0.011 * \text{EState\_VSA9}$$
$$(2)$$

where SssNH denotes the sum of the electrotopological states of the ssNH atom type, which encodes, in unison, the topology and electronic environment of such molecular fragments. EState_VSA5 is a MOE-type descriptor considering EState indices and surface area contribution: the EState VSA Descriptor 5 considers the atomic Van der Waals Surface Area contributions of atoms with EState in the range $(1.17 <= x < 1.54)$; similarly, EState_VSA9 computes the atomic Van der Waals Surface Area contributions of atoms with EState in the range $(4.69 <= x < 9.17)$. GATS7are represents the Geary autocorrelation of lag 7 weighted by Allred-Eocow electronegativity, which in essence assumes higher values when the molecule presents pairs of atoms with different electronegativities at a topological distance of 7. ETA_dBeta corresponds to the Extended Topochemical Atom delta beta descriptor (a measure of the relative unsaturation content). AATSC7Z codifies for the averaged and centered Moreau-Broto autocorrelation of lag 7 weighted by atomic number (essentially averaging the product of the atomic numbers for atom pairs located at a topological distance of 7).

The explanatory power of the best model was around 80% for the three channel subtypes. Internal validation results for the best individual classifier obtained, according to the performance of the first retrospective screen, for each channel are summarized in Table 3. The mean accuracy of the randomized models, which is virtually identical to the NOMER value in all cases, suggests a low probability of spurious correlations for the true models. Regarding the cross-validation, the mean accuracy across the folds is in all cases below 70%, suggesting that the models might be missing robustness. This seems to be confirmed by the results in the external validation. The best individual NaV1.1, NaV1.2 and NaV1.6 models showed an overall accuracy on the corresponding test sets (which consisted of 31, 57 and 31 compounds, respectively) of 74, 82, and 71%, in that order. This lack of generalizability of the individual models might have been anticipated due to the limited size of the available datasets, particularly for NaV1.1 and NaV1.6 models. The suboptimal results of the individual classifiers in the cross-validation and external validation, which insinuate some degree of overfitting, plus their rather modest metrics in the retrospective screens (Table 4) justified resorting to ensemble learning to improve robustness and predictivity.

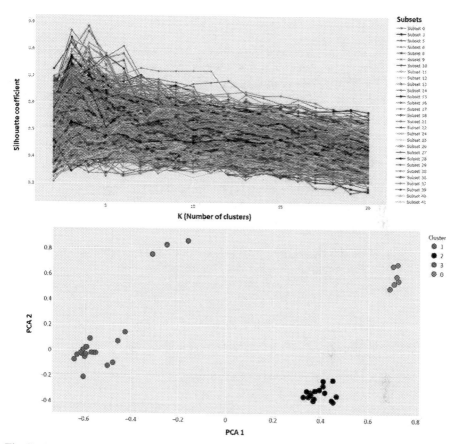

Fig. 5. Output of the RaPCA clustering procedure for NaV1.1 active compounds; the optimal value of the silhouette coefficient (0.89) was found for k = 4: (up) graph of the number of cluster vs the Silhouette coefficient; (down) scatter plot of PCA1 vs PCA2, which indicates for every molecule its belonging in each cluster.

The MIN operators consistently provided the best results across the different sodium channel subtypes, greatly improving the early and overall enrichment performance. In the case of NaV1.1 and NaV1.6, the chosen ensembles comprised 6 models, whereas in the case of NaV1.2, a 11-model ensemble was selected. Also note that, judging from the standard deviation of the enrichment metrics (obtained through bootstrapping), the behavior of the ensembles is much more robust than that of the individual models. Remarkably, the AUCROC values obtained by the MIN ensembles were higher than those obtained by RF, MLP and SVM for the three isoforms of the sodium channels, except for NaV1.6, where RF provided non-significant but higher AUCROC values than the MIN ensemble. Nevertheless, even in that case the early enrichment metrics (BEDROC, EF0.01) obtained by our ensemble were better than those obtained by RF (results not shown). All in all, our ensemble models seem to consistently provide better results than the other machine learning algorithms tested for comparison purposes.

Table 3. Accuracy of the best individual models for each sodium channel subtype in the training set, leave-group-out cross-validation and randomization test. In the case of the cross-validation and randomization tests, the mean accuracy across the 1000 rounds is informed; the standard deviation of the mean is presented within parentheses.

Channel	Training set	Cross-validation	Randomization	External validation
NaV1.1	0.80	0.66 (0.19)	0.49 (0.17)	0.74
NaV1.2	0.78	0.66 (0.14)	0.50 (0.12)	0.82
NaV1.6	0.85	0.60 (0.18)	0.49 (0.15)	0.71

Table 4. Comparison of the performance of the best individual models and the best model ensemble for each channel in the retrospective screening experiments.

Channel	Model	Retrospective screen	AUCROC	BEDROC ($\alpha = 20$)	AUPR	$EF_{0.01}$
NaV1.1	Individual model	1	0.89 (0.02)	0.29(0.05)	0.09(0.03)	6.53
		2	0.88 (0.02)	0.25(0.06)	0.11(0.04)	6.51
	6-model ensemble	1	0.94 (0.01)	0.54 (0.05)	0.21 (0.05)	9.02
		2	0.92 (0.02)	0.45 (0.06)	0.18 (0.04)	6.80
NaV1.2	Individual model	1*	0.80(0.02)	0.19(0.03)	0.08(0.02)	2.92
		2*	0.75(0.03)	0.17(0.03)	0.05(0.006)	0
	11-model ensemble	1	0.90(0.02)	0.62(0.04)	0.4(0.05)	27.40
		2	0.87(0.02)	0.47(0.04)	0.21(0.04)	13.90
NaV1.6	Individual model	1*	0.83(0.03)	0.25(0.06)	0.06(0.01)	0.70
		2*	0.82(0.03)	0.25(0.06)	0.10(0.02)	0
	6-model ensemble	1	0.89(0.04)	0.50(0.06)	0.17(0.04)	11.40
		2	0.88(0.04	0.50(0.06)	0.24(0.06)	10.14

* Statistically significant differences in comparison with the MIN ensemble ($p < 0.05$)

The NaV1.2 and NaV1.6 ensembles were then used to explore the DrugBank database for potential blockers. The score cutoff value to identify in silico hits was chosen based on PPV surface analysis. In the case of NaV1.2, the chosen cutoff value was 0.48, corresponding to a *Se* of 0.51 and a *Sp* of 0.98. For a yield of active compounds of 0.01, such cutoff value would determine a PPV of 0.20 (meaning that at least 1 in 5 in silico hits are theoretically expected to corroborate the predicted activity experimentally). For NaV1.6, we have chosen compounds with scores between 0.68 and 0.71, also providing a PPV of 0.20 for $Ya = 0.01$. Since NaV1.1 is conceived, in the framework of the present study, as an anti-target (as inhibition of this subtype of channel would aggravate Dravet phenotype), those NaV1.2 and NaV1.6 hits also predicted as NaV1.1 inhibitors were disregarded. This is graphically shown in Fig. 6, where it can be visually appreciated that, for the set of hits, the PPV for NaV1.2 or NaV1.6 substantially exceeds the PPV for NaV1.1. In this manner, 154 selective in silico hits were obtained for NaV1.2 and 33 selective in silico hits were obtained for NaV1.6.

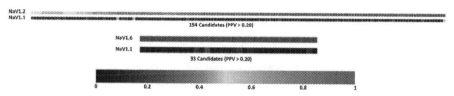

Fig. 6. The heatmaps visually display the predicted selectivity of the in silico hits. Each column represents a hit, and each row represents the *PPV* predictions for a given channel subtype (the upper row in each heatmap corresponds to the pursued target, NaV1.2 or NaV1.6, while the lower row corresponds to NaV1.1).

Table 5 and Table 6 present the *PPV* values for each channel subtype for the ten top-ranked hits for NaV1.2 and NaV1.6, respectively. It can be appreciated that the tables include compounds with different status: experimental drugs (the compound is at pre-clinical stage of development), investigational drugs (the drug has entered clinical trials) or approved drugs. Among them, investigational and, in particular, approved drugs are the ones for which a larger amount of knowledge has been collected, thus making them the most straightforward candidates to fully exploit the advantages of the drug repurposing paradigm. Analyzing the available data about the pharmacokinetics, dose range, route of administration and side effects of these candidates may serve to evaluate which deserve further consideration and research for the new pursued indication, i.e. treatment of Dravet syndrome. For instance, one of the hits, tirofiban, is an intravenous antiplatelet used at very low doses (a loading dose of 25 µg/kg, followed by an infusion at 0.15 µg/kg/min) and has bleeding as a frequent side effect [32]. All in all, thus, it makes quite a poor candidate for the treatment of a chronic condition like a childhood epilepsy. Tenofovir, in contrast, is an antiviral that is orally bioavailable and is in general well-tolerated, the most common adverse event seen in Phase 3 clinical trials being headache (although long-term use has been associated with nephrotoxicity and bone loss) [33].

Table 5. Ten top-ranked hits for Nav1.2.

DrugBank ID	Structure	PPV (0.01)	Antitarget (Nav1.1) PPV (0.01)	Status	Indication(s)
DB08270		0.606820	0.037670	Experimental	Osteoporosis
DB02200		0.606820	0.090471	Experimental	Chagas disease
DB06997		0.606820	0.042232	Experimental	Gastric carcinoma
DB06302 (Glesatinib)		0.606820	0.080588	Investigational	Lung cancer
DB15254 (RO-5126766)		0.606820	0.017874	Investigational	Kras mutant tumors
DB07333		0.606820	0.039077	Experimental	Angiogenesis for tumors
DB02051		0.606820	0.153317	Experimental	Chagas disease
DB13340 (Suloctidil)		0.606820	0.010197	Experimental	Vasodilator
DB00775 (Tirofiban)		0.562580	0.029203	Approved	Antithrombotic
DB05038 (Anatibant)		0.562580	0.016649	Investigational	Traumatic brain injuries

Table 6. Ten top-ranked hits for Nav1.6.

DrugBank ID	Structure	PPV (0.01)	Antitarget (Nav1.1) PPV (0.01)	Status	Indication(s)
DB02038		0.225441	0.022355	Experimental	Antibacterial
DB02490		0.225441	0.011677	Experimental	Creatine kinase M-type inhibitor
DB03305		0.225441	0.011222	Experimental	Neuroprotective in Parkinson's disease
DB09299 (Tenofovir alafenamide)		0.225441	0.012028	Investigational/ approved	Chronic hepatitis B
DB08395		0.225441	0.029342	Experimental	Inflammatory diseases
DB13597 (Moroxydine)		0.225441	0.018460	Experimental	Antiviral
DB12625 (Evogliptin)		0.225441	0.016784	Investigational	Type 2 Diabetes Mellitus
DB03530 (Acylated ceftazidime)		0.225441	0.011252	Experimental	Antibacterial
DB13183 (Technetium Tc-99m etifenin)		0.225441	0.011202	Experimental	Radiopharmaceutical for imaging studies
DB02463		0.225441	0.014925	Experimental	Protease-inhibitor

4   Conclusions

Linear classifiers to identify selective NaV1.2 or NaV1.6 inhibitors as potential treatments for Dravet syndrome have been derived using a combination of random subspace and forward stepwise procedures. The pool of molecular descriptors used in this work has been computed through publicly available free software; complementary, the in-house routines of the RaPCA and LUDe applicationsm as well as the datasets compiled and curated for this work, are being made available as supplementary.py files and.csv files, respectively, which maximizes the reproducibility and portability of the obtained models, and allows to freely use the same tools in future investigations.

The individual models obtained displayed moderate performance at the validation and retrospective screening steps and were considerably outperformed through ensemble learning. The so obtained meta-classifiers not only showed improved enrichment metrics in the retrospective screening campaigns, but also displayed a more robust behavior according to the standard deviation in the enrichment metrics, estimated by bootstrapping. The score cut-off values of the best-performing model ensembles were rationally optimized through inspection of Positive Predictive Value surfaces; the optimized score cutoffs were subsequently applied for the prospective screening of DrugBank, a database commonly used in computer-guided drug repurposing campaigns.

Computer-aided drug discovery represents a key strategy for the identification of novel active scaffolds in a time- and cost-efficient manner, a point especially important when pursuing novel therapeutic solutions for rare diseases, such as Dravet syndrome.

Experimental in vitro assays are to be performed in the near future to confirm our computational predictions.

Acknowledgements. All the authors thank the National University of La Plata (UNLP) and the Argentinean National Council of Scientific and Technical Research Council (CONICET). The present work was funded by The National Agency of Scientific and Technological Promotion (ANPCyT PICT 2019-1075) and Incentivos UNLP.

References

1. Catterall, W.A.: Dravet syndrome: a sodium channel interneuronopathy. Curr. Opin. Physiol. **2**, 42–50 (2018)
2. Genton, P., Velizarova, R., Dravet, C.: Dravet syndrome: the long-term outcome. Epilepsia **52**(Suppl 2), 44–49 (2011)
3. Rosander, C., Hallböök, T.: Dravet syndrome in Sweden: a population-based study. Dev. Med. Child Neurol. **57**(7), 628–633 (2015)
4. Wu, Y.W., et al.: Incidence of Dravet syndrome in a US population. Pediatrics **136**(5), e1310-1315 (2015)
5. Lochmüller, H., et al.: IRDiRC consortium assembly. The international rare diseases research consortium: policies and guidelines to maximize impact. Eur. J. Hum. Genet. **25**(12), 1293–1302 (2017)
6. Depienne, C., et al.: Spectrum of SCN1A gene mutations associated with Dravet syndrome: analysis of 333 patients. J. Med. Genet. **46**(3), 183–191 (2009)

7. Zuberi, S.M., Brunklaus, A., Birch, R., Reavey, E., Duncan, J., Forbes, G.H.: Genotype-phenotype associations in SCN1A-related epilepsies. Neurology **76**(7), 594–600 (2011)
8. Ceulemans, B.: Overall management of patients with Dravet syndrome. Dev. Med. Child Neurol. **53**(Suppl 2), 19–23 (2011)
9. de Lange, I.M., et al.: Influence of contraindicated medication use on cognitive outcome in Dravet syndrome and age at first afebrile seizure as a clinical predictor in SCN1A-related seizure phenotypes. Epilepsia **59**(6), 1154–1165 (2018)
10. Guerrini, R., Dravet, C., Genton, P., Belmonte, A., Kaminska, A., Dulac, O.: Lamotrigine and seizure aggravation in severe myoclonic epilepsy. Epilepsia **39**(5), 508–512 (1998)
11. Weuring, W.J., et al.: NaV1.1 and NaV1.6 selective compounds reduce the behavior phenotype and epileptiform activity in a novel zebrafish model for Dravet Syndrome. PLoS One **15**(3), e0219106 (2020)
12. Richards, K.L., et al.: Selective NaV1.1 activation rescues Dravet syndrome mice from seizures and premature death. Proc. Natl. Acad. Sci. USA **115**(34), E8077-E8085 (2018)
13. Yekkirala, A.S., Roberson, D.P., Bean, B.P., Woolf, C.J.: Breaking barriers to novel analgesic drug development. Nat. Rev. Drug Discov. **16**(8), 545–564 (2017)
14. Kingwell, K.: Nav1.7 withholds its pain potential. Nat. Rev. Drug Discov. **18**, 321–323 (2019)
15. Corry, B.: Physical basis of specificity and delayed binding of a subtype selective sodium channel inhibitor. Sci Rep. **8**(1), 1356 (2018)
16. Golbraikh, A., Shen, M., Xiao, Z., Xiao, Y.D., Lee, K.H., Tropsha, A.: Rational selection of training and test sets for the development of validated QSAR models. J. Comput. Aided Mol. Des. **17**(2–4), 241–253 (2003)
17. Martin, T.M., et al.: Does rational selection of training and test sets improve the outcome of QSAR modeling? J. Chem. Inf. Model. **52**(10), 2570–2578 (2012)
18. Leonard, J.T., Roy, K.: On selection of training and test sets for the development of predictive QSAR models. QSAR Comb. Sci. **25**(3), 235–251 (2006)
19. Moriwaki, H., Tian, Y.S., Kawashita, N., Takagi, T.: Mordred: a molecular descriptor calculator. J. Cheminform. **10**(1), 4 (2018)
20. Kaufman, L., Rousseeuw, P.: Finding Groups in Data: An Introduction to Cluster Analysis. Wiley, Hoboken (1990)
21. Yu, G., Zhang, G., Domeniconi, C., Yu, Z., You, J.: Semi-supervised classification based on random subspace dimensionality reduction. Pattern Recogn. **45**, 1119–1135 (2012)
22. El Habib Daho, M., Chikh, M.A.: Combining bootstrapping samples, random subspaces and random forests to build classifiers. J. Med. Imag. Health Inf. **5**(3), 539–544 (2015)
23. Gramatica, P.: On the development and validation of QSAR models. Methods Mol. Biol. **930**, 499–526 (2013)
24. Hyun, J.C., Kavvas, E.S., Monk, J.M., Palsson, B.O.: Machine learning with random subspace ensembles identifies antimicrobial resistance determinants from pan-genomes of three pathogens. PLoS Comput. Biol. **16**(3), e1007608 (2020)
25. Min, S.H.: A genetic algorithm-based heterogeneous random subspace ensemble model for bankruptcy prediction. Int. J. Appl. Eng. Res. **11**, 2927–2931 (2016)
26. Mysinger, M.M., Carchia, M., Irwin, J.J., Shoichet, B.K.: Directory of useful decoys, enhanced (DUD-E): better ligands and decoys for better benchmarking. J. Med. Chem. **55**(14), 6582–6594 (2012)
27. Zhang, Q., Muegge, I.: Scaffold hopping through virtual screening using 2D and 3D similarity descriptors: ranking, voting, and consensus scoring. J. Med. Chem. **49**(5), 1536–1548 (2006)
28. Truchon, J.F., Bayly, C.L.: Evaluating virtual screening methods: good and bad metrics for the "early recognition" problem. J. Chem. Inf. Model. **47**(2), 488–508 (2007)
29. Saito, T., Rehmsmeier, M.: The precision-recall plot is more informative than the ROC plot when evaluating binary classifiers on imbalanced datasets. PLoS ONE **10**(3), e0118432 (2015)

30. Wishart, D.S., et al.: DrugBank 5.0: a major update to the DrugBank database for 2018. Nucleic Acids Res. **46**(D1), D1074–D1082 (2018)
31. Yasri, A., Hartsough, D.: Toward an optimal procedure for variable selection and QSAR model building. J. Chem. Inf. Comput. Sci. **41**(5), 1218–1227 (2001)
32. Gargiulo, G., et al.: Cangrelor, tirofiban, and chewed or standard prasugrel regimens in patients with ST-segment-elevation myocardial infarction: primary results of the FABOLUS-FASTER trial. Circulation **142**(5), 441–454 (2020)
33. Buti, M., et al.: Tenofovir alafenamide versus tenofovir disoproxil fumarate for the treatment of patients with HBeAg-negative chronic hepatitis B virus infection: a randomised, double-blind, phase 3, non-inferiority trial. Lancet Gastroenterol. Hepatol. **1**(3), 196–206 (2016)

Implementation of Intra and Extracellular Nonperiodic Scale-Free Stimulation *in silico* for the NEURON Simulator

Heitor de Carvalho Barros Terra[1] (ID), Fernando da Silva Borges[2,3] (ID),
Marcio Flávio Dutra Moraes[4] (ID), and Vinícius Rosa Cota[1(✉)] (ID)

[1] Laboratory of Neuroengineering and Neuroscience (LINNce), Universidade Federal de São João Del-Rei, Pça. Frei Orlando, 170 – Centro, São João Del-Rei, MG 36302-600, Brazil
vrcota@ufsj.edu.br
[2] Department of Physiology and Pharmacology, State University of New York Downstate Medical Center, New York, NY 11203, USA
[3] Centro de Matemática, Computação e Cognição, Universidade Federal do ABC, Av. dos Estados, 5001 -Bangú, Santo André, SP 09210-580, Brazil
[4] Núcleo de Neurociências (NNC), Instituto de Ciências Biológicas, Universidade Federal de Minas Gerais, Av. Pres. Antônio Carlos, 6627 - Pampulha, Belo Horizonte, MG 31270-901, Brazil

Abstract. Electrical stimulation of the brain is a largely used alternative for the treatment of myriad neurological disorders. Although recognizably efficacious and safe, many details of the underlying mechanisms remain obscure. Our group devised and successfully tested, in animal models of epilepsy, a novel nonstandard form of electrical stimulation in which the intervals between pulses are randomized. Termed Nonperiodic Stimulation (NPS), it has been specifically tailored to suppress hypersynchronism supporting seizure generation. For a better understanding of the underpinnings of NPS, we sought to carry out *in silico* investigation, but we found no easy way to implement its temporal pattern in the very successful NEURON simulator, given the unconventional nature of our stimulus. In this work, we report two approaches devised and tested to implement NPS applied both intra and extracellularly using the NEURON simulator. Neuronal responses reproduced the distinct temporal patterns of stimulation in a high-fidelity fashion, while being influenced by both stimulus polarity and distance from electrode tip. These results suggest our solutions successfully implemented intra and extracellular NPS (as well as other temporal patterns of interest) and represent an early but essential step in enabling *in silico* investigation of the mechanisms of such neuromodulation method.

Keywords: NEURON platform · Intracellular · Extracellular · Electrical stimulation · NPS · Temporal-pattern

1 Introduction

Epilepsy is a serious neurological disorder affecting circa 1 to 2% of the world population [1]. Although pharmacological and surgical treatments are considerably effective,

© Springer Nature Switzerland AG 2022
P. R. d. A. Ribeiro et al. (Eds.): LAWCN 2021, CCIS 1519, pp. 119–131, 2022.
https://doi.org/10.1007/978-3-031-08443-0_8

circa 15% of the patients are unable to properly control their seizures [2]. A promising alternative in this case is the electrical stimulation (ES) of the brain, a method termed Deep Brain Stimulation (DBS), which is usually delivered as square pulses of current or voltage fired at a fixed rate to myriad different neural substrates [3]. Although DBS is a very promising neurotechnology, a less empirical and a more engineered-oriented development of such methods is much needed [4].

The design of a neuromodulation technology, for the treatment of any disorder, should always aim at reducing the energy transferred from the pulse generator to the tissue, for safety reasons and to increase the duration of batteries and electrodes [5]. Yet, virtually all DBS methods need high frequencies of operation (100 Hz and above) to properly attain therapeutic effect [6]. In fact, low frequencies have wielded controversial results in both human and animal experimentation [7]. To work around this issue, our group devised and successfully tested a novel approach of ES with robust anticonvulsant power while delivering only four pulses per second, with conventional amplitude and duration, and thus with very low energy (~0.100 μC/s) [5, 8]. Termed Nonperiod Stimulation (NPS), our method constitutes of randomizing the intervals between pulses (IPI – interpulse intervals) following a natural-like scale-free pattern in which the distribution curve of values approximates a power law of unitary exponent [9]. The rationale behind NPS is that such a temporal pattern would impair hypersynchronous processes occurring in neural circuitry known to support epileptic phenomena, while having minor effects on healthy neural function. NPS applied to the basolateral amygdala has shown robust anticonvulsant effects against seizures in both animal models of acute [8] and chronic seizures [10], and it is maxed out when applied bilaterally in an asynchronous fashion [11].

Mechanistic investigation has also been carried out to suggest that NPS is capable of disrupting aberrant synchronization within and between afferences of the basolateral amygdala, putatively by randomly (thus in an out-of-phase fashion) recruiting them and consequently impairing their coupling [12–14]. Some additional evidence corroborates this line of reasoning: 1) synchronization of brain areas is attained by means of a shared rhythmic oscillation (in contrast to non-periodic activity) [15] and; 2) scale-free stimuli mimics natural-like input that entrains single neurons and small networks in high fidelity activity [16–18]. By this token, we have recently hypothesized that the never-repeating temporal patterns in NPS easily recruits distinct microcircuits in the neighborhood of the amygdala, entraining them in healthy activity and impairing their abnormal coupling, while at the same time competing with aberrant synchronization that underlies epileptic phenomena [9].

In order to properly assess these ideas, our group set out to perform *in silico* investigations of the mechanisms underlying NPS in different levels of brain organization. Particularly, testing the response of single cells or of small networks of neurons to NPS is important considering the previously mentioned features of such temporal pattern of stimuli. A biophysically realistic model such as the Hodgkin Huxley applied to anatomically correct cells using simulation software such as NEURON (from Duke University) is an obvious choice for such investigation. Yet, considering the very unusual form of stimulation, there are no tools within the simulator to reproduce our ES methods. Thus, in this work, we sought to implement a programmable add-on to simulate nonperiodic ES both intra and extracellularly. Two different solutions were developed: 1) a *.hoc* file routine that creates a point-process for single pulse stimulation for each of the NPS pulses, and; 2) a NetPyne routine that creates NPS delivered from an extracellular point source within a small network of neurons and then performs the field propagation calculation to affect individual cells.

2 Methodology

2.1 Intracellular Stimulation Using Point-Processes

The point process is the way that NEURON uses to represent signal sources, such as localized membrane shunts, synapses, and electrodes [19]. So, one way to create a stimulus could be by using point processes. With this option in mind, our strategy was to choose a point process included in the NEURON environment that, with a specific configuration, could mimic the NPS temporal pattern.

To do that, we first created a very simple cell that would receive the stimulus. The cell created had only two compartments, a soma and an axon, both modeled by Hodgkin & Huxley equations. It is, in fact, a simplified cell to use in a computational model of the cellular level, but since the goal of this work is to implement a new wave stimulus and not to study the cellular behavior, this simple model was sufficient.

After creating the neuron, we attached the point process that would represent the electrode and stimulate the cell. The mechanism chosen to create the NPS stimulus was the "IClamp", which injects current with a constant amplitude, duration, and delay. Of particular importance here, the delay variable represents the latency period since the beginning of the stimulation in which the current will actually be injected to the cell. IClamp mechanism does not provide an option to change the interval between pulses, just delays, frequency or pre-determined distributions among which the scale-free nature of NPS is not included. Thus, instead of using one electrode that fires in the temporal pattern, our strategy was to create several electrodes in the same position and with the same duration and amplitude, but each one with a different delay. By their turn, delays corresponded to the temporal pattern of NPS according to the original algorithm of generation [8]. This strategy was implemented in a HOC language routine and we achieved it by creating a vector that saves the times that the pulses should be injected. Using a for loop with the number of iterations equals to the length of the vector, that creates one "IClamp" point process per iteration, each one receiving a delay corresponding to one element of the vector created.

Total simulation time for the intracellular ES was ten seconds (10000 ms) and the initial potential was set as −65 mV.

2.2 Extracellular Stimulation Using Field Propagation

The NEURON environment does not have an option for extracellular stimulation. The only alternative is the extracellular mechanism, which adds an additional layer to the equivalent circuit corresponding to the extracellular milieu. With this extra layer (which can be adjusted to the interest of the research), the extracellular potential can be influenced by an electric current while without it, the potential would be considered to be zero for all its extension.

In order to implement the extracellular ES, we had to use the extracellular mechanism to model an extracellular field that would be responsible for propagating the potential across all the space outside the membrane. Furthermore, since the NEURON environment does not have an option for an extracellular electrode, we also created a function to simulate the behavior of having a current injected extracellularly. This was achieved by choosing a position for the hypothetic electrode, calculating the distance between it and each cell of the network, and creating an equation that represents the decay rate of the electrical potential.

To implement all these strategies, we used the NetPyNE package and Neuron library on a colab notebook [20]. With the NetParams block from the NetPyNE package, we created a network of 50 pyramidal cells, in which 40 of them are excitatory and 10 are inhibitory (Fig. 1). The position of cells was randomly set inside a $250 \times 400 \times 250$ μm space, while the electrode position (in blue) was set to be (250, 250, 250) for x, y, and z axes respectively.

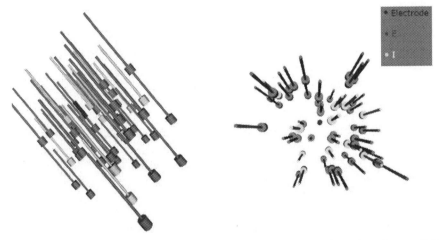

Fig. 1. Reconstruction of the network of simple neurons used for the simulation of extracellular stimulation using NetPyNE GUI. Green cells are excitatory and yellow cells are inhibitory, having their soma represented by a larger cylinder and the axon by a thinner cylinder. Electrode tip is shown at the center by a small blue cylinder. (Color figure online)

The soma compartment of each cell, inhibitory and excitatory, had the Hodgkin & Huxley and the extracellular mechanism inserted. The dendrites were modeled by the passive mechanism. The connectivity rules were set to each cell to have 0.1 probability of being connected to any other cell. Figure 2 shows the connectivity of the network. The creation of the external field was made using the "numpy.vectorize" function to insert all the calculated potential values of each cell into a vector. To insert the NPS extracellularly, we created a numpy array with the wave time stamps and multiplied it to the extracellular field. By doing this, we got a vector with different weights for each cell, multiplied by another vector with a fix amplitude for each time stamp of the NPS stimulus. A total of 5 s (5000 ms) was simulated.

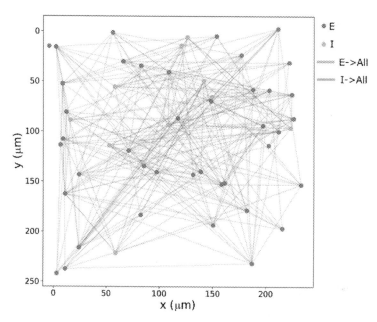

Fig. 2. Connectivity of the network created. Excitatory cells (green circles) send excitatory afferences (pink lines) to several other neurons, while inhibitory cells (yellow circles) project inhibitory afferences (blue lines), both with a 10% probability. (Color figure online)

2.3   Temporal-Patterned Stimuli

To test and compare the cellular responses to stimuli, we created three more ES temporal patterns, aside from the NPS described earlier: burst, periodic, and another form of nonperiodic stimulus, called NPSLH. The burst pattern consisted of a wave with four pulses per second and IPI of 20 ms. The periodic stimulus also had four pulses per second, but with a constant IPI of 250 ms. The NPSLH, differently from the NPS, did not have a distribution of IPI values that approximates a power law of unitary exponent, but that of a linear decay. In original animal studies, NPSLH was not effective in suppressing seizures. Histograms of IPI distributions for each of the tested temporal pattern is showed in Fig. 3.

Also, as a way to help the validation of the model created, we tested both types of current, anodic and cathodic. The cathodic intracellular stimulations should depolarize the cell and the anodic, hyperpolarize it. For the extracellular stimulations, the opposite should happen, even though both polarities can induce the firing of action potentials by different mechanisms. Moreover, as the stimulus intensity decays with distance from the tip, it is expected that neurons closer to the electrode will have a greater tendency to fire.

Intracellular current pulses had 3 nA and 100 μs of width. Extracellular pulses were 25 μs in width, but with variable amplitude (supra- and subthreshold). On both cases, there was no background noise.

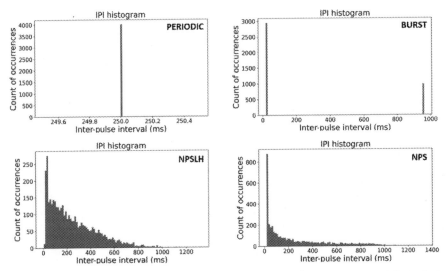

Fig. 3. Histograms of IPI distributions for each of the temporal pattern generated for both the intra and the extracellular stimulations: periodic (top left), burst (top right), NPSLH (bottom left), and NPS (bottom right).

3   Results

3.1   Single Neuron Response to Intracellular Stimulation

Responses to the intracellular stimulation are shown in Fig. 4 and in Fig. 5, which show the cellular responses for the cathodic and anodic stimulations, respectively. As Fig. 4 shows, the neuron responded in a high-fidelity one cathodic pulse (red diamonds) to one action potential fashion and, thus, faithfully reproduced the temporal-pattern being applied. Analogously, anodically-stimulated cells (Fig. 5) also responded in a one-to-one fashion. This was of course expected, given we purposefully chose a suprathreshold current applied to a simple cell without any other kind of background noise. All panels of both figures contain insets with isolated representative action potentials generated after stimulus. They are all stereotypical in morphology, with depolarization, repolarization, and hyperpolarization phases. On the other hand, only when anodic pulses are applied, action potential are preceded by a hyperpolarizing electronic potential. This suggest action potentials are fired by different mechanisms.

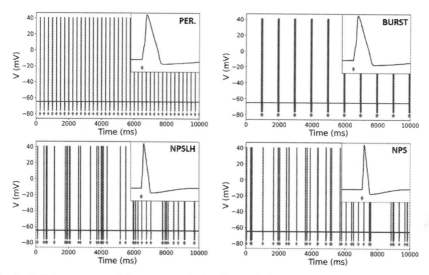

Fig. 4. Cellular response of the neuron to the four intracellular cathodic stimulation patterns. Red diamonds depict time points when stimulation pulses were applied. Insets display stereotypical action potentials generated in each case. Stimulation was periodic (top left), burst (top right), NPSLH (bottom left), and NPS (bottom right). (Color figure online)

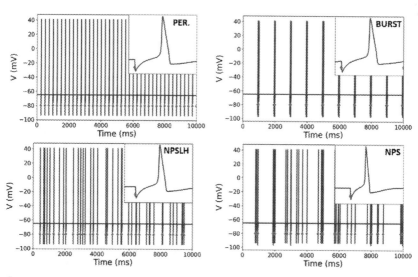

Fig. 5. Cellular response of the neuron to the four intracellular anodic stimulation patterns. Red diamonds depict time points when stimulation pulses were applied. Insets display stereotypical action potentials generated in each case. They were preceded by hyperpolarizing electrotonic potentials. Stimulation was periodic (top left), burst (top right), NPSLH (bottom left), and NPS (bottom right). (Color figure online)

3.2   Network Response to Extracellular Stimulation

Figures 6 and 7 depict the time course of the membrane potential of responsive (blue) and non-responsive (orange) cells, in terms of firing action potentials, when submitted to anodic and cathodic pulses, respectively. Notice the high-fidelity firing of action potentials to the different temporal patterns of stimulation for both cells. When undergoin anodic stimulation, while the responsive cell fires an action potential for each stimulus pulse, non-responsive cell responds only with a depolarizing subthreshold potential (Fig. 6). Insets in all of the panels show action potential waveforms in which both cells display initial depolarizing potentials, but of different magnitudes. Curiously, the burst temporal pattern has both kinds of response in the same cell, firing an action potential after the first pulse and only depolarizing electrotonic potentials for the other three pulses. One possibility is that this may be due to a polysynaptic effect in the network that causes the cancelling of potentials to a subthreshold threshold sum.

Similar results were obtained when the network was submitted to cathodic stimuli (Fig. 7). On the other hand, as insets show, both cells are preceded by a hyperpolarizing electrotonic potential. Again, burst stimulus was followed by the firing of an action potential only after the first pulse in the train. Integration of post-synaptic potentials in the network may also be in place here.

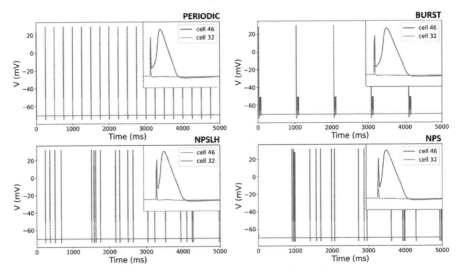

Fig. 6. Membrane potential of a responsive (blue) and a non-responsive (orange) neuron to the extracellular anodic stimulation. Notice in the insets the presence of an initial depolarizing electrotonic potential. (Color figure online)

Stimulus amplitude was chosen carefully in order to evoke action potentials in some cells and not in the other ones. In this way, we were able to show the two types of responses, sub and suprathreshold. A major determinant for this difference is the distance from the electrode tip. In order to verify this factor, we performed an additional simulation with a smaller network composed of 25 cells randomly located also inside a 250 × 400 ×

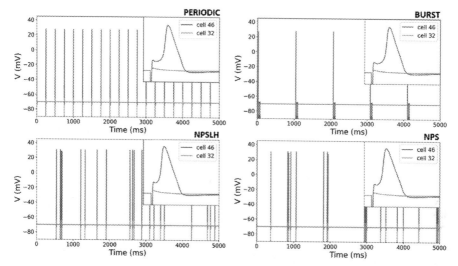

Fig. 7. Membrane potential of a responsive (blue) and a non-responsive (orange) neuron to the extracellular cathodic stimulation. Notice in the insets the presence of an initial hyperpolarizing electrotonic potential. (Color figure online)

250-µm space with an electrode positioned at (0, 0, 125) for x, y, and z axes, respectively (Fig. 8, left). Responsive (firing) cells, highlighted in thick blue, tend to be closer to the electrode tip when compared to silent cells in magenta (Fig. 8, right). Position of cells on the other axes and polysynaptic effects are additional factors here.

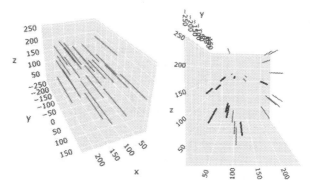

Fig. 8. A network of 25 randomly positioned neurons submitted to extracellular stimulation from a point source located in the middle of the y–z plane. Cells responding with an action potential are highlighted in blue, while non-responsive cells are depicted in magenta (right panel). Activated neurons tend to be closer to the electrode tip. (Color figure online)

4 Discussion and Conclusions

The primary objective of this work was to implement a solution to perform both intra-cellular and extracellular electrical stimulation with nonconventional temporal patterns of firing of pulses inside the NEURON simulator. The driving goal was to be able to simulate NPS and compare it to other temporal patterns used in previous *in vivo* studies and, thus, to get better insight of the mechanisms underlying the therapeutic efficacy of our neuromodulation method, given the obvious advantages of *in silico* experimentation. Considering that the time stamps of pulses in NPS (and also NPSLH) stimuli cannot be easily determined by simple mathematical formulation, there was no easy nor straightforward way to implement such computational experiment.

To the extent of our knowledge, the vast majority of therapeutic electrical neuromodulation approaches employ fixed high-frequency pulsatile methods. Only a few have tried modifying the temporal structure of stimuli to treat experimental epilepsy [5, 8, 9, 21–24] or motor disorders in pre-clinical and clinical trials [25–28]. Among these studies, at least one group has developed solid supporting theoretical work with computational neuroscience methods. A pioneering *in silico* investigation using network of oscillators has shown that stimulation, in which its temporal structure is tailored to specifically disrupt hypersynchronization, has the potential to be highly beneficial in disorders characterized by this hallmark (mainly Parkinson's disease and epilepsy) [29]. Several *in silico* studies of the same group using an approach inspired on these ideas (termed Coordinate Reset or CR) were carried out to understand the nuts and bolts of its desynchronizing effects, recently showing the relative irrelevance of the number of stimulation sites and the benefits of introducing jitter noise in inducing neural plasticity for the stabilization of synchronism levels [30–37]. Recently, they simulated networks of leaky integrate-and-fire (LIF) neurons submitted to ES with randomized temporal patterns and also locations, in a variant technique termed L/M-Random Reset [38]. They found out that such an approach induced plasticity and long-lasting effects (i.e., after stimuli terminated), while high-frequency stimuli did not. Although representing a remarkable advance in the theoretical investigation of the neurophysics of temporal structure of pulsatile neurostimulation, these studies do not provide a set of tools that can be transferred to the research on NPS. Not only temporal patterns are different, but also, they were not implemented in the NEURON simulator, which is of major importance, given the possibility of running biophysically realistic simulations.

In this work, we report initial results showing the solutions found for each type of stimulation, which were tested intracellularly on isolated neurons or extracellularly on small networks, using both cathodic and anodic pulses (known to have differential effects on neuronal activation). As expected, neurons responded according to what have been initially postulated, in a high-fidelity mode such as could be predicted by the well-established neurophysics of stimulation in a very well-controlled condition, such as this. In fact, the dependency of the nature of responses (presence of action potentials and directions of membrane voltage deflections) on the different polarities applied (cathodic and anodic) and also on the distance from electrode tip within the network of neurons were strong indicators that the implemented code is properly working. Moreover, neurons fired action potentials (or electrotonic potentials) in a high-fidelity mode reproducing the temporal pattern used for stimulation, adding further evidence that the solutions found are efficacious.

One important limitation of solutions presented here is the fact that the intracellular implementation of NPS does not scale well for longer periods of stimulation, once four new IClamp point processes have to be added for each neuron and each second. Although this is not a major concern to our own research, in which we pursue the replication of short-time *in vivo* experiments (few minutes), this may be a real issue if one is aiming at simulating many hours of stimulation and neuronal activity. In any case, we are pursuing an optimal solution for this issue, which may be attained by completely rewriting the point process using *.mod* routines. Furthermore, additional experiments could certainly help in stablishing the quality of present solutions. These includes obtaining intensity versus duration curves for the determination of rheobase current and chronaxie, delineation of activation threshold curves for anodic versus cathodic pulses, and investigation of the effects of the electrode position in relation to the cell (closer to soma or axon). On the other hand, given such experimentation is highly constrained to a sophistication of the current models of the cell and the network, it was postponed to a later phase in our studies.

In our understanding, although representing a very early stage, these initial results are of considerable importance to biophysically realistic *in silico* investigation of NPS and other nonstandard forms of electrical stimulation applied to epilepsy phenotypes, once it benefits from a very well-developed simulator in computational neuroscience. With these novel tools, we expect to be able of reproducing all the previous *in vivo* experiments, now, computationally. All code is freely available and links will be shared upon request to authors. As for the improvements and perspectives, we are already pursuing to implementing more realistic models of neuronal cells from areas of interest (e.g., basolateral amygdala, subthalamic nuclei, and hippocampal CA1) to investigate, with appropriate measures of synchronization, the application of temporally coded ES on them isolatedly or embedded in cytoarchitectonic-realistic microcircuits. We are positive that such endeavor will provide great insights into the therapeutic mechanisms underlying NPS in particular and ES in general.

Acknowledgment. We are grateful to Héctor Julian Tejada for all discussions that helped us develop this work, to Monica Bell Vila for sharing part of her code and help implementing it, and to FAPEMIG (Fundação de Amparo à Pesquisa do Estado de Minas Gerais) for the financial support.

References

1. Thurman, D.J., et al.: Standards for epidemiologic studies and surveillance of epilepsy. Epilepsia **52**, 2–26 (2011)
2. French, J.A.: Refractory epilepsy: clinical overview. Epilepsia **48**, 3–7 (2007)
3. Montgomery, E.B., Jr.: Deep Brain Stimulation Programming. Birmingham, Oxford (2010)
4. Sunderam, S., Gluckman, B., Reato, D., Bikson, M.: Toward rational design of electrical stimulation strategies for epilepsy control. Epilepsy Behav. **17**, 6–22 (2010)

5. Cota, V.R., Drabowski, B.M.B., Oliveira, J.C., Moraes, M.F.D.: The epileptic amygdala: toward the development of a neural prosthesis by temporally coded electrical stimulation. J. Neurosci. Res. **94**(6), 463–485 (2016)

6. Viswas, D., Limousin, P., Foltynie, T.: Subthalamic nucleus deep brain stimulation in Parkinson's disease: the effect of varying stimulation parameters. J. Parkinson's Dis. **7**(2), 235–245 (2017)

7. Klinger, N.V., Mittal, S.: Clinical efficacy of deep brain stimulation for the treatment of medically refractory epilepsy. Clin. Neurol. Neurosurg. **140**, 11–25 (2016)

8. Cota, V.R., Mesquita, M.B.S., Medeiros, D.C., Richardson, M.P., Williams, S., Moraes, M.F.D.: Distinct patterns of electrical stimulation of the basolateral amygdala influence pentylenetetrazole seizure outcome. Epilepsy Behav. **14**(1) (2009)

9. Cota, V.R., Oliveira, J.C., Damázio, L.C.M., Moraes, M.F.D.: Nonperiodic stimulation for the treatment of refractory epilepsy: applications, mechanisms, and novel insights. Epilepsy Behav. **121**, 106609 (2019)

10. Oliveira, J.C., Medeiros, D.C., Rezende, G.H.S., Moraes, M.F.D., Cota, V.R.: Temporally unstructured electrical stimulation to the amygdala suppresses behavioral chronic seizures of the pilocarpine animal model. Epilepsy Behav. **36**, 159–164 (2014)

11. Oliveira, J.C., Maciel, R.M., Moraes, M.F.D., Cota, V.R.: Asynchronous, bilateral, and biphasic temporally unstructured electrical stimulation of amygdalae enhances the suppression of pentylenetetrazole-induced seizures in rats. Epilepsy Res. **146**, 1–8 (2018)

12. Mesquita, M.B.S., Medeiros, D.C., Cota, V.R., Richardson, M.P., Williams, S., Moraes, M.F.D.: Distinct temporal patterns of electrical stimulation influence neural recruitment during PTZ infusion: an fMRI study. Prog. Biophys. Mol. Biol. **105**(1–2), 109–118 (2011)

13. Medeiros, D.C., Cota, V.R., Vilela, M.R.S.P., Mourão, F.A.G., Massensini, A.R., Moraes, M.F.D.: Anatomically dependent anticonvulsant properties of temporally-coded electrical stimulation. Epilepsy Behav. **23**(3), 294–297 (2012)

14. Oliveira, J.C., Drabowski, B.M.B., Rodrigues, S.M.A.F., Maciel, R.M., Moraes, M.F.D., Cota, V.R.: Seizure suppression by asynchronous non-periodic electrical stimulation of the amygdala is partially mediated by indirect desynchronization from nucleus accumbens. Epilepsy Res. **154**, 107–115 (2019)

15. Donoghue, T., Schaworonkow, N.: Methodological considerations for studying neural oscillations. Eur. J. Neurosci., 1–26 (2021)

16. Mainen, Z.F., Sejnowsky, T.J.: Reliability of spike timing in neocortical neurons. Science **268**, 1503–1507 (1995)

17. Gal, A., Marom, S.: Entrainment of the intrinsic dynamics of single isolated neurons by natural-like input. J. Neurosci. **33**(18), 7912–7918 (2013)

18. Scarsi, F., Tessadori J., Chiappalone M., Pasquale V.: Investigating the impact of electrical stimulation temporal distribution on cortical network responses. BMC Neurosci. **18**, 49 (2017)

19. Carnevale, N.T., Hines, M.L.: The Neuron Book. New Haven, Cambridge (2004)

20. Dura-Bernal, S., et al.: NetPyNE, a tool for data-driven multiscale modeling of brain circuits. Elife **8**, e44494 (2019)

21. Wyckhuys, T., Boon, P., Raedt, R., Van Nieuwenhuyse, B., Vonck, K., Wadman, W.: Suppression of hippocampal epileptic seizures in the kainate rat by Poisson distributed stimulation. Epilepsia **51**, 2297–2304 (2010)

22. Nelson, T.S., et al.: Exploring the tolerability of spatiotemporally complex electrical stimulation paradigms. Epilepsy Res. **96**, 267–275 (2011)

23. Buffel, I., et al.: The effect of high and low frequency cortical stimulation with a fixed or a Poisson distributed interpulse interval on cortical excitability in rats. Int. J. Neurol. Syst. **24**, 1430005 (2013)

24. Santos-Valencia, F., Almazán-Alvarado, S., Rubio-Luviano, A., Valdés-Cruz, A., Magdaleno-Madrigal, V.M., Martínez-Vargas, D.: Temporally irregular electrical stimulation to the epileptogenic focus delays epileptogenesis in rats. Brain Stimul. **12**, 1429–1438 (2019)
25. Dorval, A.D., Kuncel, A.M., Birdno, M.J., Turner, D.A., Grill, W.M.: Deep brain stimulation alleviates parkinsonian bradykinesia by regularizing pallidal activity. J. Neurophysiol. **104**, 911–921 (2010)
26. Birdno, M.J., Kuncel, A.M., Dorval, A.D., Turner, D.A., Gross, R.E., Grill, W.M.: Stimulus features underlying reduced tremor suppression with temporally patterned deep brain stimulation. J. Neurophysiol. **107**, 364–383 (2012)
27. Grill, W.M.: Temporal pattern of electrical stimulation is a new dimension of therapeutic innovation. Curr. Opin. Biomed. Eng. **8**, 1–6 (2018)
28. Tass, P.A., et al.: Coordinated reset has sustained aftereffects in Parkinsonian monkeys. Ann. Neurol. **72**, 816–820 (2012)
29. Tass, P.A.: A model of desynchronizing deep brain stimulation with a demand-controlled coordinated reset of neural subpopulations. Biol. Cybern. **89**, 81–88 (2003)
30. Hauptmann, C., Popovych, O., Tass, P.A.: Multisite coordinated delayed feedback for an effective desynchronization of neuronal networks. Stoch. Dyn. **5**, 307–319 (2005)
31. Hauptmann, C., Popovych, O., Tass, P.A.: Effectively desynchronizing deep brain stimulation based on a coordinated delayed feedback stimulation via several sites: a computational study. Biol. Cybern. **93**, 463–470 (2005)
32. Hauptmann, C., Tass, P.A.: Cumulative and after-effects of short and weak coordinated reset stimulation: a modeling study. J. Neural Eng. **6**, 016004 (2009)
33. Buhlmann, J., Hofmann, L., Tass, P.A., Hauptmann, C.: Modeling of a segmented electrode for desynchronizing deep brain stimulation. Front. Neuroeng. **4**, 15 (2011)
34. Ebert, M., Hauptmann, C., Tass, P.A.: Coordinated reset stimulation in a large-scale model of the STN-GPe circuit. Front. Comput. Neurosci. **8**, 154 (2014)
35. Manos, T., Zeitler, M., Tass, P.A.: How stimulation frequency and intensity impact on the long-lasting effects of coordinated reset stimulation. PLoS Comput. Biol. **14**, e1006113 (2018)
36. Kromer, J.A., Khaledi-Nasab, A., Tass, P.A.: Impact of number of stimulation sites on long-lasting desynchronization effects of coordinated reset stimulation. Chaos **30**, 083134 (2020)
37. Khaledi-Nasab, A., Kromer, J.A., Tass, P.A.: Long-lasting desynchronization effects of coordinated reset stimulation improved by random jitters. Front Physiol. **10**, 1446 (2021)
38. Khaledi-Nasab, A., Kromer, J.A., Tass, P.A.: Long-lasting desynchronization of plastic neural networks by random reset stimulation. Front Physiol. **11**, 1843 (2020)

In silico Investigation of the Effects of Distinct Temporal Patterns of Electrical Stimulation to the Amygdala Using a Network of Izhikevich Neurons

João Pedro Silva e Oliveira[1] , Victor Rafael Pereira Discacciati[1] ,
Daniel de Castro Medeiros[2] , Márcio Flávio Dutra Moraes[2] , Grace S. Pereira[2] ,
Keite Lira de Almeida França[2] , and Vinícius Rosa Cota[1](✉)

[1] Laboratory of Neuroenegineering and Neuroscience (LINNce), Universidade Federal de São João Del-Rei, Pça. Frei Orlando, 170 – Centro, São João Del-Rei, MG 36302-600, Brazil
vrcota@ufsj.edu.br
[2] Núcleo de Neurociências, Departamento de Fisiologia e Biofísica, Universidade Federal de Minas Gerais, Av. Antônio Carlos, 6627 – Campus Pampulha, Belo Horizonte, MG CEP 31270-901, Brazil

Abstract. Computational modeling is a powerful tool to investigate the mechanisms of neural function. This work model *in silico* the effect of experimental electrical stimulation on a neuronal network of the basolateral amygdala. Starting from the premise that different temporal patterns of stimulation affect in different ways the behavior of neural circuits involved in the genesis of epilepsy and seizures, we tested the hypothesis that non-periodic electrical stimulation (NPS) has a desynchronizing or suppressing effect on the origin of synchronization. The basolateral amygdala was modeled with three firing patterns present in Izhikevich's neurons. The obtained data were analyzed and compared with the effect of other temporal patterns of electrical stimulation. The results indicates that different temporal patterns reflect different timing for the origin of synchronization, but also suggest that the already proven mechanism of NPS, is not on a microcircuit level, but possibly on a macroscopic level of forebrain networks.

Keywords: Epilepsy · Basolateral amygdala · Ictogenesis · Non-Periodic Electrical Stimulation (NPS) · Izhikevich

1 Introduction

1.1 General

Electrical stimulation of neural tissue is a promising alternative for the treatment of different neurological disorders in cases when first-line treatment methods (pharmacological, surgical, behavioral, etc.) fail to provide proper control of symptoms or to deliver long-lasting effects [1]. One such application is the usage of electrical stimulation (ES) delivered to the central nervous system (Deep Brain Stimulation – DBS) to suppress

© Springer Nature Switzerland AG 2022
P. R. d. A. Ribeiro et al. (Eds.): LAWCN 2021, CCIS 1519, pp. 132–152, 2022.
https://doi.org/10.1007/978-3-031-08443-0_9

seizures in patients with refractory epilepsy [2]. While with varying electrical parameters and targets within the brain, most if not all different methods of pulsatile ES (DBS included) are delivered in a high-frequency manner (pulses fired at 80 Hz or more), given the majority of studies showed that application of low frequencies results in controversial (or neutral at best) effects [3]. On the other hand, the carefully engineering of ES strategies should always pursue the lowest frequencies possible [4]. Such solutions would wield therapeutic effect with minimum amounts of energy being transferred from the power supply of an implantable pulse generator to the neural tissue, which implies increased safety and extended longevity of batteries and electrodes [5].

To approach this issue, our group proposed and successfully tested in animals a non-standard form of ES, termed nonperiod stimulation (NPS), as a means to treat epilepsy with a very low count of pulses per second, only four. Based on the rationale that seizures are a network-level hypersynchronous phenomena originating from a condition of tissue hyper-excitability, NPS was specifically designed to impair neural synchronization by delivering its pulses across time in a random fashion, in which the interpulse intervals (IPI) display a natural-like scale-free distribution that follows a power-law of unitary exponent [6]. This would putatively break aberrant oscillations and thus suppress seizures with minor impact on basal neural function. In an original work, we tested NPS in animals submitted to acute seizures induced by pentylenotetrazole (PTZ) and compared it to controls and three other temporal patterns of ES: periodic (fixed 250 ms IPI), 50 Hz *Bursts*, and a different form of IPI randomization termed NPSLH [7]. Even though all patterns had the very same low number of pulses per second (four) and same electrical parameters, thus same energy, only NPS was capable of increasing latencies for animals to display convulsive behavior during controlled PTZ injection, demonstrating its anticonvulsant effect. NPS also showed beneficial effects on an animal model of Temporal Lobe Epilepsy (a frequently refractory form of the disease) [8] and that it is most efficacious when applied to both amygdalae in an asynchronous fashion [9]. Finally, mechanistic investigation suggested that NPS suppresses seizures by inducing a naturally-randomized recruitment of nodes receiving afferences from the amygdala, which impairs aberrant synchronization across ictogenic neural circuitry such as the limbic system and others involving areas of the forebrain, midbrain, and hindbrain [10–12].

In order to further investigate this hypothesis, our group set out to test NPS *in silico*, given the obvious and well known ethical and methodological advantages of computational models of the brain [13]. Although accumulated evidence suggests the therapeutic mechanisms rely on circuits in the meso to macroscale, the group is testing a wide range of brain-organization levels, from single biophysically realistic neurons to the neurodynamics of the whole brain. In this work, we present the first *in silico* results of NPS applied to a microcircuit resembling the cytoarchitectonics of the basolateral amygdala. We chose to construct the network using different types of Izhikevich neurons, once it is a model praised for its capacity of reproducing several different kinds of neuronal firing behaviors with small computational complexity [14, 15]. Ictogenesis was modeled by gradually changing the synaptic weights of the network across time, while the different types of ES were implemented using the external input current term of the Izhikevich model.

2 Methodology

2.1 Network of Izhikevich Neurons

Izhikevich's model is a nonlinear integrate-and-fire type model. This model combines computational efficiency and the ability to produce rich firing patterns exhibited by real biological neurons [14, 15], making it biophysically realistic and ideal for large-scale simulations. The model can be described by the following equations:

$$v' = 0.04v^2 + 5v + 140 - u + I \qquad (1)$$
$$u' = a(bv - u) \qquad (2)$$

$$if\ v \geq 30\ mV\ ,\ then\ \begin{cases} v \leftarrow c \\ u \leftarrow u + d \end{cases} \qquad (3)$$

where $v(t)$ is the membrane voltage; $u(t)$ is the recovery variable and; I is the input current, i.e., the external stimulus that the neuron receives, which can be background activity or the response of another neuron. In addition, parameter a describes the time scale of the recovery variable; b describes the sensitivity of the recovery variable (u); parameter c describes the resting potential of the membrane; and d describes the reset of the recovery variable after firing. Here, these equations were computationally solved by applying the Euler method.

The present study consisted in modeling a neuronal circuit *in silico* (Fig. 1), which presented cytoarchitecture similar to that of the basolateral amygdala (~70,000 neurons), including the proportion between the main cell types present in this region. The implementation represented a biologically plausible simulation capable of presenting firing patterns and oscillations similar to those of the synchronous and asynchronous forebrain states observed in this region [13, 14, 16]. The network was composed of 1200 neurons (scale of 1:60) [14], divided into three subpopulations: main cells with adaptation (PNa); main cells with continuous spiking (PNc); and the fast-firing interneurons (FSI) [13]. Thus, according to the study by Feng *et al.* (2019) neurons were categorized being 64% PNa (n = 768), 26% PNc (n = 312) and 10% FSI (n = 120). These cells were assigned with the firing patterns commonly found in electrophysiological recordings in the basolateral amygdala. The class of excitatory neurons (PNa and PNc) was assigned the patterns regular firing (RS) and chattering (CH) neurons, respectively. In turn, the inhibitory neurons (FSI) mimic the low firing threshold (LTS) neurons [15, 16]. This network was made to be recurrent with all-to-all connections, where all neurons connect to each other with randomly distributed synaptic weights. The network implementation was chosen and evaluated in terms of biological plausibility and considering previous works that used the same network architecture [14–19] or that compared different topologies, realistic or scaled, in the structuring of neural networks [20–22]. The entire study was developed based on an adapted version of the MATLAB® code provided by Izhikevich (2003) [15].

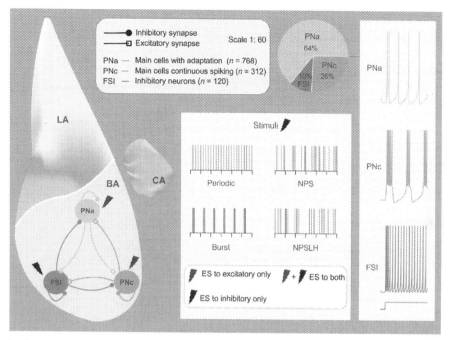

Fig. 1. Basolateral Amygdala (BA) model. The neural network implemented for this simulation study was based on the Izhikevich formalism and was performed in a reduced scale (1:60) [14], that is, with 768 main cells with adaptation (PNa) indicated by a green circle, 312 main cells continuous spiking (PNc) indicated by a blue circle, and 120 inhibitory neurons (FSI) indicated by a red circle (illustration in the left). The relative proportions of the three cell types were obtained from Feng *et al.* (2019) (top panels) [13]. PNa and PNc cells provide excitatory inputs to other cells, while FSI neurons are inhibitory. This network was made to be recurrent with all-to-all connections, where PNa, PNc and FSI were connected among themselves and with each other. Sample recordings from neurons in the current injection are shown in the righ panel. Four Stimulus temporal patterns were developed according to the experiments performed by Cota and collaborators (2009) [7]: (1) periodic stimulation with interpulse intervals (IPIs) of 250 ms; (2) bursts with IPI of 20 ms; (3) non-periodic stimulation (NPSLH) with pseudo-randomized IPIs, following the linear decay histogram and; (4) non-periodic stimulation (NPSIH, or just NPS) with pseudo-randomized IPIs, following the inverse decay histogram (power-law with unitary exponent) (bottom panel). In all cases, the amplitudes were kept the same for all cases. Furthermore, all temporal patterns of stimulation always trigger four pulses per second. LA: lateral amygdala; CA: central amygdala; ES: electrical stimulation.

2.2   Induction of Ictogenesis

First, the network with the parameters described in Table 1 was adjusted, so it displayed a gamma rhythm-modulation, a frequency that is commonly present in electrographic recordings in physiological conditions [23]. This adjustment was done by empirically modifying the synaptic weights. At first, the excitatory neurons received a maximum weight of 0.5 and the inhibitory neurons a maximum weight of 1, maintaining the configuration in Izhikevich's study [15, 16]. Thus, the firing rate of the inhibitory population was increased in comparison to that of the excitatory population [23]. However, this combination of weights returned an already hypersynchronized network, so the inhibitory synaptic weight was raised to the minimum necessary for the network not to exhibit this aberrant activity.

Table 1. Network model parameters

Parameters	PNa	PNc	FSI
Number of neurons	768	312	120
a	0.02	0.02	0.02
b	0.2	0.2	0.25
c	−65	−50	−65
d	8	2	2
s (max)	0.5	0.5	−3.5
v	−65	−50	−65

To simulate the process of ictogenesis, a gradual modification (increment or decrement) of 0.01% was made in the synaptic weights at each iteration (1 ms) and, therefore, modifying the excitatory or inhibitory tonus. With this, the network makes a gradual transition from the normal state to an aberrant synchronous activity arising from increased excitability. The four experiments to achieve this transition were: (1) increased synaptic weights in A-type excitatory neurons (PNa); (2) increased synaptic weights in C-type excitatory neurons (PNc); (3) increased synaptic weights in all excitatory neurons (PNa and PNc); (4) reduced synaptic weights in inhibitory neurons (FSI). The normal activity was modeled by random distribution with the following maximum synaptic weights: 0.5 PNa, 0.5 PNc, and −3.5 FSI. In this way, and considering a total time of 10000 ms, the subpopulation that would suffer changes in their synaptic weights would end each experiment with twice the initial weight, or with a zero weight for experiment 4.

These changes promoted by the gradual modification of synaptic weights in the simulation protocol allowed us to study the influence of the relationship between excitation/inhibition in the network that is associated with the generalized change in the amygdala, as well as in pharmacological maneuvers used in our *in vivo* experiments [7] using nonspecific GABAergic antagonists or pilocarpine, a nonselective muscarinic agonist.

2.3 Temporal-Patterned Stimuli

Stimulus temporal patterns were developed according to the experiments performed by Cota and collaborators (2009) [7]. The present study applied 4 patterns of ES: (1) periodic stimulation with interpulse intervals (IPIs) of 250 ms; (2) bursts with IPI of 20 ms;

(3) non-periodic stimulation (NPSLH) with pseudo-randomized IPIs, following the linear decay histogram and; (4) non-periodic stimulation (NPSIH, or just NPS) with pseudo-randomized IPIs, following the inverse decay histogram (power-law with unitary exponent). In all cases, the amplitudes were kept the same for all cases. Furthermore, all temporal patterns of stimulation always trigger four pulses per second. Figure 2 shows the histograms of the inter-pulse intervals (IPIs) for each type of stimulation implemented [7].

The total simulation time was 10 s for each experiment performed, and the stimulations were applied from the beginning for each of the stimulated groups. These stimulations were developed in subroutines that returned a stimulation matrix (stim), with dimensions of the number of neurons [PNa; PNc; FSI] vs. simulation time [ms]. In this way, the matrix was filled with zeros and, at the time of stimulation, the column was filled with the pre-set amplitude. This stim matrix is added to the input current (parameter I of Eq. 1), which represents external inputs.

In this study we used a randomized distribution of stimulation amplitudes between 5 and 15 mV, and these parameters were obtained empirically. Finally, we ran simulations in which electrical stimulation differentially affects neuronal types, in order to represent different situations of the electrode position in relation to the amygdala cytoarchitecture. We simulated: 1) stimulation of only excitatory neurons (PNa and PNc), separately or together; 2) only inhibitory neurons (FSI) and; 3) the whole set of neurons.

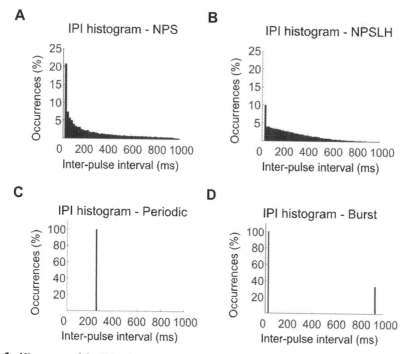

Fig. 2. Histogram of the IPIs of the stimulations implemented in the experiments (MATLAB®). A) NPS stimulation; B) NPSLH stimulation; C) Periodic stimulation; D) Burst stimulation.

2.4 Experimental Protocol and Assessment of Effects on Synchronization

For each experiment presented in this paper, 10 trials were performed under all conditions for each stimulation pattern to obtain statistical power ($1 - \beta = 0.915$ with a critical $F = 2.579$ for an effect of 0.6 and $p < 0.05$. Performed using the *G Power software – version 3.1.9.7*), totaling 600 simulations. From the neuronal firing, the following were calculated: 1) the percentage of neurons firing simultaneously (time window of 10000 ms); 2) the simplified local field potential (LFP), represented by the sum of the membrane potentials of the excitatory neurons over time and; 3) the frequency spectrum obtained by the Fast Fourier Transform on the LFP. From these analyses, we manually collected data such as the time to the first hypersynchronous event (spike), the occurrence and number of spike clusters and of their spikes, the latency to onset of sustained synchronization, and the intervals between events. For this evaluation, the periods in which the network exceeded a threshold of three times the standard deviation of the baseline activity were considered as spikes. A synchronization criterion of 400 ms minimum-time between spikes was established to validate whether the interval between events belonged to a synchronized state or not. To characterize as a synchronization cluster, the network should exhibit at least two spikes within the synchronization criterion followed by a long low neuronal activity.

Statistical analysis was performed based on the mean and standard error of the mean (SEM) obtained in each experiment, with the help of IBM SPSS Statistics program. Data normality was analyzed by the Shapiro-Wilk test and statistical significance of the comparative analysis was performed using one-way ANOVA followed by Tukey test for multiple comparisons ($p < 0.05$). The association between the stimulated groups and the presence of a spike cluster was performed by Fisher's exact test, which is usually used for small samples.

2.5 Interspike Intervals (ISI) and Coefficient of Variation (CV)

Neural networks have the ability to change from one state of activity to another by modifying the external frequency that feeds the network's activity, or by altering the balance between excitation and inhibition. Brunel (2000, 2001) carried out, in an analytical way, the categorization of the different states that a network with sparse limits can be adopted, so the greater the width of the distribution of interspike intervals (ISI), the more irregular the network [21, 22]. Aiming to quantify the variability of the neuronal firings, the ISI was defined as the time interval between two consecutive spikes [24]:

$$ISI = td_{t+1} - td_t \tag{4}$$

where td_t is the time of the *m*-th neuronal fire. For a given spike train, the average ISI was given by:

$$\langle ISI \rangle = \frac{1}{N_{spk} - 1} \sum_{i=1}^{N_{spk}} ISI \tag{5}$$

where N_{spk} is the number of spikes.

The coefficient of variation (CV) of the ISI was defined from the ratio between the standard deviation σ_{ISI} of the ISI and the mean ISI [25]:

$$CV = \frac{\sigma_{ISI}}{ISI} \tag{6}$$

Considering that Poisson processes produce CV = 1, values of CV < 1 determine that the firings of a given neuron are less regular, while values of CV > 1 imply regular firings. CV values close to 0 indicate regular spikes, while bursting patterns results in CV ≥ 0.5 [24, 25].

3 Results

The network created to model a circuit in the basolateral amygdala was capable of presenting a state of synchronous irregular firing [21]. Figure 3 shows a normal firing pattern, that is, the network presents the dominant gamma rhythm (above 20 Hz) [26]. Panels on the right confirm the idea that the network does not exhibit a characteristic hypersynchrony present in epilepsy electrographic recordings.

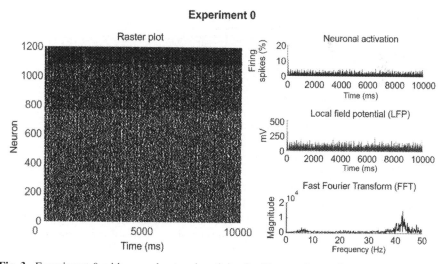

Fig. 3. Experiment 0 with normal network activity. In this experiment there was no change in synaptic weights and the network does not show any level of hypersynchronism. Raster Plot of network with maximum synaptic weights: S = 0.5 PNa; 0.5 PNc and −3.5 FSI. Here and in all raster plots of this study, neurons are aligned in sequence in the y-axis as PNa (rows 1 to 768), PNc (rows 769 to 1080), and FSI (rows 1081 to 1200).

Basolateral amygdala is an ideal system for the exploration of the biophysical rationales of physiological and pathophysiological oscillations and thus the basic mechanisms underlying the cellular basis of the phenomenal local field potential oscillations and normal-ictal transitions [27]. Figure 4 shows the four possible ways to achieve high

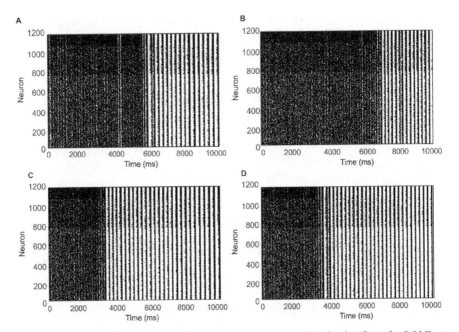

Fig. 4. Samples of the four strategies for obtaining network synchronization from the 0.01% step modification in synaptic weights (no stimulation). Maximum synaptic weights used: 0.5 PNa; 0.5 PNc and −3.5 FSI. A) Raster Plot of Experiment 1: Increase in synaptic weights in PNa; B) Raster Plot of Experiment 2: Increase in synaptic weights in PNc; C) Raster Plot of Experiment 3: Increase in synaptic weights in PNa and PNc; D) Raster Plot of Experiment 4: Reduction in synaptic weights in FSI inhibitory neurons.

levels of synchronization. All forms of tampering with synaptic weights resulted in a transition from synchronous irregular to synchronous regular states.

An important detail that contributed to the validation of the model was that all four experiments displayed oscillations in the delta (0 to 4 Hz) or low theta (4 to 8 Hz) ranges as the fundamental frequency (Fig. 5) [26]. This rhythm is found in *in vivo* studies in animals with pharmacologically induced seizures and is mainly determined by spiking rates at (4 to 5 events per second) [7]. It is worth noting that this rhythm arose naturally, without any changes to adjust the network in this direction.

It is believed that experiment 4 (Fig. 5), where there is a loss of inhibitory tone, is the experiment that better reflects reality because it is considered a fundamental factor in the generation of epileptic phenomena. Of particularly interest to us, in our work seizures were induced by means of decreasing inhibitory tonus via administration of PTZ, which is a GABAergic antagonist.

Figure 6 depicts the results of the analysis of the first hypersynchronous event and the results of the onset of sustained synchronization obtained in experiment 1 (increased synaptic weights of PNa) with the various conditions tested.

When all neurons were stimulated, only the burst stimulation significantly decreases the time for appearance of the first spike when compared to the no stimulation group only (Fig. 6A). When considering stimulation only of inhibitory neurons, burst decreases the

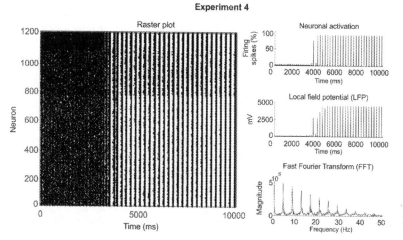

Fig. 5. Experiment 4 with aberrant network activity. In this experiment, there was a reduction in inhibitory synaptic weights. The network shows hypersynchronism. Raster plot of network with maximum synaptic weights: S = 0.5 PNa; 0.5 PNc and −3.5 FSI

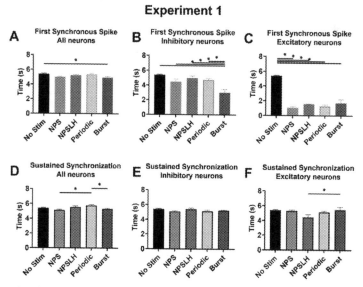

Fig. 6. Synchronization results for all stimulation conditions across ictogenesis induced by increasing PNa synaptic weights. Panel shows the time of the first spike and the onset of sustained synchronization obtained in experiment 1. A) Time of first spike in which all neurons were stimulated; B) Time of first spike in which only inhibitory neurons were stimulated; C) Time of first spike in which only excitatory neurons were stimulated; D) Onset of sustained synchronization in which all neurons were stimulated; E) Onset of sustained synchronization in which only inhibitory neurons were stimulated; F) Onset of sustained synchronization in which only inhibitory neurons were stimulated. Significant differences are indicated by an asterisk.

time for the first spike in comparison to all other groups, while these others groups do not induce any changes (Fig. 6B). Finally, when only excitatory neurons are stimulated, all groups induce a significant decrease in comparison to the non-stimulated group (Fig. 6C).

Regarding the onset of sustained synchronization, stimulation of all neurons differentially modulated the network for the periodic pattern when compared to NPS and burst (Fig. 6D). This increase of time is of unclear significance. On the other hand, when stimulation target is broken down, only NPSLH (but not NPS, nor periodic) induced a decrease for onset of sustained synchronization in comparison to burst.

Only a few simulations displayed isolated spike clusters and to test whether different patterns modulated these synchronous events, number of experiments resulting in clusters (number of occurrences) was assessed using Fisher's exact. Table 2 shows that there was no association between stimulations and the presence of spike clusters when all neurons were stimulated. On the other hand, periodic and burst stimuli seem to generate fragmentation, although mildly, of synchronization when inhibitory neurons were targeted. Additionally, all patterns induced fragmentation of synchronization when only excitatory neurons were stimulated.

Table 2. Count of occurrences of spike clusters from Experiment 1

Count of occurrences	All Neurons				
	No Stim	NPS	NPSLH	Periodic	Burst
Yes	0	1	1	4	0
No	10	9	9	6	10
Fisher's exact test	$X^2_{(4)} = 7.298$; p = 0.64				
Count of occurrences	Inhibitory				
	No Stim	NPS	NPSLH	Periodic	Burst
Yes	0	0	0	3	4
No	10	10	10	7	6
Fisher's exact test	$X^2_{(4)} = 10.085$; p = 0.015				
Count of occurrences	Excitatory				
	No Stim	NPS	NPSLH	Periodic	Burst
Yes	0	8	10	9	7
No	10	2	0	1	3
Fisher's exact test	$X^2_{(4)} = 27.805$; p = 0.000003				

Figure 7 presents the results obtained with experiment 2, increasing the synaptic weights in C-type excitatory neurons (PNc). Here, results are analogous to experiment 1, but somehow toned down (no differences when all neurons are stimulated; Fig. 7A and Fig. 7D). As before, time for the appearance of the first spike was significantly decreased under burst stimulation, when only inhibitory neurons were targeted (Fig. 7B), but were decreased by all patterns when only excitatory neurons were affected (Fig. 7C). Finally, time for onset of sustained synchronization was affected (increased) only by burst stimulus targeted at excitatory neurons (Fig. 7F).

Experiment 2

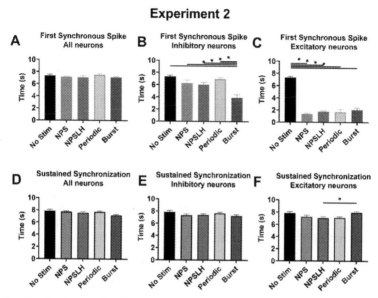

Fig. 7. Synchronization results for all stimulation conditions across ictogenesis induced by increasing PNc synaptic weights. Panel shows the time of the first spike and the onset of sustained synchronization obtained in experiment 2. A) Time of first spike in which all neurons were stimulated; B) Time of first spike in which only inhibitory neurons were stimulated; C) Time of first spike in which only excitatory neurons were stimulated; D) Onset of sustained synchronization in which all neurons were stimulated; E) Onset of sustained synchronization in which only inhibitory neurons were stimulated; F) Onset of sustained synchronization in which only inhibitory neurons were stimulated.

Table 3 presents Fisher's exact test for occurrence of spike clusters in experiment 2. Again, there seems to be no association between stimulations and the presence of spike clusters when all neurons and also when only inhibitory neurons were stimulated. On the other hand, all patterns induced fragmentation when excitatory neurons were targeted.

In experiment 3 (Fig. 8), increase in synaptic weights in all excitatory neurons (PNa and PNc), results repeat those of experiment one: time for the appearance of the first spike was significantly decreased under burst stimulation only, when inhibitory neurons were targeted (Fig. 8B), but were decreased by all patterns (but burst significantly less) when only excitatory neurons were affected (Fig. 8C). No differences were observed when all neurons were stimulated (Fig. 8A). In the same vein, there were no significant differences regarding onset of sustained synchronization in the first two conditions (all neurons stimulated, Fig. 8D and inhibitory neurons stimulated, Fig. 8E). Curiously, NPSLH pattern only significantly decreased, in comparison to all other groups, onset time for sustained synchronization when all neurons are targeted (Fig. 8F).

Table 3. Count of occurrences of spike clusters from Experiment 2

Count of occurrences	All Neurons				
	No Stim	NPS	NPSLH	Periodic	Burst
Yes	3	4	4	2	0
No	7	6	6	8	10
Fisher's exact test	$X^2_{(4)} = 6.254$; $p = 0.223$				
Count of occurrences	Inhibitory				
	No Stim	NPS	NPSLH	Periodic	Burst
Yes	3	2	4	2	5
No	7	8	6	8	5
Fisher's exact test	$X^2_{(4)} = 3.043$; $p = 0.664$				
Count of occurrences	Excitatory				
	No Stim	NPS	NPSLH	Periodic	Burst
Yes	3	9	8	9	10
No	7	1	2	1	0
Fisher's exact test	$X^2_{(4)} = 14.387$; $p = 0.002$				

Next, the results of Fisher's exact test for experiment 3 are presented (Table 4). As in experiment 2, the test shows that there is no association between stimulations and the presence of spike clusters when all neurons were stimulated and when only inhibitory neurons were stimulated. Also, as in experiment 2, the test showed that all patterns induced fragmentation of sustained synchronization.

Experiment 4, reduction of synaptic weights in inhibitory neurons (FSI), displayed results very analogous to those of experiment 2 regarding time for appearance of the first synchronous spike (Figs. 9A, 9B, and 9C). Conversely, effects on sustained synchronization were much more diverse in this alternative form of induction of ictogenesis. In this case, both nonperiodic stimuli (NPS and NPSLH) induced a decrease in the onset time, compared to all other groups, when all neurons were stimulated (Fig. 9D). On the other hand, only NPSLH had such an effect, and compared only to no-stimulation condition and periodic pattern, when inhibitory neurons were targeted. Finally, and in line with this previous finding, NPSLH only induced a decrease of onset times when compared to all other stimulation patterns when they were applied to excitatory neurons (Fig. 9F).

Finally, the phenomenon of fragmentation of synchronization was more prevalent in relation to previous ones, as showed by the Fisher's exact test for experiment 4 (Table 5).

There is an association between stimuli and the presence of spike clusters in all the conditions tested. While burst stimulation seems to induce clusters when applied to all neurons or inhibitory only neurons, all stimulation patterns seem to do so when applied to excitatory only neurons.

Experiment 3

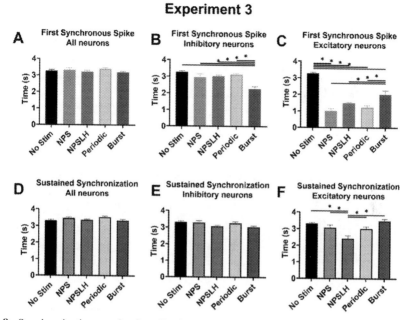

Fig. 8. Synchronization results for all stimulation conditions across ictogenesis induced by increasing PNa and PNc synaptic weights. Panel shows the time of the first spike and the onset of sustained synchronization obtained in experiment 3. A) Time of first spike in which all neurons were stimulated; B) Time of first spike in which only inhibitory neurons were stimulated; C) Time of first spike in which only excitatory neurons were stimulated; D) Onset of sustained synchronization in which all neurons were stimulated; E) Onset of sustained synchronization in which only inhibitory neurons were stimulated; F) Onset of sustained synchronization in which only inhibitory neurons were stimulated.

Table 4. Count of occurrences of spike clusters from Experiment 3

Count of occurrences	All Neurons				
	No Stim	NPS	NPSLH	Periodic	Burst
Yes	0	1	0	1	2
No	10	9	10	9	8
Fisher's exact test	$X^2_{(4)} = 3.355$; p $= 0.783$				
Count of occurrences	Inhibitory				
	No Stim	NPS	NPSLH	Periodic	Burst
Yes	0	0	0	2	2
No	10	10	10	8	8
Fisher's exact test	$X^2_{(4)} = 4.952$; p $= 0.197$				
Count of occurrences	Excitatory				
	No Stim	NPS	NPSLH	Periodic	Burst
Yes	0	8	7	8	6
No	10	2	3	2	4
Fisher's exact test	$X^2_{(4)} = 18.882$; p $= 0.001$				

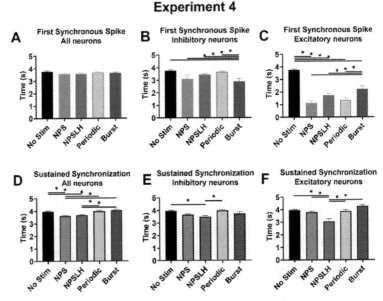

Fig. 9. Synchronization results for all stimulation conditions across ictogenesis induced by reduction FSI synaptic weights. Panel shows the time of the first spike and the onset of sustained synchronization obtained in experiment 4. A) Time of first spike in which all neurons were stimulated; B) Time of first spike in which only inhibitory neurons were stimulated; C) Time of first spike in which only excitatory neurons were stimulated; D) Onset of sustained synchronization in which all neurons were stimulated; E) Onset of sustained synchronization in which only inhibitory neurons were stimulated; F) Onset of sustained synchronization in which only inhibitory neurons were stimulated.

Table 5. Count of occurrences of spike clusters from Experiment 4

Count of occurrences	All Neurons				
	No Stim	NPS	NPSLH	Periodic	*Burst*
Yes	1	0	1	4	7
No	9	10	9	6	3
Fisher's exact test	$X^2_{(4)} = 15.351$; p $= 0.002$				
Count of occurrences	Inhibitory				
	No Stim	NPS	NPSLH	Periodic	*Burst*
Yes	1	1	1	5	7
No	9	9	9	5	3
Fisher's exact test	$X^2_{(4)} = 13.725$; p $= 0.005$				
Count of occurrences	Excitatory				
	No Stim	NPS	NPSLH	Periodic	*Burst*
Yes	1	8	5	9	7
No	9	2	5	1	3
Fisher's exact test	$X^2_{(4)} = 16.266$; p $= 0.002$				

Table 6. ISI and CV of the experiments.

Stimulation	Pattern of electrical stimulation	Experiment 1 ISI (mean ± SEM) (ms)	CV	Experiment 2 ISI (mean ± SEM) (ms)	CV	Experiment 3 ISI (mean ± SEM) (ms)	CV	Experiment 4 ISI (mean ± SEM) (ms)	CV
All neurons	No Stim	260.7 ± 2.20	0.1109	228.5 ± 4.75	0.1960	253.9 ± 1.84	0.1166	239.3 ±1.94	0.1273
	NPS	259.8 ± 2.92	0.1513	220.4 ± 2.68	0.1197	251.3 ± 1.62	0.1026	235.0 ±1.34	0.0925
	NPSLH	260.6 ± 2.61	0.1287	226.0 ± 3.28	0.1477	253.5 ± 1.51	0.0951	234.8 ±1.16	0.0801
	Periodic	256.5 ± 2.04	0.0997	222.6 ± 3.29	0.1456	253.0 ± 1.57	0.0984	236.5 ±1.42	0.0952
	Burst	256.2 ± 2.04	0.1060	225.6 ± 3.61	0.1835	252.7 ± 1.62	0.1028	237.3 ±1.25	0.0823
Inhibitory neurons	No Stim	260.7 ± 2.20	0.1109	228.5 ± 4.75	0.1960	253.9 ±1.84	0.1166	239.3 ± 1.94	0.1273
	NPS	260.4 ± 2.49	0.1293	231.7 ± 5.44	0.2450	252.8 ± 1.67	0.1064	236.8 ± 1.32	0.0907
	NPSLH	261.2 ± 2.35	0.1175	228.7 ± 4.72	0.2153	251.7 ± 1.71	0.1118	237.7 ± 1.55	0.1066
	Periodic	257.5 ± 2.48	0.1301	230.9 ± 4.78	0.2017	252.6 ± 1.65	0.1060	238.8 ± 1.55	0.1021
	Burst	260.2 ± 2.32	0.1189	228.4 ± 4.82	0.2252	253.5 ± 1.81	0.1170	240.4 ± 1.99	0.1319
Excitatory neurons	No Stim	260.7 ± 2.20	0.1109	228.5 ± 4.75	0.7960	253.9 ± 1.84	0.1166	239.3 ± 1.94	0.1273
	NPS	253.1 ± 1.95	0.1275	240.6 ± 10.87	0.4800	247.8 ± 2.01	0.1337	230.6 ± 1.54	0.1078
	NPSLH	254.4 ± 2.45	0.1391	213.0 ± 4.86	0.2582	249.3 ±2.10	0.1444	233.4 ± 1.61	0.1169
	Periodic	257.7 ± 2.77	0.1447	240.3 ± 7.06	0.3164	249.0 ±1.80	0.1192	238.3 ± 1.87	0.1240
	Burst	252.3 ± 2.33	0.1224	215.0 ± 3.96	0.1726	251.4 ± 1.97	0.1248	235.6 ± 1.73	0.1129

Complementary analysis of the ISI and the CV was carried out to investigate the patterns of activities of the simulated networks. Table 6 shows, in detail, the values found for ISI and CV in all simulated scenarios (Figs. 6–9 D–F). The ISI analysis showed significant differences only in Experiments 2 and 4, both with stimulation of excitatory neurons. In Experiment 2, an increase in ISI (213.0 ms to 240.0 ms) and CV (0.2582 to 0.3164) during periodic stimulation, in comparison to NPSLH, was observed. In Experiment 4, a significant reduction in ISI was observed in the NPS and NPSLH groups (230.6 ms and 233.4 ms, respectively) when compared to the No Stimulation group (239.3 ms). Finally, an increase in this parameter in periodic stimulation when compared to NPS (230.6 ms to 238.3 ms) was also observed. In these simulations, the CV was between 0.1078 and 0.1273.

The variations found in both the ISI and the CV indicated that the activities correspond to regular synchronous dynamics with CV < 0.5. For these values, the mean of the ISI is large, that is, far above the threshold, and the standard deviation σ is comparatively small, characterizing a neuronal dynamic that is close to deterministic with an almost periodic firing. These states have been observed as a self-sustained activity in networks, which results naturally from the recurrently generated fluctuations intrinsic to the dynamics of the system to display characteristics consistent with both experimental [28] and simulation data [24, 25].

4   Discussion and Conclusions

Although insufficient to derive definitive conclusions regarding the effects of distinct patterns of ES in general and of NPS in particular in the occurrence and nature of hypersynchronous phenomena, present results add novel evidence supporting the rationale that the temporal structure of stimulus is a major determinant of neuronal response, including in therapeutic approaches [6, 7, 29–33]. In fact, a prevalent result seen here were different modulation effects (increases and decreases) in all studied metrics (time to first spike, onset of transition to a synchronous regular state (hypersynchronism), induction of fragmentation, ISI, and CV) that depended on the temporal pattern being applied to the network. Of particularly interest to us, effects of NPS and NPSLH were different in several experimental conditions, even though both are nonperiodic, with randomly generated IPI, differing only in their distributions. It is important to highlight that NPS and NPSLH also displayed different anticonvulsant effects on animal experimentation (NPSLH had none). On top of that, even this simple model of the basolateral amygdala undergoing ictogenesis by alteration of single parameters (synaptic weights) was enough to give rise to the property of differentiating the subtle distinction between NPS and NPSLH. We believe it is remarkable that such feature emerges in such a simple system as the model described here.

The network used in these simulations was capable of producing a synchronous irregular state with gamma-oscillating activity [13, 34] when synaptic weights remained unmodified. This provided initial validation regarding its neurobiological plausibility. Additionally, by changing synaptic weights, we were able to induce transitions to synchronous regular (or hypersynchronous) states, that showed a realistic spiking activity in the 4–5 Hz rate. In fact, the gradual variation of synaptic weights disturbing the excitatory versus inhibitory balance over time used here is similar to approaches of other studies, in which alterations in the synaptic connectivity weight were performed to investigate plastic changes [35–37] and also to induce ictogenesis in the network [38]. In any case, modeled ictogenesis exhibited several aspects observed experimentally by our group [7] and that were predicted in previous theoretical studies [14, 17, 21, 35, 36], such as synchronous and asynchronous behavior of activity and changes in the balance between inhibition and excitation at the microcircuit level. Moreover, similar findings were also seen in the basolateral amygdala kindling model [27], where oscillations in the delta (0–4 Hz) or low theta (4–8 Hz) ranges were found in both normal and seizure conditions. In these experiments, multi-unit discharges increased with higher seizure staging, but remained phase-locked to the delta waves in local field potentials. This induced alternations between burst inhibitory (FSI neurons) and principal neurons (PNa and PNc) activity, in which spike and inter-pulse intervals may concurrently set a wavelength for delta frequencies. Finally, among the strategies to induce transition to synchronous regular states in the network of this work, it is the decrease of inhibitory synaptic weights. This directly relates to the mechanisms underlying a very common and useful animal model employed for the screening of new antiepileptic drugs or of novel therapeutics, pentylenotetrazole (PTZ)-induced acute seizures. In fact, most of our previous results has been obtained using such approach.

There are not many studies that report different patterns of ES applied to the basolateral amygdala on ictogenesis [14, 18], since most investigations carried out in this region focused on its role in conditioning and fear [39–41]. Focusing on the role of ES on suppression and initiation of sustained synchronization, several studies have also indicated that ES has the ability to modulate seizures [42–44]. In particular, responsive stimulation, in which stimuli is applied to an epileptic region when the seizure has been detected or predicted, has the ability to suppress ongoing seizures, even if the suppression effect occurs stochastically or locally [45].

We were not able to see any desynchronization effects of NPS in the present results. On contrary, while it was neutral in many situations tested, in other times it actually decreased onset time for hypersynchronous phenomena. Although counter-intuitive in the face of the well-established therapeutic properties of NPS, this was somehow expected. First, it is important to notice that such latency-decreasing effect was not a particularity of NPS as it was always accompanied by similar effects of other temporal patterns (Figs. 6 to 9). Second, our original guess was that NPS would manifest its therapeutic effects on higher levels of brain organizations, such as polysynaptic neural circuits of even in the coupling of large-scale networks, not in the microcircuit level [6]. In line with this, previous findings with animal models actually suggest that NPS may induce cross-frequency synchronization between oscillations in the delta and the ripple bands [46], the latter being functionally related to microcircuit activity. Yet, and as corroborated with present finding, it was important to assess effects of NPS on microcircuits, once these could have an impact on larger scale circuits. Taken together, results may corroborate the notion that ictogenesis is not a trivial ubiquitous process of neural hypersynchronization. Conversely, seizure generation probably relies on a loss of proper and intricate coordination of myriad synchronization processes [47], including local (high-frequency) desynchronization and long-range (low-frequency) synchronization.

Any model is a simplification of reality. Particularly, in the case of a mathematical models, when simulations are planned, reductionism can be considered a rule to carry out a reliable computational implementation and provide guidance for experimental investigations, aiming to unravel the intricate interdependence between the various mechanisms that are capable of sustaining or suppressing the seizure. In this sense, despite the present work being able to represent different temporal patterns that reflect different times for the origin of synchronization, it is of central importance to repeat these experiments in an expanded version of this model, which includes in silico reproductions of other areas in the temporal lobe or maybe even across the forebrain, midbrain, and hindbrain. To see if this is feasible using Izhikevich neuron models is still an open issue for us.

Acknowledgment. We are grateful to Conselho Nacional de Desenvolvimento Científico e Tecnológico (CNPq) for financial support. This chapter is dedicated to the memory of author Keite L. A. França who passed away a few weeks after having contributed extensively to this work and its final acceptance.

References

1. Semprini, M., et al.: Technological approaches for neurorehabilitation: from robotic devices to brain stimulation and beyond. Front. Neurol. **9**, 212 (2018). https://doi.org/10.3389/fneur. 2018.00212. PMID: 29686644; PMCID: PMC5900382
2. Theodore, W.H., Fisher, R.S.: Brain stimulation for epilepsy. Lancet Neurol. **3**(2), 111–118 (2004)
3. Klinger, N.V., Mittal, S.: Clinical efficacy of deep brain stimulation for the treatment of medically refractory epilepsy. Clin. Neurol. Neurosurg. **140**, 11–25 (2016)

4. Sunderam, S., Gluckman, B., Reato, D., Bikson, M.: Toward rational design of electrical stimulation strategies for epilepsy control. Epilepsy Behav. **17**, 6–22 (2010)

5. Cota, V.R., Drabowski, B.M., de Oliveira, J.C., Moraes, M.F.: The epileptic amygdala: toward the development of a neural prosthesis by temporally coded electrical stimulation. J. Neurosci. **94**(6), 463–485 (2016). https://doi.org/10.1002/jnr.23741

6. Cota, V.R., de Oliveira, J.C., Damázio, L.C.M., Moraes, M.F.: Nonperiodic stimulation for the treatment of refractory epilepsy: applications, mechanisms, and novel insights. Epilepsy Behav. **121**, 106609 (2019). https://doi.org/10.1016/j.yebeh.2019.106609

7. Cota, V.R., Medeiros, D.C., Vilela, M.R., Doretto, M.C., Moraes, M.F.: Distinct patterns of electrical stimulation of the basolateral amygdala influence pentylenetetrazole seizure outcome. Epilepsy Behav. **1**, 26–31 (2009). https://doi.org/10.1016/j.yebeh.2008.09.006

8. de Oliveira, J.C., Medeiros, D.C., Rezende, G.H.S., Moraes, M.F., Cota, V.R.: Temporally unstructured electrical stimulation to the amygdala suppresses behavioral chronic seizures of the pilocarpine animal model. Epilepsy Behav. **36**, 159–164 (2014). https://doi.org/10.1016/j.yebeh.2014.05.005

9. de Oliveira, J.C., Maciel, R.M., Moraes, M.F., Cota, V.R.: Asynchronous, bilateral, and biphasic temporally unstructured electrical stimulation of amygdalae enhances the suppression of pentylenetetrazole-induced seizures in rats. Epilepsy Res. **146**, 1–8 (2018). https://doi.org/10.1016/j.eplepsyres.2018.07.009

10. Mesquita, M.B., Medeiros, D.C., Cota, V.R., Richardson, M.P., Williams, S., Moraes, M.F.: Distinct temporal patterns of electrical stimulation influence neural recruitment during PTZ infusion: an fMRI study. Prog. Biophys. Mol. Biol. **105**(1–2), 109–118 (2011). https://doi.org/10.1016/j.pbiomolbio.2010.10.005

11. Medeiros, D.C., Cota, V.R., Vilela, M.R., Mourão, F.A., Massensini, A.R., Moraes, M.F.: Anatomically dependent anticonvulsant properties of temporally-coded electrical stimulation. Epilepsy Behav. **23**(3), 294–297 (2012). https://doi.org/10.1016/j.yebeh.2012.01.004

12. de Oliveira, J.C., Drabowski, B.M.B., Rodrigues, S.M.A.F., Maciel, R.M., Moraes, M.F., Cota, V.R.: Seizure suppression by asynchronous non-periodic electrical stimulation of the amygdala is partially mediated by indirect desynchronization from nucleus accumbens. Epilepsy Res. **154**, 107–115 (2019). https://doi.org/10.1016/j.eplepsyres.2019.05.009

13. Feng, F., et al.: Gamma oscillations in the basolateral amygdala: biophysical mechanisms and computational consequences. eNeuro. **6**(1) (2019). https://doi.org/10.1523/ENEURO.0388-18.2018

14. Pena, R.F.O., Zaks, M.A., Roque, A.C.: Dynamics of spontaneous activity in random networks with multiple neuron subtypes and synaptic noise. J. Comput. Neurosci. **45**(1), 1–28 (2018). https://doi.org/10.1007/s10827-018-0688-6

15. Izhikevich, E.M.: Simple model of spiking neurons. IEEE Trans. Neural Netw. **14**(6), 1569–1572 (2003)

16. Izhikevich, E.M.: Which model to use for cortical spiking neurons? IEEE Trans. Neural Netw. **15**(5), 1063–1070 (2004)

17. Hojjatinia, S., Aliyari Shoorehdeli, M., Fatahi, Z., Hojjatinia, Z., Haghparast, A.: Improving the Izhikevich model based on rat basolateral amygdala and hippocampus neurons, and recognizing their possible firing patterns. Basic Clin. Neurosci. **11**(1), 79–90 (2020)

18. Liu, Y., Grigorovsky, V., Bardakjian, B.: Excitation and inhibition balance underlying epileptiform activity. IEEE Trans. Biomed. Eng. **67**(9), 2473–2481 (2020)

19. Wang, Y., Shi, X., Cheng, B., Chen, J.: Synchronization and rhythm transition in a complex neuronal network. IEEE Access **8**, 102436–102448 (2020). https://doi.org/10.1109/ACCESS.2020.2997879

20. De Blasi, F.: Simulation of large scale neural networks for evaluation applications. Neurons and Cognition (q-bio.NC); Signal Processing (eess.SP). arXiv:1805.08626 [q-bio.NC] (2018)

21. Brunel, N.: Dynamics of sparsely connected networks of excitatory and inhibitory spiking neurons. J. Comput. Neurosci. **8**, 183–208 (2000)
22. Brunel, N., Wang, X.J.: Effects of neuromodulation in a cortical network model of object working memory dominated by recurrent inhibition. J. Comput. Neurosci. **11**(1), 63–85 (2001)
23. Keeley, S., Byrne, Á., Fenton, A., Rinzel, J.: Firing rate models for gamma oscillations. J. Neurophysiol. **121**(6), 2181–2190 (2019)
24. Protachevicz, P.R., et al.: Noise induces continuous and noncontinuous transitions in neuronal interspike intervals range. Indian Acad. Sci. Conf. Ser. **3**, 1 (2020)
25. Destexhe, A.: Self-sustained asynchronous irregular states and up–down states in thalamic, cortical and thalamocortical networks of nonlinear integrate-and-fire neurons. J. Comput. Neurosci. **27**(3), 493–506 (2009)
26. Steriade, M.: Thalamocortical oscillations in the sleeping and aroused brain. Science **262**(5134), 679–685 (1993)
27. Chou, P., Wang, G.H., Hsueh, S.W., Yang, Y.C., Kuo, C.C.: Delta-frequency augmentation and synchronization in seizure discharges and Telencephalic transmission. iScience **23**(11), 101666 (2020)
28. Burton, S.D., Ermentrout, G.B.: Urban, N.N.: Intrinsic heterogeneity in oscillatory dynamics limits correlation-induced neural synchronization. J. Neurophys. **108**(8), 2115–2133 (2012)
29. Grill, W.M.: Temporal pattern of electrical stimulation is a new dimension of therapeutic innovation. Curr. Opin. Biomed. Eng. **8**, 1–6 (2018)
30. Birdno, M.J., Kuncel, A.M., Dorval, A.D., Turner, D.A., Gross, R.E., Grill, W.M.: Stimulus features underlying reduced tremor suppression with temporally patterned deep brain stimulation. J. Neurophysiol. **107**, 364–383 (2012)
31. Tass, P.A., et al.: Coordinated reset has sustained aftereffects in Parkinsonian monkeys. Ann. Neurol. **72**(5), 816–820 (2012). https://doi.org/10.1002/ana.23663
32. Khaledi-Nasab, A., Kromer, J.A., Tass, P.A.: Long-Lasting desynchronization of plastic neural networks by random reset stimulation. Front. Physiol. **5**(11), 622620 (2021). https://doi.org/10.3389/fphys.2020.622620
33. Khaledi-Nasab, A., Kromer, J.A., Tass, P.A.: Long-lasting desynchronization effects of coordinated reset stimulation improved by random jitters. Front. Physiol. **10**, 1446 (2021)
34. Buzsáki, G., Wang, X.J.: Mechanisms of gamma oscillations. Ann. Rev. Neurosci. **35**, 203–225 (2012)
35. Butz, M., Steenbuck, I.D., van Ooyen, A.: Homeostatic structural plasticity increases the efficiency of small-world networks. Front. Synaptic Neurosci. **6**, 7 (2014)
36. Butz, M., Wörgötter, F., van Ooyen, A.: Activity-dependent structural plasticity. Brain Res. Rev. **60**, 287–305 (2009)
37. Oliveira, L.D.R., Gomes, R.M., Santos, B.A., Borges, H.E.: Effects of the parameters on the oscillation frequency of Izhikevich spiking neural networks. Neurocomputing **337**, 251–261 (2019)
38. Rich, S., Chameh, H.M., Rafiee, M., Ferguson, K., Skinner, F.K., Valiante, T.A.: Inhibitory network bistability explains increased interneuronal activity prior to seizure onset. Front. Neural Circuits **13**, 81 (2020)
39. Rescorla, R.A., Wagner, A.R.: A theory of Pavlovian conditioning: variations in the effectiveness of reinforcement and non-reinforcement. In: Black, A., Prokasy, W.F. (eds.) Classical Conditioning II: Current Research and Theory, pp. 64–99. Appleton-Century-Crofts, New York (1972)
40. Balkenius, C., Morén, J.: Emotional learning: a computational model of the Amygdala. Cybern. Syst. **32**, 611–636 (2001)
41. Kim, D., Pare, D., Nair, S.S.: Assignment of model amygdala neurons to the fear memory trace depends on competitive synaptic interactions. J. Neurosci. **33**, 14354–14358 (2013)

42. Mina, F., Benquet, P., Pasnicu, A., Biraben, A., Wendling, F.: Modulation of epileptic activity by deep brain stimulation: a model-based study of frequency-dependent effects. Front. Comput. Neurosci. **7**, 94 (2013)
43. Ewell, L.A., Fischer, K.B., Leibold, C., Leutgeb, S., Leutgeb, J.K.: The impact of pathological high-frequency oscillations on hippocampal network activity in rats with chronic epilepsy. Elife **22**, 8 (2019)
44. Ashourvan, A., et al.: Model-based design for seizure control by stimulation. J Neural Eng. **17**(2) (2020)
45. Ahn, S., Jo, S., Jun, S.B., Lee, H.W., Lee, S.: Prediction of the seizure suppression effect by electrical stimulation via a computational modeling approach. Front. Comput. Neurosci. **11**, 39 (2017)
46. Oliveira, J.C., Rodrigues, S.M.A.F., Maciel, R.M., Réboli, L.A., Cota, V.R.: Evolução temporal do hipersincronismo fase-amplitude no modelo de crises epilépticas induzido por pentilenotetrazol. I Latin American Workshop on Computational Neuroscience (LAWCN) (2017)
47. Jiruska, P., de Curtis, M., Jefferys, J.G., Schevon, C.A., Schiff, S.J., Schindler, K.: Synchronization and desynchronization in epilepsy: controversies and hypotheses. J. Physiol. **591**(4), 787–97 (2013). https://doi.org/10.1113/jphysiol.2012.239590

Software and Hardware
Implementations in Neuroscience

Brain Connectivity Measures in EEG-Based Biometry for Epilepsy Patients: A Pilot Study

Bruna M. Carlos[1,2]([⊠]) [iD], Brunno M. Campos[3] [iD], Marina K. M. Alvim[3] [iD], and Gabriela Castellano[1,2] [iD]

[1] Neurophysics Group, "Gleb Wataghin" Institute of Physics, University of Campinas, Campinas, SP 13083-859, Brazil
b235624@dac.unicamp.br
[2] Brazilian Institute of Neuroscience and Neurotechnology (BRAINN), Campinas, SP 13083-859, Brazil
[3] Laboratory of Neuroimaging (LNI), School of Medical Sciences, University of Campinas, Campinas, SP 13083-859, Brazil

Abstract. The use of electroencephalography (EEG) signals for biometrics purposes has gained attention in the last few years, and many works have already shown that it is possible to identify a person based on features extracted from these signals. In this work we focus on four functional connectivity measures (magnitude-squared and imaginary coherence, motif synchronization and space-time recurrence) for the classification of 10 epilepsy patients with recorded resting-state EEG signals, to compare and discuss different methodologies. We perform the analysis by slicing the signals of at least 2 trials for each subject in epochs of 3 and 10 s, filtering the data in the ranges of 1 40 Hz and 1 100 Hz, building reference and test vectors from the connectivity measures and labeling each test vector to a subject using the minimal Euclidean distance from the feature vectors. The best classification rates were obtained with magnitude-squared coherence and motif synchronization, for the data segmented in epochs of 10 s and filtered between 1 40 Hz. All the measures with the signal filtered in the same range obtained an accuracy equal or higher than 80%, a result that can be enhanced with more complex classifiers.

Keywords: EEG-based biometry · Epilepsy · Brain connectivity

1 Introduction

Electroencephalography (EEG) based biometry is a growing area of research [1,2] for user recognition in security systems, since it provides signals that can only be

Supported by FAPESP (São Paulo Research Foundation; grants 2020/16571-0, 2017-25795-7 and 2013-07559-3), CAPES (Coordination for the Improvement of Higher Education Personnel) and CNPq (National Council for Scientific and Technological Development).

P. R. d. A. Ribeiro et al. (Eds.): LAWCN 2021, CCIS 1519, pp. 155–169, 2022.
https://doi.org/10.1007/978-3-031-08443-0_10

obtained from live individuals and varies according to different types of stimuli. The first works on the subject [3, 4] proposed the use of spectral decomposition as a measure for identification, and an accuracy of almost 90% was obtained in [4]. Since then other methodologies were applied, combining different tasks and feature extraction methods. Some combinations were able to achieve 100% of accuracy, such as the use of averaged event-related potential (ERP) from visual stimulation [5], correlation between ERPs elicited by a rapid serial visual presentation (RSVP) [6] and spectral coherence (COH) from resting-state with eyes open and closed [7]. Some effects caused by the increase in the number of subjects, their gender or modification in the age group are discussed in [8], and show that accuracy levels can strongly rely on these parameters, which indicates the need for more works with diverse populations and methodologies on the subject.

On the other hand, EEG has been one of the most used neuroimaging techniques to aid in the diagnosis of epilepsy [9]. This is mainly due to its relatively lower cost, portability and high temporal resolution, compared to other techniques. The EEG exam can detect physiological manifestations underlying epileptic activity, although only interictal epileptiform discharges (IEDs) are of clinical use [9]. In addition, it has been suggested that epilepsy interferes with functional brain networks [10–13]. These networks are characterized through functional connectivity analysis, where a similarity measure is used to compare activity time series from different brain regions (for a review, see, e.g., [14]). Recently, Nentwich et al. showed that EEG functional connectivity is subject-specific and depends on the phenotype [15]. They report that the connectivity patterns they found were more similar across tasks than across individuals, and state that "functional connectivity can be used as a diagnostic metric to assess individuals" [15].

In this context, the aim of this work was to perform an individual characterization of epilepsy patients using different connectivity measures and methodologies, and compare their performances in a biometry scenario. Magnitude-squared coherence (COH) has already been used for EEG biometry in [7], achieving 100% accuracy, and the use of other measures such as imaginary coherence (ICOH), motif-synchronization (MS) [16] and space-time-recurrence (STR) [17] are proposed here along with COH. In addition to these measures, we also vary the pre-processing steps for the signals, performing filtering in the intervals 1–40 Hz and 1–100 Hz and segmentation in epochs of 3 s and 10 s. The frequency band 1–40 Hz was chosen due to its common use in connectivity studies as it covers the low frequency bands, especially the alpha band whose alterations have been associated with epilepsy [18, 19]. The 1–40 Hz range was also used in another EEG based authentication study [7]. The second frequency band, 1–100 Hz, was chosen so that its higher frequency is close to the maximum available frequency considering the sampling rate 250 Hz. As for the epoching choices, the 10 s segmentation was used based on previous works in the area [6, 7, 20]. The smaller segmentation was chosen to be 3 s as it is the lower interval that gives more precise estimations of coherence in low frequencies, and it is recommended for security systems with a required true acceptance rate equal or higher than 90% [6]. As a result, four methodologies were applied for each measure, producing sixteen different classifiers. This is a pilot study; at this point, we did not yet investigate the association between epilepsy phenotype and EEG connectivity.

2 Subjects, Materials and Methods

2.1 Data Acquisition and Pre-processing

Scalp EEG signals were obtained from volunteer epilepsy patients undergoing pre surgical evaluation in the Neuroimaging Laboratory (LNI) at Unicamp. EEG data were acquired in resting state condition simultaneously with functional magnetic resonance imaging (fMRI) data, using a magnetic resonance (MR) compatible EEG system (BrainProducts GmbH, München, Germany), consisting of two BrainAmp MRplus amplifiers and a 64-electrode brain cap (including one electrocardiogram electrode), with electrodes positioned following the 10/10 system [21]. The sampling rate was 5 kHz, with reference on FCz and ground on AFz.

The criteria for inclusion in the study were a total acquisition time larger or equal to 600 s and a number of epileptiform events, which were marked by neurophysiologists, smaller than 30. From that, we selected signals from ten subjects (mean age 41.9 ± 12.3, 6 female). The EEG signals were collected in a single session (day) for each subject, and all the selected subjects had two or more acquisitions during the same session (trials). Table 1 shows the number of trials used for each patient and their diagnosis, which can be temporal lobe epilepsy (TLE) or frontal lobe epilepsy (FLE), and the respective affected brain hemisphere.

Table 1. Number of trials of each patient and diagnosis when available.

Patient	Trials	Diagnosis
1	3	Bilateral TLE with left predominance
2	3	FLE (unknown side)
3	3	Left TLE
4	3	Left TLE
5	3	Right TLE
6	3	Left TLE
7	3	Left TLE
8	3	Right TLE
9	3	Left TLE
10	2	Left TLE

The steps of the pre-processing were the following: MR gradients artifact correction using MR trigger syncronism; average artifact subtraction correction; balistocardiogram correction for the scalp channels; downsampling the data to 250 Hz and discarding epileptiform events and the ECG channel, in order to retain only signals with regular brain activity. A manual cleaning and an independent component analysis (ICA) decomposition were also performed to discard noisy fragments and to remove blink components from the data, respectively. The ICA decomposition and the rejection of components were made with the fastICA algorithm and the ICLabel extension [22], both implemented in EEGLAB [23]. EEG data were then re-referenced to the average of all electrodes, and filtered in the frequency ranges of 1–40 Hz and 1–100 Hz. Since we wanted a total of 600 s of signal, we first selected 300 s from the first trial of each patient to compose the training dataset. Then, for the patients with two trials we selected 300 s from the second trial, and for the remaining patients we selected 150 s from the second and 150 s from the third trials to compose the test dataset. Finally, these segments were divided into epochs of 3 s and 10 s.

The study was approved by the ethics committee of our institution (CAAE 16715319.9.0000.5404, CEP-UNICAMP), and all subjects signed an informed consent form prior to data acquisition.

2.2 Connectivity Measures

Coherence. Coherence is a measure that quantifies the level of similarity between signals with respect to their frequency and amplitude [24]. It is a common technique to study brain connectivity from EEG signals since it gives the synchrony in a chosen specific frequency range between distinct regions of the brain. The magnitude-squared coherence between two signals i and j for a frequency f is given by the formula

$$COH_{ij}(f) = \frac{|S_{ij}(f)|^2}{S_{ii}(f)S_{jj}(f)}, \tag{1}$$

where S_{ij} is the cross spectral density between the two signals and S_{ii} and S_{jj}, the spectral density for each of them. Another common way to express coherence is using its imaginary part, which can prevent the contamination of the signals from volume conduction [25]. The expression for the imaginary coherence now depends on the imaginary part of the cross spectral density, and is given by

$$ICOH_{ij}(f) = \frac{Im(S_{ij}(f))}{\sqrt{S_{ii}(f)S_{jj}(f)}}. \tag{2}$$

To build the reference vectors, the magnitude-squared and imaginary coherence were calculated for each epoch of the first trial ($n = 30$ epochs for segments with 10 s and $n = 100$ epochs for segments with 3 s) over the frequency ranges 1–40 Hz and 1–100 Hz. The analysis was performed with Brainstorm [26], an open-source application for analysis and processing of brain recordings, with a maximum frequency resolution of 1 Hz and an overlap of 50% for power spectral density (PSD) estimation. The resultant coherence matrices were then averaged over the n epochs and over the frequencies, resulting in a vector 2016×1 ($2016 = [N(N-1)/2 + N]$, where $N = 63$ is the number of electrodes) for each subject. For the test vectors, COH and ICOH were calculated for each epoch from the second trial or the second and third trials, and the coherence matrices were averaged only over the frequencies. This method resulted in $n = 100$ and $n = 30$ test vectors 2016×1 for epochs of 3 and 10 seconds, respectively, for each subject and frequency range.

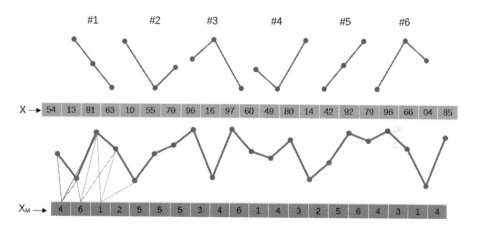

Fig. 1. Transformation of a randomly generated signal X into a series of motifs X_M, with unitary lag.

Motif-Synchronization. The motif technique considers an original signal X as a sequence of predetermined elementary patterns that are used to transform the signal into a sequence of labels X_M, as depicted in Fig. 1. This method was originally proposed to perform a study on permutation entropy in EEG data [27], and a more recent work proposed the use of motifs for a connectivity measure, called Motif-Synchronization [16]. The objective of the method is to obtain the synchrony between the signals of two sources by counting the simultaneous appearance of the defined patterns. After performing the transformation of the signal, the following variable is evaluated for each pair of sources

$$c_{XY} = \max \left(\sum_{i=1}^{L_m} J_i^{\tau_0}, \sum_{i=1}^{L_m} J_i^{\tau_1}, \ldots, \sum_{i=1}^{L_m} J_i^{\tau_n} \right), \tag{3}$$

where

$$J_i^\tau = \begin{cases} 1, & \text{if } X_M(i) = Y_M(i+\tau) \\ 0, & \text{else.} \end{cases} \tag{4}$$

In the expressions above, L_m is the number of selected points from the time series and τ is the time delay ranging from $\tau_0 = 0$ to a maximum value τ_n to be chosen. The connectivity matrix is then obtained from the synchronization degree of each pair, given by

$$Q_{XY} = \frac{\max(c_{XY}, c_{YX})}{L_m}, \tag{5}$$

that can assume values between 0 (no synchronization) and 1 (maximum synchronization).

For this work, we performed the transformation of the original signals to motifs using three points patterns and unitary lag, in which the two last points of a pattern overlap with the next one (see Fig. 1). The maximum delay was considered to be $\tau_n = 4$, corresponding to 16 ms in the data. The $n = 100$ (for epochs with 3 s) and $n = 30$ (for epochs with 10 s) connectivity matrices from the first trial were averaged to form the reference vector (of dimensions $N^2 \times 1$) and the matrices from the second trial or the second and third trials were used as test vectors.

Space-Time Recurrence. The space-time recurrence technique for connectivity is based on recurrence plots (RP) [17], a powerful tool in the analysis of complex systems that indicates the level of proximity between dynamical states. The recurrence in space and time for a pair of signals can be computed as [28]

$$STR_{ij}(\epsilon, t) = \theta(\epsilon - \|x_i(t) - x_j(t)\|_1), \tag{6}$$

where θ is the Heaviside function, ϵ a threshold value for the distance and t the index of the sample (time). For N sources of signals, we have a $N \times N \times T$ matrix, with T the total number of samples. To obtain a recurrence for a time period, we can define a density matrix of the form

$$Den_{ij} = \frac{1}{T} \sum_{t=1}^{T} STR_{ij}(\epsilon, t), \tag{7}$$

which assumes values from 0 to 1 and gives a space-time recurrence average through time.

For this work, the density matrix (7) was used to build the reference and test vectors for classification. Since Den is symmetric, only the entries below the diagonal and the diagonal were used, resulting in vectors of 2016×1 as in the coherence measures. For the reference vectors, the density matrices of all epochs from the first trial were averaged, and the matrices from epochs of the other trials were considered as test vectors. Although many methods for the choice of the distance threshold value have been proposed [29,30], in this work the values of ϵ for each case were chosen according to the best classification results.

2.3   Classification

Once the reference and test vectors were built and labeled to their respective subjects, the method of classification for all the connectivity measures was performed in the same way. First, the Euclidean distance between each of the i test vectors and j reference vectors was calculated by the expression

$$D_{ij} = \|\boldsymbol{t}_i - \boldsymbol{r}_j\|_2. \tag{8}$$

This distance matrix has the dimensions $n \times N_{subjects}$, where $n = 30$ for epochs with 10 s, $n = 100$ for epochs with 3 s and $N_{subjects} = 10$. For every test vector, the minimum distance obtained was associated with the respective subject, and the classification results compared to the original labels. The accuracy was then given by the ratio between the number of correct classifications and n.

3   Results and Discussion

As can be seen in Figs. 2, 4, and 5, the connectivity matrices for COH, MS and STR present subtle variations that are not easily distinguishable, at least visually. The imaginary coherence maps exhibit more variety as can be seen in Fig. 3, where the maps generated by data segmented into epochs of 10 s have lower values in general.

The classification accuracies are presented in Table 2. It can be seen that COH, ICOH and MS vary strongly with the range of filtering chosen, with a difference of up to 24% in classification accuracy for COH. The variation for STR is less significant, but the accuracies for the filtering range 1–40 Hz are still better. These results indicate that the most relevant signals for subject distinction are contained in the lower frequency bands, including the α and β bands which are related to relaxed awareness and concentration [31]. A more restricted filtering also provides the elimination of possible high-frequency artifacts that can harm the quality of the data.

As for the epoch size, the 10 s segmentation resulted in higher accuracy in the majority of the cases, producing a difference of at most 5% for MS and STR. A better performance was expected with the segmentation in 10 s, since the connectivity measures from larger periods of time are less susceptible to be disrupted by momentary movement artifacts and cognitive processes. However,

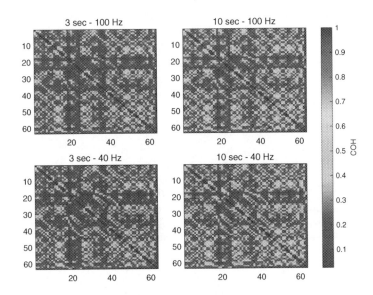

Fig. 2. Connectivity matrices for the reference vector from subject 1, with values of the magnitude-squared coherence (1) (COH).

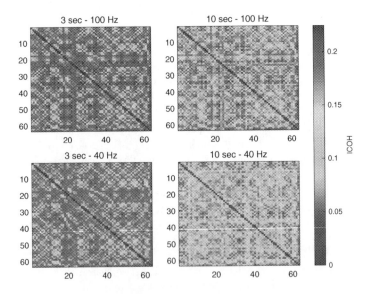

Fig. 3. Connectivity matrices for the reference vector from subject 1, with values of the imaginary coherence (2) (ICOH).

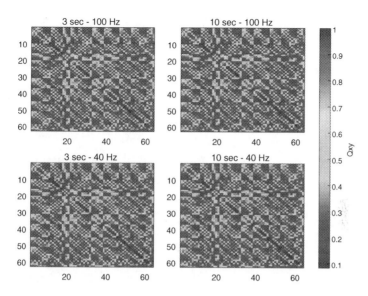

Fig. 4. Connectivity matrices for the reference vector from subject 1, with values of the degree of synchronization Q_{xy} (5) using MS.

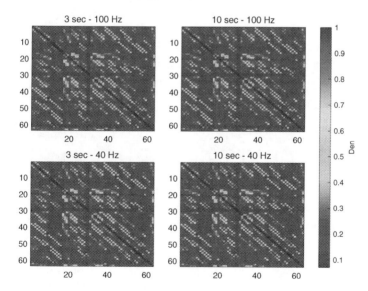

Fig. 5. Connectivity matrices for the reference vector of the first subject, with values of the density matrices (7) using STR (the off-diagonal entries were rescaled from 0 to 1 for a better visualization).

some of the accuracies for 3 s were still higher, and periods longer than 10 s can be studied to verify if this improvement is relevant.

Table 2. Classification accuracy (in percentage) obtained from the different measures. The parentheses in the STR line contain the values for ϵ that gave the best accuracy.

Measure	1–40 Hz		1–100 Hz	
	3 s	10 s	3 s	10 s
COH	93.7	94.7	72.3	70.7
ICOH	84.9	80.0	75.2	67.3
MS	91.6	91.7	81.0	86.0
STR	86.3 (5.0e−7)	91.3 (3.3e−7)	85.1 (0.19)	91.0 (0.19)

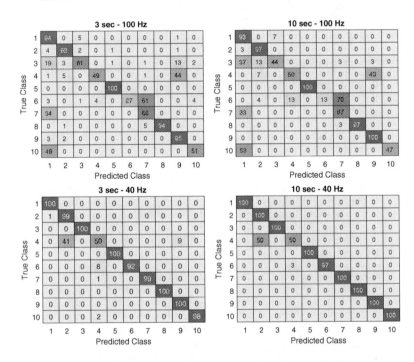

Fig. 6. Confusion matrices for the classifiers with COH measures. A row contains the percentage of the samples from one class attributed to each of the classes.

The good performance of magnitude-squared coherence corroborates the results of [7], where high accuracies were obtained with both eyes-closed and eyes-open acquisitions. To the best of our knowledge, no other works used MS or STR for EEG-based biometry, but both measures have already been used in connectivity studies [16,28] and generated good results. Our results for MS reveal that this measure is a good candidate to perform distinction between subjects, alongside with COH.

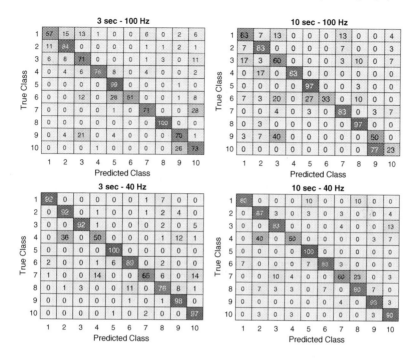

Fig. 7. Confusion matrices for the classifiers with ICOH measures. A row contains the approximate percentage of the samples from one class attributed to each of the classes.

As can be seen in the confusion matrices in Figs. 6, 7, 8 and 9, the patients 3, 4, 6, 9, and 10 have a correct classification smaller or equal to 50% for at least one of the connectivity measures. Patient 4 has the lower hit rates in general, and is more related to patients 9 and 2 in some of the measures. The rest of the patients with worse ratings are related to different subjects depending on the connectivity measure. Alongside this, the patterns of classification seem to repeat for the same measure and filtering range, and not vary too much for the different epoch segmentation.

Relevant limitations of this work were the number of subjects whose EEG signals were appropriate for our analysis and the use of EEG signals acquired jointly with fMRI data, which have more artifacts than regularly acquired signals. However, the data used are maintained for diverse scientific purposes, which includes EEG-fMRI investigation of epilepsy patients, a goal towards which we believe this work will be useful in the future.

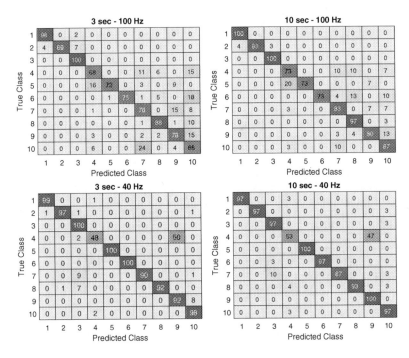

Fig. 8. Confusion matrices for the classifiers with MS measures. A row contains the approximate percentage of the samples from one class attributed to each of the classes.

4 Conclusion

The approach proposed here had the intention to study different connectivity measures and methodologies for EEG-based biometry of epilepsy patients, and to compare their performances. For our subjects and method of classification, COH and MS measures obtained from epochs of 10 s extracted from the original signals filtered in the 1–40 Hz range resulted in the highest classification accuracy. We also found that STR and MS can result in classifications as good as or even better than COH and ICOH, depending on the methodology and pre-processing steps.

A first modification in the continuation of this work will be to include a larger number of subjects, which can make the results more reproducible and reliable. Other improvements include the use of more robust classification methods, exploration of the lag parameter for MS, which was held constant here, and to determine which electrodes are more relevant for classification, in order to reduce the dimensions of feature and test vectors. Finally, once we are able to increase patient sample, a future direction will be to explore the association between epilepsy phenotype and diagnosis with EEG functional connectivity.

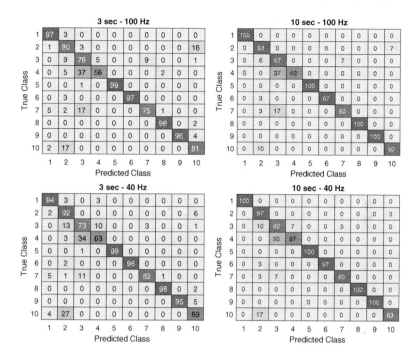

Fig. 9. Confusion matrices for the classifiers with STR measures. A row contains the percentage of the samples from one class attributed to each of the classes.

References

1. Jayarathne, I., Cohen, M., Amarakeerthi, S.: Survey of EEG-based biometric authentication. In: 2017 IEEE 8th International Conference on Awareness Science and Technology (iCAST), pp. 324–329 (2017)
2. Jalaly Bidgoly, A., Jalaly Bidgoly, H., Arezoumand, Z.: A survey on methods and challenges in EEG based authentication. Comput. Secur. **93**, 101788 (2020)
3. Berkhout, J., Walter, D.O.: Temporal stability and individual differences in the human EEG: an analysis of variance of spectral values. IEEE Trans. Biomed. Eng. BME **15**(3), 165–168 (1968)
4. Stassen, H.: Computerized recognition of persons by EEG spectral patterns. Electroencephalogr. Clin. Neurophysiol. **49**(1), 190–194 (1980)
5. Ruiz-Blondet, M.V., Jin, Z., Laszlo, S.: CEREBRE: a novel method for very high accuracy event-related potential biometric identification. Trans. Info. For. Sec. **11**(7), 1618–1629 (2016)
6. Chen, Y., et al.: A high-security EEG-based login system with rsvp stimuli and dry electrodes. IEEE Trans. Inf. Forensics Secur. **11**, 1 (2016)
7. Rocca, D., et al.: Human brain distinctiveness based on EEG spectral coherence connectivity. IEEE Trans. Biomed. Eng. **61**(9), 2406–2412 (2014)
8. Svetlakov, M., Hodashinsky, I., Slezkin, A.: Gender, age and number of participants effects on identification ability of EEG-based shallow classifiers. In: Ural Symposium on Biomedical Engineering, Radioelectronics and Information Technology (USBEREIT), pp. 350–353 (2021)

9. Smith, S.J.M.: EEG in the diagnosis, classification, and management of patients with epilepsy. J. Neurol. Neurosurg. Psychiatry **76**(suppl 2), ii2–ii7 (2005)
10. Smith, S.J.M.: Functional and structural brain networks in epilepsy: what have we learned? Epilepsia **54**, 1855–1865 (2013)
11. Elshahabi, A., Klamer, S., Sahib, A.K., Lerche, H., Braun, C., Focke, N.K.: Magnetoencephalography reveals a widespread increase in network connectivity in idiopathic/genetic generalized epilepsy. PLoS ONE **10**, e0138119 (2015)
12. Englot, D.J., et al.: Global and regional functional connectivity maps of neural oscillations in focal epilepsy. Brain **138**(8), 2249–2262 (2015)
13. Li Hegner, Y., et al.: Increased functional meg connectivity as a hallmark of MRI-negative focal and generalized epilepsy. Brain Topogr. **31**, 863–874 (2018)
14. Bastos, A.M., Schoffelen, J.M.: A tutorial review of functional connectivity analysis methods and their interpretational pitfalls. Front. Syst. Neurosci. **9**, 175 (2016)
15. Nentwich, M., et al.: Functional connectivity of EEG is subject-specific, associated with phenotype, and different from FMRI. Neuroimage **218**, 117001 (2020)
16. Rosário, R.S., Cardoso, P.T., Muñoz, M.A., Montoya, P., Miranda, J.G.V.: Motif-synchronization: a new method for analysis of dynamic brain networks with EEG. Physica A **439**, 7–19 (2015)
17. Marwan, N., Carmen Romano, M., Thiel, M., Kurths, J.: Recurrence plots for the analysis of complex systems. Phys. Rep. **438**(5), 237–329 (2007)
18. Pyrzowski, J., Siemiński, M., Sarnowska, A., Jedrzejczak, J., Nyka, W.M.: Interval analysis of interictal EEG: pathology of the alpha rhythm in focal epilepsy. Sci. Rep. **5**, 16230 (2015)
19. Stoller, A.: lowing of the alpha-rhythm of the electroencephalogram and its association with mental deterioration and epilepsy. J. Ment. Sci. **95**(401), 972 (1949)
20. Chuang, J., Nguyen, H., Wang, C., Johnson, B.: I think, therefore I Am: usability and security of authentication using brainwaves. In: Adams, A.A., Brenner, M., Smith, M. (eds.) FC 2013. LNCS, vol. 7862, pp. 1–16. Springer, Heidelberg (2013). https://doi.org/10.1007/978-3-642-41320-9_1
21. Chatrian, G.E., Lettich, E., Nelson, P.L.: Modified nomenclature for the "10%" electrode system. J. Clin. Neurophysiol. **5**, 183–186 (1988)
22. Pion-Tonachini, L., Kreutz-Delgado, K., Makeig, S.: ICLabel: an automated electroencephalographic independent component classifier, dataset, and website. Neuroimage **198**, 181–197 (2019)
23. Delorme, A., Makeig, S.: EEGLAB: an open source toolbox for analysis of single-trial EEG dynamics including independent component analysis. J. Neurosci. Methods **134**(1), 9–21 (2004)
24. Andres, F.G., Gerloff, C.: Coherence of sequential movements and motor learning. J. Clin. Neurophysiol. **16**, 520–527 (1999)
25. Nolte, G., Bai, O., Wheaton, L., Mari, Z., Vorbach, S., Hallett, M.: Identifying true brain interaction from EEG data using the imaginary part of coherency. Clin. Neurophysiol. **115**, 2292–2307 (2004)
26. Tadel, F., Baillet, S., Mosher, J., Pantazis, D., Leahy, R.: Brainstorm: a user-friendly application for MEG/EEG analysis. Comput. Intell. Neurosci. **2011**, 879716 (2011)
27. Olofsen, E., Sleigh, J., Dahan, A.: Permutation entropy of the electroencephalogram: a measure of anaesthetic drug effect. Br. J. Anaesth. **101**(6), 810–821 (2008)
28. Rodrigues, P.G., Filho, C.A.S., Attux, R., Castellano, G., Soriano, D.C.: Space-time recurrences for functional connectivity evaluation and feature extraction in motor imagery brain-computer interfaces. Med. Biolog. Eng. Comput. **57**(8), 1709–1725 (2019). https://doi.org/10.1007/s11517-019-01989-w

29. Zbilut, J.P., Webber, C.L.: Embeddings and delays as derived from quantification of recurrence plots. Phys. Lett. A **171**(3), 199–203 (1992)
30. Zbilut, J., Zaldivar-Comenges, J.M., Strozzi, F.: Recurrence quantification based-Liapunov exponents for monitoring divergence in experimental data. Phys. Lett. A **297**, 173–181 (2002)
31. Sanei, S., Chambers, J.A.: EEG Signal Processing. Wiley, Chichester (2007)

A Multiplatform Output Stage for the Development of Current-Fixed Electrical Stimulators Applied to Neural Electrophysiology

Maikon L. Santos[1] (ID), João D. Nolasco[2], and Vinícius R. Cota[1]([⊠]) (ID)

[1] Laboratory of Neuroengineering and Neurosciences – LINNce,
Federal University of São João del-Rei - UFSJ, São João del Rei, Brazil
vrcota@ufsj.edu.br
[2] Department of Electrical Engineering UFSJ – DEPEL,
Federal University of São João del-Rei - UFSJ, São João del Rei, Brazil

Abstract. Electrical stimulation of neural tissue is a well-established method in neurosciences for the investigation of neural function, neurological disorders, and neuromodulation therapies. Although one can easily find a great variety of off-the-shelf equipment for such experimentation, recent developments of the field, such as a precision neuroengineering approach to stimuli waveforms and closed-loop paradigms, are putting a lot of pressure on current available designs. In fact, many times, scientists fall short of implementing their novel non-conventional stimulation protocols on commercially available apparatuses and need to develop their own device. While the popularization of microcontroller boards made it easy and cheap to design and build highly flexible control units for electrical stimulators, output stages with proper voltage and current output compliances, controlled by multiple low-cost platforms are largely missing. In this work we report a new inexpensive design of a PWM-controlled output stage capable of producing current-fixed mono or biphasic pulses (i.e., it does not change even if output impedance varies) with enough power to sufficiently excite neural tissue. Electrical tests confirmed that the circuit is capable of producing highly stable current pulses of different amplitudes and morphologies (cathodic, anodic, or biphasic), with a null dead time (interval between phases). Although we have tested the design using and Arduino Leonardo controller board, it is expected that any platform capable of generating PWM pulses will work just as well .

Keywords: Electrical stimulation · Neural electrophysiology · Fixed current · Output stage

1 Introduction

Electrical stimulation (ES) of excitable tissue is a widely used method for the treatment of diverse neurological disorders and also extensively for neuroscience experimentation [1]. This last application includes brain slices electrophysiology, long term potentiation (LTP) and plasticity induction, behavioral modulation, electrolytic lesions, and also

© Springer Nature Switzerland AG 2022
P. R. d. A. Ribeiro et al. (Eds.): LAWCN 2021, CCIS 1519, pp. 170–185, 2022.
https://doi.org/10.1007/978-3-031-08443-0_11

experimental epileptic seizure suppression. Recently, novel techniques use simultaneous recordings to trigger responsive ES in closed-loop experiments. Such approach opens up new possibilities for studies in neuroscience, creating new biohybrid approaches [2] in which tissue excitability is controlled in real-time [3] to benefit, for instance, patients with epilepsy [4]. Effects and applicability of ES in neural tissue are now largely known and comprehensive reviews can be found in [5, 6].

Laboratory ES equipment is often composed of complex machinery, based on many different designs and usually with high costs, being very difficult to customize to novel paradigms of stimulation. This is mostly due to intellectual property reasons, but also to a general closed innovation strategy of production, marketing, and commercialization [7]. Yet, this is particularly concerning given that the neuromodulation field is currently entering a new age of precision engineering in which every aspect and parameter of the stimulation waveform matters, not only the target substrate or firing frequency. In particular, non-rhythmic temporal patterns of stimulation is an aspect of increasing importance [8]. For instance, our group has been successfully developing and testing a promising technique for the treatment of refractory epilepsy, termed Non-Periodic Electrical Stimulation (NPS), which consists in the application of ES with random intervals between pulses and low mean frequency (4 Hz) [9, 10]. Usually, electrical stimulus applied with short symmetrical square biphasic pulses of voltage or current, and fired at high frequency (usually >100 Hz), has an anticonvulsive effect in the control of epilepsies, while at low frequencies it does not [11]. Yet, the same therapeutic effect can be obtained by applying lower frequencies and with less energy, causing less damage to tissues, if a temporal pattern such as NPS is used [12]. Thus, very high flexibility and freedom to customize stimuli is largely desirable in ES hardware design supporting neuromodulation research.

Older implementations of electrical stimulator hardware were solely based on oscillator systems (quartz crystal-driven frequency dividers and counters, timer ICs, etc.) in order to generate fixed rates for the firing of pulses. This design strategy made it very complex to implement ES strategies which deviated from a fixed frequency paradigm. On the other hand, modern, microcontroller-based architectures largely enabled a great variability of waveform generation capabilities. The popularization of microcontrollers of all kinds with comprehensive sets of programmable properties, including those with open-source design (open-source hardware) such as Arduino, contributed a lot to popularize and to lower the costs of development and acquisition [13]. With this sort of technology, it became easy to develop control units for ES equipment, which are capable of controlling multiple aspects of the pulsatile stimulation, including frequency, temporal pattern, pulse width, number and polarity of phases, etc.

Although such approach to the development of stimulator designs offers great versatility in an easy and inexpensive manner, output generated from controllers are not tailored to properly affect neurons. This is due to several reasons: 1) microcontrollers operate on a positive-only power supply (e.g. 0 to 5 V), while both cathodic and anodic (or both of them at the same time) pulses are largely desirable; 2) digital circuit output voltage pulses will yield different currents according to the output impedance, while experimental ES is better carried out with fixed values of electric currents (i.e. it does not change even if impedance varies), and; 3) digital circuits do not comply to power levels needed for tissue excitation.

In this work, we present an inexpensive electronic circuit design that generates mono or biphasic fixed-current pulses controlled with PWM commands for proper timing and it is thus compatible with any microcontroller platform with such capabilities. We describe its working and the results of a simple implementation to show its output compliance.

2 Materials and Methods

2.1 Electronic Circuit Design

The software used to develop and simulate the circuit was LTspice, which is free. Figure 1 depicts the final diagram.

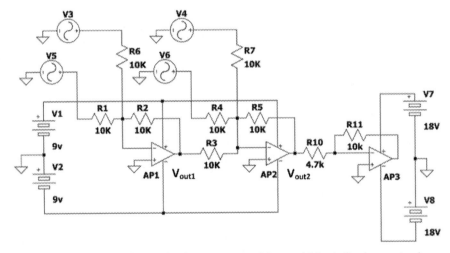

Fig. 1. Electronic circuit diagram for the output stage. Mono or biphasic fixed-current pulses are created from PWM control signals (V3, V4, V5, and V6) by summator circuits and a voltage to current converter.

V3, V4, V5 and *V6* sources are microcontroller PWM signals which are summed and subtracted in the circuit to generate outputs of interest, which can be monophasic (only positive or negative) or also biphasic (positive and negative) pulses. The selective presence or absence of each of the PWM signals will determine the output morphology. Moreover, their timing will define pulse width, firing rate (if in a fixed frequency), and the temporal pattern.

To analyze the circuit, first consider operational amplifier represented by AP1, connected in the adder configuration with the voltages *V3* and *V5* as inputs. That is, in this configuration, AP1 will add *V3* and *V5* and, since all resistors in this stage are 10 KΩ, there will be no amplification of the signal as this is not the intention. This is represented by Eq. 1 below ($R1 = R2 = R6 = 10$ KΩ) before and after simplification.

$$V_{out1} = -\left(\frac{R2}{R1}V_5 + \frac{R2}{R6}V_3\right) = -(V3 + V5) \tag{1}$$

The voltage output V_{out1} is also the input of the second operational amplifier AP2, which is also wired as an adder together with V4 and V6. Analogously to what has been done to Eq. 1, we can easily derive V_{out2} in Eq. 2.

$$V_{out2} = -\left(\frac{R5}{R3}V_{out1} + \frac{R5}{R4}V_6 + \frac{R5}{R7}V_4\right) = -(-(V3 + V5) + V4 + V6) \quad (2)$$

Equations 3 and 4 below are just algebraic rearrangements of Eq. 2.

$$V_{out2} = ((V3 + V5) - V4 - V6) \quad (3)$$

$$V_{out2} = (V5 - V4) - (V6 - V3) \quad (4)$$

Notice that Eq. 4 describes the subtraction of two other subtractions. This can be interpreted as voltage signals for the positive (V5–V4) and the negative (V6–V3) phases of stimulation waveform. Moreover, each subtraction is put in place in such a way that while one PWM signal (V5 or V6) is used to generate the main wave, the other one (V3 or V4) is used to limit it.

Finally, operational amplifier AP3 receives the signal according to the configuration made by the user and generated by the controller regarding the number and polarity of phases, frequency and pulse duration. The electronic circuit was designed to generate fixed electrical currents. That is, even if conditions change from animal to animal, such as the resistance of the brain tissue, the current remains at the programmed value. For this, AP3 is wired in the voltage-to-current converter configuration.

The input current i_1 depends only on the operation voltage of the controller (usually 5 V), maintained across AP1 and AP2 circuits, and the resistor R10. By its turn, the output current i_{out}, or i_2 in the diagram of Fig. 2 below, is equal to i_1 (there is no current entering the inverter terminal of the operational amplifier due to its high impedance), which is obtained through Eq. 5. Therefore, even when the output impedance is changed, the current remains the same, that is, constant and determined only by resistor R10. Specifically, for R10, this can be a potentiometer or a board with resistors, with a selector switch, for example, where it is possible to select different currents.

$$i_{out} = -\frac{V_{out2}}{R10} \quad (5)$$

The entire process described and detailed in Eqs. 1 to 5 for generating the signals (anode and cathode) is illustrated in Fig. 3. In this Figure we have that the first pulse generated is given by V5–V4 (anodic pulse). The second pulse is given by V6–V3 (cathodic pulse). That is, V5 and V6 are the main waves and V3 and V4 cut the main waves according to the desired pulse width for a given frequency. Finally, in the last wave, there is the sum of these signals in the second amplifier, (V5–V4) and (V6–V3), with a 180° shift for the second pulse, resulting in the wave that will be amplified in the last stage, in AP3.

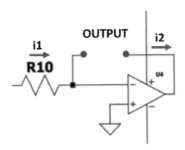

Fig. 2. Voltage to current operational amplifier circuit used to generate fixed-current pulses. Output current (i_{out} or i_2) is equal to i_1 which is dependent only upon R10 and the voltage at its left node, which is 5 V pulsed (Eq. 5).

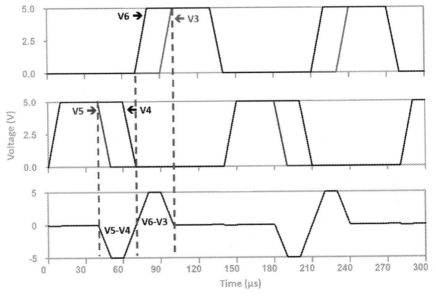

Fig. 3. A biphasic cathodic-first pulse is created from summation and subtraction of PWM signals according to Eq. 4. Signal $V4$ is subtracted from $V5$ to create the cathodic pulse after an inversion (top row). Analogously, $V3$ is subtracted from $V6$ to create the anodic pulse (middle row). These partial signals are summed to create V_{out2} which will be converted to a current-fixed signal (bottom row).

2.2   Circuit Tests

To establish the limits and characteristics of the circuit, electrical tests were carried out. The first and most important was the constant current test, which aimed at verifying the stability of the output current, regardless of the output resistance found (simulating the variability between experiments). We know that in a typical application of extracellular ES, the stimulated impedance may vary between 1 KΩ and 10 KΩ, these values being represented by resistor $R11$. Here, we used the following values for $R11$: 1 KΩ, 4.02 KΩ,

6.19 KΩ, 8.25 KΩ and 10 KΩ. It is important to note that, although both stimulated tissue and the electrolyte-electrode interface are not pure resistive, current testing and calibration is usually performed upon pure resistive loads.

A total of 23 different resistors for R10 were used, yielding output currents from 15 μA to 1.2 mA. Table 1 presents all the values used, as well as the calculated/expected currents (according to Eq. 5). The multimeter used for this test was the Agilent U1241B and to generate the PWM waves, the Arduino Leonardo was used. We selected very long pulses to facilitate readouts.

Another test performed was the polarity test, in order to verify if the circuit is really generating negative and/or positive pulses. The polarity test certifies via oscilloscope that the output signal is responding to the commands for choosing the pulses. Finally, the dead time of the circuit, which is the time interval between the end of one phase and the start of the next phase in a biphasic pulse, was verified. The oscilloscope used for these tests was the Agilent DSO-X 2002A model.

Table 1. Resistance values used for R10 during testing.

Nominal current (μA)	Resistor *R10* (KΩ)	Calculated current (μA)
1200	4,02	1243,78
1000	4,7	1063,83
900	5,6	892,86
800	6,19	807,75
700	7,15	699,30
600	8,25	606,06
500	10	500,00
400	12,1	413,22
350	14	357,14
300	16,9	295,86
250	20,5	243,90
200	24,9	200,00
150	33,2	150,60
100	44,2	113,12
90	56,2	88,97
80	61,9	80,97
70	71,5	69,93
60	78,7	63,53

(*continued*)

Table 1. (*continued*)

Nominal current (μA)	Resistor $R10$ (KΩ)	Calculated current (μA)
50	100	50,00
40	120	41,67
30	150	33,33
20	240	20,83
15	360	13,89

2.3   Circuit Assembly

In order to carry out all the tests, the circuit was assembled on a protoboard. The operational amplifier used was the TL071 which has among its characteristics a low voltage - noise ratio (0.003%) and a good slew rate (13 V/μs). This 8-pin integrated circuit can be powered with voltages up to + 18 V (+Vdc) and − 18 V (−Vdc). In addition, it features 1.4 mA supply current, 75 dB common mode rejection ratio, and 3 MHz gain bandwidth

Fig. 4. Electrical stimulator circuit assembled on protoboard. The Arduino board was used to create the PWM pulses for these tests, but any other compatible platforms can also be used. Potentiometers on the bottom-left of the protoboard are used to control pulse width and frequency. The operational amplifier-based circuitry for the integration of PWM signals into a biphasic (or monophasic) fixed-current pulse is seen on the superior portion of the protoboard.

(GBP). However, we make it clear that any other operational amplifier with similar characteristics can also be used. The resistors are all precision, that is, they have a maximum of 1% error in relation to their face values and their power is 1/8 W. It is important to highlight that resistor value should always be tested with a multimeter prior to assembly in order to increase circuit reliability. For the generation of PWM signals, an Arduino Leonardo was used. Frequencies as well as the pulse widths were informed to Arduino by 10 KΩ potentiometers connected to analog inputs. To make all the interconnections on the protoboard, AWG 26 cables (jumpers) were used. The sources *V1* and *V2* and also *V7* and *V8* in the diagram of Fig. 1 are DC power supplies of +9 V, −9 V, +18 V, −18 V respectively, as well as the circuit reference. The font used to supply this was the Agilent U9031A model. Figure 4 shows the circuit in question with the components used.

Here we used of Arduino Leonardo for convenience and simplicity, but any other circuit capable of generating a PWM signal could also be employed. The Arduino code for these tests is freely available upon request to authors. All tests were performed only on an electronic bench and no animal experimentation was carried out at this point of development for ethical reasons.

3   Results

3.1   Positive and Negative Current Test

With the proposed circuit, it is possible to stimulate with monophasic or biphasic pulses. For this reason, it is necessary to check the positive and negative currents separately. Tables 2 and 3 present the results found for positive and negative currents, respectively, applied to different output loads.

Table 2. Stimulation currents for positive pulse.

Possible currents (μA)	1 KΩ	4,02 KΩ	6,19 KΩ	8,25 KΩ	10 KΩ	Variation / error (%)
1243,78	1252	1247	1245	1240	1239	1,04 / 0,07
1063,83	1068	1064	1062	1058	1050	1,70 / 0,32
892,86	902	896	894	890	885	1,90 / 0,06
807,75	810	805	804	800	795	1,87 / 0,62
699,30	702	697	695	692	686	2,30 / 0,71
606,06	609	605	604	600	595	2,32 / 0,57
500,00	505	500	500	495	491	2,81 / 0,36
413,22	415	413	413	405	400	3,67 / 0,98
357,14	360	355	355	350	347	3,68 / 1,06
295,86	302	298	295	291	288	4,75 / 0,36

(*continued*)

Table 2. (*continued*)

Possible currents (μA)	1 KΩ	4,02 KΩ	6,19 KΩ	8,25 KΩ	10 KΩ	Variation / error (%)
243,90	250	245	243	241	240	4,10 / 0,04
200,00	208	205	202	197	195	6,45 / 0,70
150,60	154	153	152	149	148	3,97 / 0,40
113,12	115	112	110	110	108	6,31 / 1,91
88,97	92	90	90	88	86	6,73 / 0,26
80,97	83	82	81	79	77	7,46 / 0,71
69,93	72	70	70	68	67	7,20 / 0,76
63,53	64	63	63	62	61	4,79 / 1,49
50,00	51	50	50	47	47	8,16 / 2,04
41,67	43	42	41	40	39	9,76 / 1,63
33,33	34	33	33	33	32	6,06 / 1,00
20,83	22	22	21	21	20	9,43 / 1,75
13,89	15	15	14	14	14	6,94 / 3,54

The mean error of measured currents to calculated values were below 1% for the majority of currents, positive and negative pulses, but achieving a maximum of 3.54% and 3.66% for a current of 15 μA, positive and negative pulses respectively. The mean of the total variation of the positive current is 4.93% and for the negative current, it is 4.60%.

Table 3. Stimulation currents for negative pulse

Possible currents (μA)	1 KΩ	4,02 KΩ	6,19 KΩ	8,25 KΩ	10 KΩ	Variation / error (%)
1243,78	1245	1239	1238	1238	1235	0,81 / 0,39
1063,83	1059	1057	1055	1054	1048	1,04 / 0,88
892,86	897	892	890	888	885	1,35 / 0,28
807,75	807	803	802	799	795	1,50 / 0,82
699,30	695	692	691	687	685	1,45 / 1,35
606,06	605	603	602	599	596	1,50 / 0,84
500,00	500	496	495	493	490	2,02 / 1,05
413,22	413	410	408	405	400	3,19 / 1,48
357,14	357	354	353	350	345	3,41 / 1,52
295,86	300	295	293	291	290	3,40 / 0,70

(*continued*)

Table 3. (*continued*)

Possible currents (μA)	1 KΩ	4,02 KΩ	6,19 KΩ	8,25 KΩ	10 KΩ	Variation / error (%)
243,90	247	244	242	240	238	3,72 / 0,70
200,00	205	200	199	197	195	5,02 / 0,40
150,60	152	149	149	147	145	4,72 / 1,48
113,12	115	112	112	110	108	6,28 / 1,54
88,97	91	90	88	87	85	6,80 / 0,87
80,97	82	80	80	79	77	6,28 / 1,72
69,93	72	70	70	68	67	7,20 / 0,76
63,53	64	63	62	61	60	6,45 / 2,47
50,00	51	50	49	48	48	6,10 / 1,63
41,67	42	41	41	39	39	7,43 / 3,14
33,33	34	34	33	32	31	9,15 / 1,62
20,83	22	21	21	20	20	9,62 / 0,14
13,89	14	14	13	13	13	7,46 / 3,66

Figures 5 and 6 is a graphical depiction of results obtained for the positive and negative current tests, respectively. A total of 46 currents were measured, being 23 positive pulses and 23 negative pulses. Both tables and figures help to demonstrate how currents are stable across loads of different resistance values.

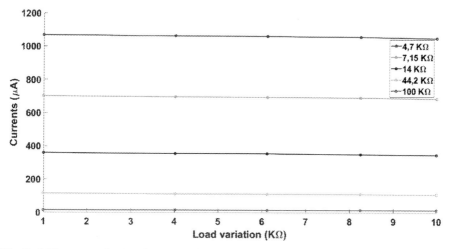

Fig. 5. Different amplitudes of output positive pulse currents generated by the circuit by varying *R10* (see color coding and image inset) as applied to different loads varying from 1 KΩ to 10 KΩ. Notice that amplitude values remain highly constant across load variation.

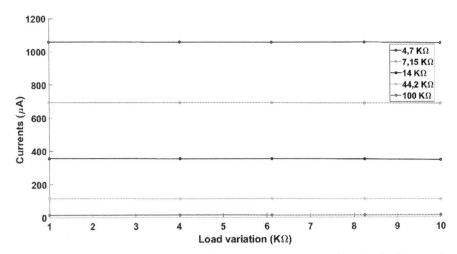

Fig. 6. Different amplitudes of output negative pulse currents generated by the circuit by varying *R10* (see color coding and image inset) as applied to different loads varying from 1 KΩ to 10 KΩ. Notice that amplitude values remain highly constant across load variation.

3.2 Polarity Test

For this test, we simply checked if there are two pulses and if they obey the triggers turning on or off according to the user's handling.

To perform this test, a frequency of 2 Hz and a pulse width of 512 μs was chosen. Figure 7 shows the two pulses together, that is, in the biphasic configuration. In Fig. 8, the negative pulse was deactivated, leaving the output signal as a monophasic positive pulse.

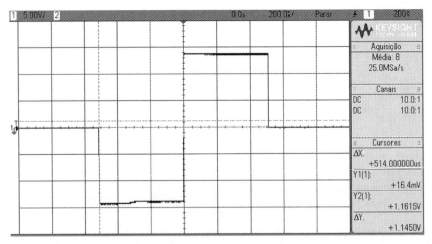

Fig. 7. Screenshot from the oscilloscope for the polarity test configured for a biphasic pulse of 512 μs duration (each phase) fired at 2 Hz.

Finally, in Fig. 9, the positive pulse was deactivated, making the circuit be single-phase with a negative pulse at the output.

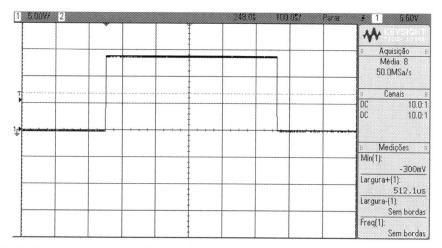

Fig. 8. Screenshot from the oscilloscope for the polarity test configured for 512 μs monophasic positive-only pulse fired at 2 Hz.

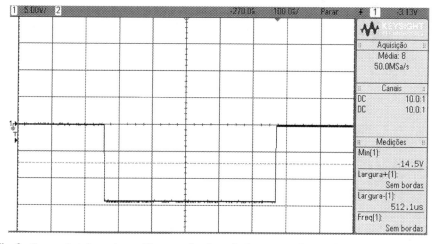

Fig. 9. Screenshot from the oscilloscope for the polarity test configured for 512 μs monophasic negative-only pulse fired at 2 Hz.

3.3   Dead Time Test

Using the same frequency and the same pulse width, Fig. 10 depicts a biphasic pulse in a larger timescale (5 ms/div). Figure 11 has a faster timescale (500 ns/div), where it is already possible to see that there is a rate of change, but the dead time is still not seen. Finally, in Fig. 12 (100 ns/div), it is already possible to say that the dead time of the circuit is very close to zero.

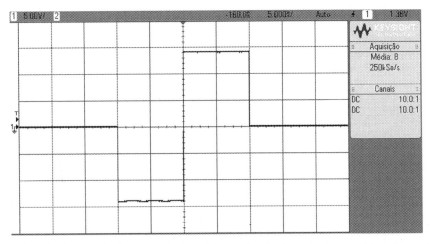

Fig. 10. A biphasic pulse (negative-first) used for testing dead time between phases observed at a 5 ms per division scale.

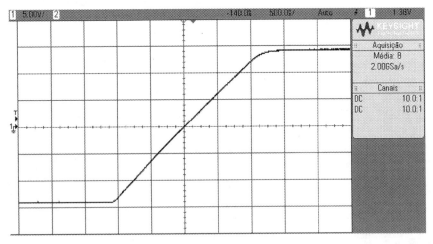

Fig. 11. A biphasic pulse (negative-first) used for testing dead time between phases observed at a 500 ns per division scale.

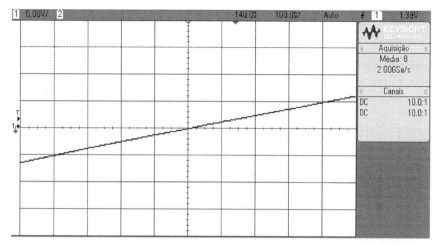

Fig. 12. A biphasic pulse (negative-first) used for testing dead time between phases observed at a 100 ns per division scale. There is no noticeable dead time.

4 Discussions and Conclusions

This article presented an inexpensive electronic circuit capable of delivering electrical stimulation current-fixed pulses as it is done in several fields of electrophysiology research. Simplified and very low cost, the circuit obtained good results in its electrical tests and confirmed that it can be fully controlled using only PWM signals.

The first test was the constant current, which kept its variation below 10% for each pulse (anodic or cathodic). Largest errors found are related to currents of 15 μA and does not exceed 4% in both pulses (Tables 2 and 3). As these values are found in the lowest currents, where any slight variation causes a large percentage of error, it is expected that the largest error is associated with them. Therefore, the constant current test showed that the circuit maintains its current fixed, even if the output impedance changes.

Another test performed was the polarity test, which, regardless of frequency and pulse width, can be chosen between positive and negative (anodic or cathodic). There are studies that need single-phase pulses and others that need biphasic pulses and thus, a circuit was developed in which it is possible to choose the polarity and number of phases. This test validated the choice of polarity according to the user's need.

The dead time found is practically zero, that is, there is no noticeable delay time between the voltage variation between the phases of the biphasic pulse. Even with the time scale in the order of nanoseconds, it was still not possible to verify the existence of dead time.

Additional testing must be carried out before the output stage can be used in animal experimentation. For instance, it is important to know how current values hold for long-term stimulation protocols. Furthermore, it is highly necessary to assess the stimulator performance in terms of reliability of pulse width and firing frequency according to the commanded values and also in the long run. Finally, it is also of paramount importance to evaluate efficiency and efficacy of the circuit with animal experimentation. On the other hand, all these criteria will be influenced also by the controller platform chosen. For this reason, such experimentation was not carried in the study, which has the goal of assessing the output stage separately. Follow up development and investigation on these issues are already being performed by our group with promising preliminary results and will be reported soon.

Here, we tested the output stage using pure resistive loads, while in a real experimental scenario, current pulses will be applied to impedances with also a capacitance part too (inductances are usually negligible). Consequently, current pulses flowing in the neural tissue will not be perfectly square and its shape (particularly speed of decay) will depend on the capacitance seen by the output stage. By its turn, this depends on factors such as stimulation target (e.g., gray vs. white matter) and electrode characteristics. Researchers should always be aware of such confounding factors when performing neural stimulation experiments. It is important to notice, on the other hand, that these issues are true for any stimulation equipment, given that they arise from the physical nature of tissue and the electrolyte-electrode interface.

Virtually all electrical stimulators used in research purposes across Latin America and other underdeveloped regions are manufactured and sold by private companies operating abroad and thus, have mostly high cost. Prices are also vulnerable to market fluctuations that affect the foreign currency and its exchange ratio. On top of that, taxes and importation fees impose even further difficulties in the access of such apparatuses. With this circuit together with any hardware capable of generating PWM, it is possible to start implementing simple but versatile ES protocols for research in electrophysiology. Here, the controller hardware used was the Arduino Leonardo. However, it would also be possible with any other Arduino board or other controllers, such as ESP32, ESP 8266, and even a Raspberry Pi system.

Acknowledgments. This study was financed in part by the Coordenação de Aperfeiçoamento de Pessoal de Nível Superior - Brasil (CAPES) - Finance Code 001.

References

1. Schomer, D.L., da Silva, F.H.L.: Niedermeyer's electroencephalography. Book **1**, 535 (2011)
2. Buccelli, S., et al.: A neuromorphic prosthesis to restore communication in neuronal networks. iScience **19**, 402–414 (2019). https://doi.org/10.1016/j.isci.2019.07.046
3. Gluckman, B.J., Nguyen, H., Weinstein, S.L., Schiff, S.J.: Adaptive electric field control of epileptic seizures. J. Neurosci. **21**(2), 590–600 (2001). https://doi.org/10.1523/jneurosci.21-02-00590.2001
4. Tcheng, T., Morrell, M.: Responsive neurostimulation for epilepsy. Neuroengineering (2007). https://doi.org/10.1201/9780849381850.ch5
5. Tehovnik, E.J.: Electrical stimulation of neural tissue to evoke behavioral responses. J. Neurosci. Methods **65**(1), 1–17 (1996). https://doi.org/10.1016/0165-0270(95)00131-X
6. Theodore, W.H., Fisher, R.S.: Brain stimulation for epilepsy. Lancet Neurol. **3**(2), 111–118 (2004). https://doi.org/10.1016/S1474-4422(03)00664-1
7. Santos, M.L., Silva, H.R., Cota, V.R.: Construindo um Open Source Hardware: da ideia ao negócio – um estudo da obra de Alicia Gibb. In: Online Proceedings of LAWCN 2019, pp. 75–98 (2019). https://www.lawcn.com.br/files/proceedingsfinal.pdf

8. Grill, W.M.: Temporal pattern of electrical stimulation is a new dimension of therapeutic innovation. Curr. Opin. Biomed. Eng. **8**, 1–6 (2018). https://doi.org/10.1016/j.cobme.2018.08.007

9. Medeiros, D.D.C., et al.: Anatomically dependent anticonvulsant properties of temporally-coded electrical stimulation. Epilepsy Behav. **23**(3), 294–297 (2012). https://doi.org/10.1016/j.yebeh.2012.01.004

10. Cota, V.R., de Oliveira, J.C., Damázio, L.C.M., Moraes, M.F.D.: Nonperiodic stimulation for the treatment of refractory epilepsy: applications, mechanisms, and novel insights. Epilepsy Behav. **121** (2021). https://doi.org/10.1016/j.yebeh.2019.106609

11. Udupa, K., Chen, R.: The mechanisms of action of deep brain stimulation and ideas for the future development. Prog. Neurobiol. **133**, 27–49 (2015). https://doi.org/10.1016/j.pneurobio.2015.08.001

12. Cota, V.R., Medeiros, D.D.C., Vilela, M.R.S.D.P., Doretto, M.C., Moraes, M.F.D.: Distinct patterns of electrical stimulation of the basolateral amygdala influence pentylenetetrazole seizure outcome. Epilepsy Behav. **14**(1 SUPPL. 1), 26–31 (2009). https://doi.org/10.1016/j.yebeh.2008.09.006

13. Cota, V.R., Aguiar, C.L., de Souza Neto, B., Benegas, M.: Open-source hardware as a model of technological innovation and academic entrepreneurship. Innov. Manag. Rev. **17**(2), 177–195 (2020). https://doi.org/10.1108/INMR-06-2018-0036

Neuroengineering – Science and Technology

Physiological Self-regulation Using Biofeedback Training: From Concept to Clinical Applicability

Karina Aparecida Rodrigues[1], João Vitor da Silva Moreira[1],
Daniel José Lins Leal Pinheiro[1], Ana Teresa Contier[1], Esper Cavalheiro[1],
and Jean Faber[1,2(✉)]

[1] Escola Paulista de Medicina, Departamento de Neurologia e Neurocirurgia, Universidade Federal de São Paulo, São Paulo, São Paulo, Brazil
jean.faber@unifesp.br
[2] Instituto de Ciência e Tecnologia, Universidade Federal de São Paulo, São José dos Campos, São Paulo, Brazil

Abstract. For a better rescuing of people with disabilities, it is crucial the development of new assistive technologies and therapeutic methods to rehabilitate people with some disabilities to integrate them to a complete social life. A very promising tool is the physiological self-regulation protocols based on biofeedback training. Biofeedback protocols are based on the premise that it is possible to learn how to self-modulate specific aspects of the body's physiological activity. A biofeedback system is composed of input physiological information and output sensorial stimuli information in a real-time closed-loop process that allows patients to modulate a target physiological (dys)function. The application of biofeedback protocols has been widely studied and used in different clinical practices such as orthopedic, neurological, physiological, and cognitive conditions. This review focuses on the main aspects concerning the system arrangement and protocols of stimulation in biofeedback approaches, from its basic principles of operation to its clinical application in different contexts, with emphasis on sensorimotor and cognitive deficits.

Keywords: Self-regulation · Biofeedback · Neurofeedback · Brain machine interface · Brain computer interface · Rehabilitation

1 Introduction

In the last decade, different protocols based on closed loop self-regulation training have been applied as a new experimental and clinical approach, with great therapeutic potential (Neblett 2016; Bunderson 2014; Kawase et al. 2017; Schweisfurth et al. 2016; Ramos-Murguialday et al. 2013; Shokur et al. 2016). Currently, there are many different systems and protocols, but all of them start from the same common biofeedback principles (Hodgson et al. 2014; Kawase et al. 2017; Dosen et al. 2015; Reiter et al. 2016; Seáñez-González et al. 2016).

Technically, the concept of biofeedback can designate two complementary parts - (*i*) a physical system, relative to the construction/integration of physical components, device

P. R. d. A. Ribeiro et al. (Eds.): LAWCN 2021, CCIS 1519, pp. 189–214, 2022.
https://doi.org/10.1007/978-3-031-08443-0_12

architecture, statistical techniques, and type of signal recording, and (*ii*) a protocol, relative to the process and training that the patients will be submitted to recover or improve the physiological target (dys)functions. The biofeedback system depends on the type of physiological signal that will be recorded, such as the brain, heart, muscle, etc. It is characteristically composed of a set of electronic devices, arranged in a specific and ergonomic way to optimally record the physiological activity related to the target function, to treat and produce in real time the set of stimuli (feedbacks) to the patient. It also contains a computational processing that implements statistical techniques to enable the processing of all signal features associated with a software (in general, with a friendly interface) to allow the responsible clinician/researcher and the patient choose and command all parameters (Neblett 2016; Fazli et al. 2012; Sarasola-Sanz et al. 2017; Xie et al. 2013).

Concerning biofeedback as a protocol, it must be elaborated according to specific conditions of interest, with the premise of explicit or implicit learning through operant conditioning. It means that, as the target activity is recorded, the patient receives some sensory feedback and/or reward, for example, by performing a game-type task (such as rotating a virtual cube, and translating a vertical bar), reinforcing positively or negatively the patient's behavior and the physiological function that generates the desired activity (Sterman and Egner 2006). This physiological activity modulation is guided by a specific protocol design that in a closed loop stimulates the patient's senses (visual, tactile, or auditory) according to a signal-stimulus mapping (Neblett 2016).

Biofeedback protocols have shown success in the clinical treatment of different comorbidities, such as attention-deficit/hyperactivity disorder (ADHD) (Reiter et al. 2016), stroke (Carvalho 2019; Stanton et al. 2017), epilepsy (Sterman and Egner 2006), urinary incontinence (Herderschee et al. 2013), and tension-type headache (Bendtsen et al. 2010). However, although biofeedback training has already been widely used as a rehabilitation tool, the precise mechanisms and neural bases underlying the self-learning are not entirely well known. Evidence from studies on neurofeedback (Gunkelman and Johnstone 2005; Yucha and Montgomery 2008) has indicated that learning to self-modulate certain physiological information possibly involves permanent changes in the central nervous system (CNS) (Sitaram et al. 2017), which can support the application of this therapeutic approach in different scenarios.

Given the importance of a better understanding of the therapeutic options available that can help people with disabilities to return to their functional and social activities as soon as possible, and the increasing and promising use of biofeedback training, this study reviewed the key aspects of this technique, from its basic concepts and principles of operation to its application in different clinical contexts, especially in the conditions of sensorimotor or cognitive deficits.

2   Principles of System Operation

Besides the clinical environment, ergonomic structure, and electronic configuration/arrangements of a biofeedback system, one of the most important parts of the system consists in the way and choice of signal features selected as inputs of the system to optimize the physiological modulation. Input signals contain the physiological information that will be self-modulated. This information needs to be recorded and converted into digital data to be processed and analyzed in real time and finally provide a feedback to the user through some sensory modality from which it is possible to learn to control/modulate the physiological information in question (Neblett 2016) (Fig. 1).

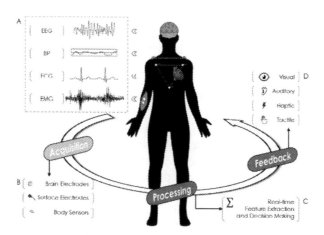

Fig. 1. Overview of biofeedback. A biofeedback system involves data acquisition from one or more physiological modalities, the real-time processing of these signals, and feedback, which is given through some sensory modality. From this cycle, it is possible to learn how to self-modulate the desired activity through training. A) Examples of different acquisition techniques that can be used: electroencephalography (EEG) to record large-scale neural activity, biomechanical parameters (BP) to acquire information about body movements, electrocardiography (ECG) to record cardiac electrical activity, and electromyography (EMG) to record muscle electrical activity. B) Examples of sensors used in different acquisition techniques, which might be invasive or non-invasive. C) Real-time data processing, which includes signal filtering, feature extraction, and decision making to provide feedback. D) Feedback delivery by stimulation of one or more sensory modalities.

2.1 Inputs

Input signals of a biofeedback system can be directly or indirectly measured from any physiological activity that reflects the interaction of our body with the environment. There are many techniques available to provide measurements of physiological activities in different contexts (Castelnuovo et al. 2016; Ma et al. 2015; Mihara and Miyai 2016; Moleiro and Cid 2001; Rao 2011), such as sensors to estimate biomechanical parameters, electromyography (EMG), electrocardiography (ECG or EKG), and electroencephalography (EEG). Other techniques can also be used, such as functional magnetic resonance (fMRI), functional near-infrared spectrum (fNIRS), magnetoencephalography (MEG), etc. However, most of these types of measurements are expensive and not practical for real-time procedures, which restricts their uses.

Biomechanical Signals. Biomechanical signals are commonly used to measure movements and postural patterns. These patterns can be estimated using several sensors or devices, such as motion sensors (inertial sensors, potentiometers, and accelerometers) (Kent et al. 2015), ground reaction force platforms (Schenck and Kesar 2017), or cameras (Valdés and Van der Loos 2018).

Electronic devices, such as accelerometers and gyroscopes (Kent et al. 2015), which measure acceleration and angular velocity, respectively, can be found either separately or in combination, composing a system known as an Inertial Measurement Unit (Morrison 1987). Additionally, pressure and force sensors also make part of the setup to measure biological signals associated with motion and displacement (Schenck and Kesar 2017). These sensors typically transduce angular rotation along three axes (pitch, roll, and yaw) into a time series of electrical potential amplitude, according to the body displacements in time and space.

Biomechanical signals are used in different protocols due to their intuitive use and low cost, such as training people with spinal cord injury (SCI) (Seáñez-González et al. 2016) or as part of the treatment of people with low back pain (Kent et al. 2015). Different studies have also demonstrated efficiency in using reaction force platforms as biofeedback systems to improve gait (Schenck and Kesar 2017) or for balance training when associated with visual feedback and functional electrical stimulation in the elderly (Li et al. 2018). Camera-based systems are generally used to perform body-tracking, which is obtained via markers placed on anatomical references on the patient's body, allowing a body-dynamic representation in a three-dimensional coordinate system (Amadio et al. 1999). A recent study showed that the use of biofeedback with cameras was efficient in respiratory training for healthy people (Heerink et al. 2018). Valdés and Van der Loos 2018 also showed that this type of input associated with multimodal feedback may be interesting to reduce body compensation after stroke (Valdés and Van der Loos 2018).

Electromyography (EMG). Electromyography is a technique that measures bioelectrical responses produced by muscle activity, via depolarization of the muscle membrane during contraction over time (Basmajian and De Luca 1985). The technique is performed by applying electrodes on the surface of the skin using contact electrodes or intramuscularly via a needle. The device that performs EMG is the electromyograph and the reading is called the electromyogram. EMG signals inform the level of activation or order of muscle recruitment and also can be used to analyze the biomechanics of motion (Konrad 2005).

This technique pioneered biofeedback training for people to learn how to relax their muscles (Budzynski and Stoyva 1969). EMG biofeedback protocols have been applied to different clinical conditions, such as improvement of upper-limb functionality in patients with hemiparesis (Armagan et al. 2003), upper-limb training for children with cerebral palsy (Yoo et al. 2017), and sensory-motor recovery for people after peripheral nervous surgeries (Sturma et al. 2018). In terms of the use of an electrophysiological signal as an input to the biofeedback system, EMG is also the technique most found in the clinical environment.

Electrocardiography (ECG) and Heart Rate Variability (HRV). Electrocardiography measures the variation of electric cardiac activity over time. ECG is recorded through electrodes placed on the skin surface using bipolar acquisition or more derivations (Houghton and Gray 2008). The recorded signals represent the sum of action potentials in multiple cardiac muscle cells, which provides information on the propagation of the electric wave through the cardiac chambers that underlies the heart contraction dynamic (Silverthorn 2010). There are many ECG indexes associated with heart dynamics, however heart rate (HR) is one of the simplest and most used metrics (Holm et al. 2010; Ivanov et al. 2004). It essentially reports an average of heartbeats in the right time window and helps to evaluate, for instance, moments of bradycardia and tachycardia (Houghton and Gray 2008).

Another important biological signal is the activity of the autonomic nervous system (ANS). In essence, the ANS is the primary mechanism related to flight-or-flight responses, and it is governed by the activity of two paths, the parasympathetic (vagal nervous), and sympathetic nervous, where they present competitive (but complementary) actions (Gordan et al. 2015). Besides the regulation of physiological functions such as digestion, respiratory rate, and pupillary action, one of the most important physiological function modulated by the ANS is the HR (Borresen and Lambert 2008). Thus, it is possible to extract ANS activity through a correlation with heart rate variability (HRV) by evaluating how the heartbeat intervals vary over time and to infer which branch of the ANS is more active (Dong 2016).

Studies have shown that the use of biofeedback systems that utilizes HR as input signals can reduce heart arrhythmias as well as a reduction in the systolic blood pressure by modulating the HR (Moleiro and Cid 2001). While biofeedback systems using HRV can be useful in the treatment of respiratory diseases, such as asthma (Lehrer et al. 2004), coronary heart disease (Nolan et al. 2005), and stress (Shusterman 2005).

There are still many other possible inputs applicable to biofeedback systems, such as the use of respiratory parameters, ultrasound images (Giggins et al. 2013), and galvanic skin response (Nagai et al. 2019). Any physiological characteristics measurable over time by a biosensor can, in principle, be used in a biofeedback system and be proposed a specific biofeedback clinical protocol to modulate some signal-feature related to a target physiological condition (Giggins et al. 2013). In addition, several combinations can be made between these techniques, seeking more robustness, speed, and clinical efficacy.

2.1.1 Central Nervous System Activity

When using neural activity as input information, the biofeedback system is called neurofeedback (Gunkelman and Johnstone 2005; Yucha and Montgomery 2008). This unlocks a great possibility for directly training the brain and its ascending and descending communication pathways under various conditions (Frolov et al. 2017; Hodgson et al. 2014; Ramos-Murguialday et al. 2013; Shokur et al. 2016). Usually, the training is based on brain information recorded by EEG, or fMRI and fNIRS. Regardless of the way brain information is acquired, there is a possibility, through training of the participant, to self-modulate certain brain activities and bring functional benefits to which this activity is related.

Electroencephalography (EEG). In neurofeedback, the most used method of acquisition in the research environment and clinical area is EEG (Hohmann et al. 2016). An EEG essentially records cortical electrical activity changes over time by measuring the sum of electrical fields generated by oscillations of post-synaptic potential (Buzsáki et al. 2012). When the recording is performed directly on the cortex surface, sub- or over-dural, this technique is called electrocorticography (ECoG). An ECoG signal has, in general, a better resolution and more specificity on the activity over spatial cortex regions (Kaiju et al. 2017). For non-invasive EEG, the electrodes are positioned on the scalp of the subject, following an international system of placement (Tatum et al. 2016). In a general way, the neural activity in the brain is supported by a variety of neuronal oscillations, characterized by their frequency ranges and anatomical locations, and widely correlated with cognitive and behavioral states (Buzsáki and Watson 2012). Several studies use the information from theses oscillations to investigate brain dynamics, synchronicity, or to establish neurofeedback protocols, wherein the patients are trained to modulate their brain activity according to an objective and clinical conditions (Orndorff-Plunkett et al. 2017), such as rehabilitation of people with motor deficits or cognitive arising from stroke (Cho et al. 2015), SCI (Shokur et al. 2016), or even for cognitive training in healthy people (Gomez-Pilar et al. 2014), and other conditions such as ADHD (Hodgson et al. 2014) and post-traumatic stress disorder (PTSD) (Peniston and Kulkosky 1991).

Functional Magnetic Resonance Imaging (fMRI). The fMRI technique allows measuring the intrinsic relaxation time of a material, after the application of a magnetic field, revealing differences in its composition. The generated image allows exploring anatomical structures of soft tissues with high spatial resolution, which is not possible using X-ray and tomography (Watanabe et al. 2017). Associated with this signal it is possible to extract information about differences in blood flow in biological systems, usually through the technique blood-oxygen-level dependent (BOLD) imaging, which may be related to metabolic changes in the brain and consequently to neural activity (Logothetis et al. 2001). Therefore, despite the use of fMRI being far more expensive and complex than EEG, there are many studies using fMRI in biofeedback protocols for chronic pain control (DeCharms et al. 2005), training people with stroke (Liew et al. 2016), and modulation of cognitive functions (Caria et al. 2007; Yoo et al. 2006). The great advantage of the fMRI technique is its accuracy concerning spatial-temporal parts in the brain. It means that, if well applied, a neurofeedback protocol using fMRI could, in principle, modulate a specific signal from a very particular internal brain region (DeCharms 2008).

Functional Near-Infrared Spectroscopy (fNIRS). The fNIRS technique is a method to assess the activation state of cortical areas in the brain by applying light pulses with a wavelength near the infrared electromagnetic spectrum on the region of interest (Coyle et al. 2004). The neural tissue can present different absorption rates according to the balance of oxygenated and deoxygenated hemoglobin in the local capillaries. It means that the BOLD technique is frequently used to correlate neural metabolic activity (Richard et al. 2011). Furthermore, compared to traditional neuroimaging technology, fNIRS is non-invasive, safe, portable, and has a significantly lower cost (Mihara and Miyai 2016). One of the first studies with fNIRS in neurofeedback protocols was conducted by Coyle et al. (2004), where the participants performed a movement of grasping a ball with their hand or imagined themselves performing this task. From their measurements, it was possible to observe an increase of oxygen flow in the cerebral area corresponding to that movement (the portion of the motor cortex related to hand control) (Coyle et al. 2004). Clinical protocols applying fNIRS started to be explored in the last few years, such as for better motor control of people with severe hemiparesis after stroke (Mihara et al. 2013).

For neurofeedback approaches, there are still several other types of techniques and signals that can be used, such as MEG (Buch et al. 2008) and invasive multielectrodes (Benabid et al. 2019). Furthermore, it also possible to make different combinations of these techniques, according to interest and accessibility (Fazli et al. 2012; Keynan et al. 2016). The main limitation to use or integrate some of these techniques is the high cost of device acquisition and protocol complexity. Therefore, when compared to those, EEG is still the most used in clinical practice (Gruzelier 2014).

2.2   Features from Input Signals

After selecting the type of signal that will be recorded, the next step is to choose what features of this signal optimize the target physiology activity and how these features will be changed to ensure the intended physiological modulation (Anzai 2012; Bishop 2006). Here, we will especially focus on the electrophysiological signals most used in biofeedback and neurofeedback systems, recorded through EMG, ECG/HRV, and EEG, and on the image acquisition techniques (fMRI and fNIRS) (Fig. 2).

Electromyography (EMG). The intensity of muscle activity, related to contraction or relaxation, is very well represented through the amplitude of the EMG signals over time. Therefore, if the objective is just to detect the level of activation of muscle groups, to look at the amplitude variation over time is enough. In this case, the most common features to be calculated and analyzed are total power, signal root mean square (RMS), maximum/minimum amplitude values, and average/median amplitude values (that overpass a threshold); all of them calculated along with buffer window (that can be the whole buffer) (De Luca 2006). Depending on the protocol, sometimes it is necessary to identify more precisely the shape and firing rates of some motor units, which can be important in cases of some neuromuscular disorders, it is necessary to look after some spectral signatures of these units and use their features in the classification process (Reaz et al. 2006).

Electrocardiography (ECG) and Heart Rate Variability (HRV). The signal generated by the ECG record forms waves and complexes related to electrical and muscular activity of the heart are known as PQRST complexes. The first approach in these cases is to detect the peak of one of these complexes and through them calculate the HR and HRV. Generally, it uses the peak R due to its prominence. Once detected, the peak R, and the precise time associated with its occurrence, it is possible to calculate both, HR and HRV. For HR, it is enough to count the number of R peaks in a specific interval of time (Houghton and Gray 2008).

Through the HRV it is possible to infer the variability associated with the HR. HRV is commonly calculated using a related ECG time series, called tachogram (Clifford 2002), defined by the temporal distance of each R–R interval. The tachogram is not calculated with the R amplitude values but with its time stamps. Once the tachogram is in hand,

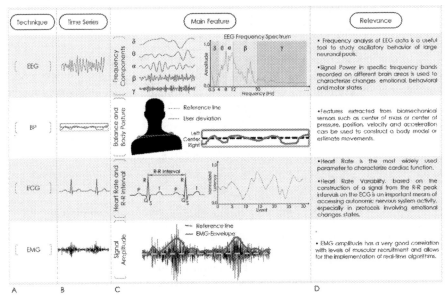

Fig. 2. The first step in defining a biofeedback system is to determine which physiological activities will be trained, and A) which acquisition techniques will be used for recording, such as EEG, BP, ECG, EMG B) The next step is to understand how this signal changes over time, and then C) which characteristics of that signal can best represent the physiological modality of interest D) Relevance of each feature given the choice of a technique. For example, in order to train brain activity and record it using EEG, the best way to extract information from this signal is to separate it into different frequency bands, commonly referred to as "brain rhythms". These rhythms vary largely depending on where they are registered, and in respect to different behaviors or movement states. Else, if the idea is to train motion control of a body segment or balance, we can use biomechanical parameters, often using information from the center of mass, center of pressure, position, velocity, or acceleration. Another possibility is training based on self-modulation of the autonomic nervous system, which is widely used in protocols involving emotional behavioral changes by HRV. Finally, as exemplified, we can also train muscle control (to learn to either relax or contract a particular muscle), and this muscle activity can be easily represented by the amplitude of the signal over time.

it is possible to extract different features, both in time and frequency domain, that are used to characterize cardiac and autonomic functions (Hejjel and Roth 2004).

Examples of HRV features in time domain are as follows: standard deviation of normal-to-normal beats, defined as the standard deviation of RR intervals; standard deviation of averages normal-to-normal, which corresponds to standard deviation of slow variabilities; and RMS of the successive differences, which mainly refers to abrupt variations of HRV (Clifford 2002). HRV features in the frequency domain uses some spectral technique on the tachogram (usually the parametric technique autoregressive model since tachograms generally are small time series and techniques based on the Fourier analysis become unstable). The main HRV signal features in the frequency domain are power spectrum density of frequency, power of low frequency (LF), high frequency (HF), and the ratio between them (LF/HF), which are related to autonomic balances of the nervous system (Őri et al. 1992). The HF spectrum (0.15 to 0.4 Hz) is related to parasympathetic or vagal activity and also called the respiratory band since it corresponds to the HR variations associated with respiratory cycles (Hernando et al. 2016). In addition, despite the LF spectrum (0.05 to 10 Hz) described as being related to sympathetic activity, this relationship is not completely precise. Currently, several studies have shown that independently of HF modulation LF power seems to be more related to baroreflex function than cardiac sympathetic tone (Hayano 2019).

This is one of the most complex signals to be used in a biofeedback approach. The main problem concerning biofeedback protocols using HRV is the short interval of time that every biofeedback system imposes to process the signal in real time. It means that all biofeedback systems have only a small period to extract all informative features to decode and transduce it to a sensory stimulus. However, working with short time intervals in a HRV from ECG recordings may be insufficient, and one needs to be careful with this type of protocols (Acharya et al. 2006).

Electroencephalography (EEG). The EEG recordings often investigate the information associated with the frequency domain, since it shows the brain presents specific frequency ranges, called rhythms, associated with specific regions and conditions. By convention, they are defined as Delta (0.5–4 Hz), Theta (4–8 Hz), Alpha (8–12 Hz), Beta (12–30 Hz), and Gamma (>30 Hz) (Buzsáki 2009). For spontaneous EEG recordings, the neural oscillatory activity is better represented by these frequency bands than by amplitude over time. The most used methods that work on the spectrum of frequency are mainly based on the calculus of power, coherence, and phase lag of these rhythms (Vaid et al. 2015).

A widely used brain rhythm in neurofeedback protocols is the sensorimotor rhythm (SMR). There are some divergences concerning the actual frequency range of oscillation related to this rhythm (Stern 2005; Pfurtscheller et al. 2006). The literature points out that this rhythm in humans varies between 9 and 13 Hz (Pfurtscheller et al. 2006), but in neurofeedback or Brain Computer-Interface (BCI) protocols broader frequency ranges are normally used, reaching up to 30 Hz (Naros et al. 2016; Pfurtscheller et al. 2006; Zich et al. 2015).

The SMR rhythm is a result of the interaction between thalamic nuclei and the sensorimotor cortex. It is characterized by the resting activity of the motor-sensory thalamocortical pathway. In this way, the power associated with the frequency range of SMR is higher in resting conditions and lower during an execution, preparation, or imagination of some motor act (Sterman and Egner 2006). Such aspects make this rhythm the best choice in neurofeedback protocol or BCI, especially in motor deficit conditions, in which users are trained to imagine a certain movement and self-modulate this activity to suppress the power of the SMR (Frolov et al. 2017; Pfurtscheller et al. 2006; Ramos-Murguialday et al. 2013). Another current possible clinical application is for people with pharmacoresistant epilepsy. There is evidence of training to self-modulate the power of the SMR (in this case, learning how to increase it, since they want to reduce motor activity); there is a change on the excitability threshold of the cortical sensorimotor-thalamus pathway and, consequently, a reduction on the number of crises (Finley et al. 1975; Sterman 2000; Sterman and Egner 2006; Wyler et al. 1979).

Motor imagery protocols, typically use two types of stimuli—(i) event-related synchronization (ERS), which is related to an SMR increase in power and present after the end of movement or imagination, related to inhibitory cortical activity, and (ii) event-related desynchronization (ERD), which occurs during the imagination of a specific movement, associated with a decreasing in SMR power (Neuper et al. 2009).

Furthermore, other possibilities for neurofeedback protocols with EEG is to use slow cortical potentials (SCP) (Mayer et al. 2016; Studer et al. 2014) and directed evoked potentials (Silvoni et al. 2016). SCP referred as the specific cortical activity of post-synaptic potentials of large cell assemblies, usually identified with a frequency range less than 1 Hz, also provided by the thalamocortical circuitry (Neske 2016). SCP is essentially characterized by periods of intense high (up states) and low (down states) levels of activity, where these fluctuations are the core of a neurofeedback protocol using SCP (Mattia and Sanchez-Vives 2019; Timofeev 2011). Finally, evoked potentials protocols generate the type of signals that are more in phase training with the sensory stimulus. In these protocols, the neural activities observed are yielded due to a synchronized external stimulus that evokes a specific neural response (Bentley et al. 2016; Güntekin and Başar 2016). The neural response characteristic of an evoked potential protocol has some specific peaks in the waveform of the signal, which will be used as an input feature in the neurofeedback system.

Functional Magnetic Resonance Imaging (fMRI) and Functional Near-Infrared Spectroscopy (fNIRS). Regarding imaging analysis, we highlight the BOLD technique used in both fMRI and fNIRS (DeCharms et al. 2005; Richard et al. 2011). The differences in blood oxygenation detected are related to metabolic changes in the brain and consequently to neural activity (Logothetis et al. 2001). Therefore, the signal analyzed with these techniques refers to a temporal-scale of the neurophysiological activity slower than electrophysiological responses, and the main aimed feature, usually analyzed, is the amplitude variation of the signal over time (Murta et al. 2015). Furthermore, in this type of activity, it is important to investigate the real BOLD activity from non-BOLD drifts, which can occur due to respiration artefacts, for example (Evans et al. 2015).

It is worth emphasizing that it is possible to use more than one feature from a collected signal and integrate features from different physiological activities measures (Fazli et al. 2012; Keynan et al. 2016). However, it is necessary to pay attention to the efficacy of that integration regarding the real-time computational processing, as well as the classification accuracy and their importance to the physiological changes sought by clinical biofeedback protocols.

3   Real-Time Signal Processing

Once they choose all input signals and their features of interest, it is crucial to determine which statistical approach will be used to perform the pattern identification and data classification. This step is correlated with the previous one, in the sense that the extracted features will have a direct influence on the type of statistical tool required for optimal pattern recognition and computational cost.

In a general way, any statistical technique seeks an optimal line able to discriminate two or more probability distributions related to a specific feature. Once some perturbation occurs, it is expected (as an alternative hypothesis) that this alteration will produce some statistical difference in their probability distributions (Bishop 2006). Therefore, in a biofeedback protocol, it is expected that some statistical features associated with the physiological activity recorded will be modulated, and differentiate itself from the baseline activity, during the target task.

In this way, the chosen features of a signal corresponding to the processed dataset that will be used to distinguish the observed physiological patterns related to a specific behavior, intention, or response. This processed dataset constitutes the so-called 'feature space', wherein the patterns are classified (Bishop 2006). From this, it is then selected a classifier, or some multifactorial statistical method, which can identify, in real time, the different changes promoted by the task protocol on the physiological signal features (Van Drongelen 2018). Depending on the protocol signal to record and chosen feature, it is only necessary to apply a simple comparison between the baseline activity and the activity during the stimulus exposition. If the signal-feature evaluated overpassed some predefined threshold, the task is considered accomplished, and a new threshold is imposed. This procedure is performed until the intended activity level is achieved.

However, some neuro/biofeedback protocols are complex and require more sophisticated techniques to compare different sets of features in real time. The application of a classifier can be done by using supervised methods, involving a training data set, semi-supervised methods where part of data is labeled and the other is not, or unsupervised methods where the dataset has no label, and it classifies via data clustering. The labels are indicators of the particular state that an event is related to and are used to assess the precision of a classifier during training by comparing the rate of correct predictions according to the data label (Bishop 2006). Additionally, the applied mathematical tools can be based on linear or nonlinear equations to perform class discrimination. All these techniques are known as machine learning methods that correspond to a branch of artificial intelligence. Some of the most used and known techniques in this context include linear and quadratic discriminant analysis, support vector machine, partial least square, naïve Bayes, network Bayes, tree classifier, and k-means (Anzai 2012).

In summary, the major consideration to be made in respect to the data processing cycle in biofeedback systems is to promote an efficient autoregulation. All of the steps have to be performed within a physiological time constraint, it is usually referred between 250 ms and 300 ms (Mizuno et al. 2011; Felsinger et al. 1947; Grice et al. 1948), to guarantee a physiological time of response, allowing the user to interpret the stimulus happening in real time.

4   Output Signals: Feedback Stimulation

There are several ways to associate a physiological signal to sensory stimulation. The choice of how a sensory stimulus is presented to a user must consider the clinical condition and the best way to represent the physiological information being trained, that is, feedback must be contingent (Sitaram et al. 2017). A stimulus can be presented isolated, independently, or integrated with other stimuli, such as in a video game, for instance

(Giggins et al. 2013, Caria et al. 2007; Donovan et al. 2016; Shokur et al. 2016; Weber et al. 2011).

Auditory Stimulus. In the case of auditory feedback, this can be integrated by varying different parameters such as tone, volume, sound type, and duration. Auditory stimuli are easy to implement and present a relatively short time of processing in the brain, with a wide informational bandwidth (Robertson et al. 2009). This type of biofeedback is mainly used in animal research (Koralek et al. 2012) and has been also proven effective in human clinical conditions for training of sensorimotor skills, for example (Donovan et al. 2016). The integration of different sensory modalities seems to elicit a better perceptual experience, for instance, using the auditory feedback related to a target-based task increases the accuracy of visual perception (Boyer et al. 2016).

Visual Stimuli. Regarding visual stimuli, the biofeedback protocols can be performed with different types of contents, such as images, videos, and virtual games, which can be displayed on a computer, cell phone, tablet screen, or in a virtual or augmented reality environment. Important care must be taken not to present excessive visual stimulation, since it can work as a distractor instead of a modulation guide of the physiological target function (Sterman and Egner 2006). In general, for visual stimulation, it is presented to the user as a specific visual target, as a point or line, that must be reached using a cursor represented by another point or line (Wolpaw et al. 1991; Zapała et al. 2017). It is common to use bars to represent the effort of the user (Caria et al. 2007; Weber et al. 2011), for instance, more concentrated or contracted muscles will increase the size of the bar. The hot-cold color intensity of an image is also often used to represent the modulation of brain activity training in a neurofeedback protocol (Hwang et al. 2009). Additionally, texts and photos can also be used as a reward when the task is completed (Zapała et al. 2017).

In recent years, with the popularization of virtual reality (VR) devices, there has been an increase in the number of studies applying VR as a tool in biofeedback protocols, allowing for immersive and more realistic perception (Riener et al. 2006). The number of resources and degree of freedom that a VR device can provide in a biofeedback protocol is much bigger than by using a regular two-dimensional screen. For example, it can provide new possibilities of therapeutic games and reproduce environments related to real daily activities in an interactive and pleasant task (Bunderson 2014). Many previous studies have already used VR devices in biofeedback protocols, for instance, people with amputation to train the movement control of a limb or virtual prosthesis (Blana et al. 2016; Bunderson 2014), people with SCI who see and control an avatar walking on different texture floors (Shokur et al. 2016), or to improve the dynamic balance of stroke patients (Kim et al. 2016).

Augmented reality (AR) environments also follow the same track as VR, however its concept and technology are slightly more recent. The principle behind its functioning is to use image processing as a tool to extract and identify properties of the natural (and real) surrounding environment and use that information to superimpose interactive virtual objects (Azuma 1993). The use of augmented reality in biofeedback protocols has already been tested by people with neurological diseases such as Parkinson's and stroke (Kim et al. 2016) or for gait training of people with orthopedic diseases (Karatsidis et al.

2018). This technology shows high potential as a personal gadget; it does not limit the user's perception of the real world, but it adds new features into it.

Tactile Stimuli. The term haptic, often used when talking about tactile sensation/perception, refers to a more encompassing concept, which involves the relationship between the sensations produced internally by the body itself and its interaction with the environment, including modalities such as pressure, vibration, or even temperature as well as kinematic and kinesthetic information that is involved in the perception of body movements and acting forces (Burton 1993; West and Gibson 1969). In this way, haptic feedback amplifies the concept of tactile stimulation by extending the emulation of sensations considering other modalities around sensorial information.

This type of stimulus also has been well explored and can be provided as a touch feeling using vibratory stimuli applied directly to the skin or by electrical stimulation (Farina and Aszmann 2014; Hellman et al. 2015). Additionally, biofeedback systems with vibrotactile stimulation have already been used under some conditions, such as balance training in people with Parkinson's disease (Lee et al. 2018) and gait training in people after stroke (Ma et al. 2017), with associated feedback in a VR environment with vibrotactile stimuli to represent different floor textures and gait phases in patients with SCI (Shokur et al. 2016).

Considering the variety of sensory stimuli that can be used as feedback, there is a great possibility of integrating them in different applications to provide the most relevant information to the user, and consequently, optimize the treatment and improve outcomes.

5 Biofeedback Training Protocols

Training protocols must be constructed according to the clinical condition to be modulated, considering the advantages and limitations of the system itself. However, regardless of the profile of people who will perform the training with a biofeedback protocol, there is a basic premise that is critical - operant conditioning (Sterman and Egner 2006).

Associative learning can be divided into two approaches, classical and operant conditioning. The classical conditioning occurs through the association between an environmental stimulus and a natural stimulus. The association between them results in a learned and automatic/involuntary response. The classical example was given by Ivan P. Pavlov where every time he presented meat to a dog, he played a bell. After some trials, the dog associated the meat with the bell sound in such a way that if the bell was played, the dog started to salivate (Pavlov 1927). In operant conditioning, there is an association between behavior and a consequence of this behavior. Certain behavior can be reinforced positively (addition of a favorable event) or negatively (removal of unfavorable events), favoring a specific behavior. Alternatively, the same behavior can be punished positively (presentation of an unfavorable event) or negatively (removal of a favorable event), disfavoring the repetition of this behavior. A good example is given by Burrhus F. Skinner, recognized as the father of operant conditioning. He taught a dove to turn itself around by applying the reward/punishment principles of operant conditioning (Skinner 1938).

In this way, the biofeedback protocol should be planned such that the participant gradually succeeds in the proposed task. Hence, at first, a minimum of control over the trained physiological activity is considered satisfactory and reinforcement is given to the participant, for the criterion to consider the task completed to be progressively increased. In general, contingent feedback itself already works as a form of reinforcement, however motivational stimuli can also be used as a reward. Although, the latency between response and contingent feedback/reward must be immediate; ideally approximately less than 250/300 ms of time is required for learning development (Mizuno et al. 2011;Felsinger et al. 1947; Grice et al. 1948). In terms of neurophysiology, the base nucleus circuitry seems to play an important role in the development of reinforcement learning. Additionally, there is much evidence indicating that the activity of dopaminergic neurons in the substantia nigra and cholinergic interneurons in the striatum are involved in the processing of this information (Kandel et al. 2014) (Fig. 3).

6 Underlying Mechanisms

Although it is unclear which are the exact biological mechanisms that support learning provided by the use of biofeedback protocols, some studies have sought to understand how biofeedback mediated by self-modulation can lead to specific physiological, neural, and behavioral changes (Bouton et al. 2016; Hochberg et al. 2006). In a review, Sitaram et al. (2017) proposed some theories and models to explain learning from the use of neurofeedback and its underlying mechanisms: operant or instrumental learning, motor learning, dual-process theory, awareness theory, global workspace theory, and skill learning (Sitaram et al. 2017). From this perspective, any learning achieved using a neurofeedback protocol seems to involve associative learning. Behaviorally, associative learning is mainly based on classical and operant conditioning (Kandel et al. 2014). Neurobiologically, the main known mechanism associated with any learning–memory process is long-term potentiation (LTP) (Cooke and Bear 2012). Essentially, LTP is the persistent strengthening of synapses in neuronal networks that exhibit specific activity patterns. Additionally, this synaptic strengthening between neurons reinforces signal transmission between neurons. This relationship is at the core of the principles formulated by Donald Hebb in 1949, to explain how the brain favored some neural connections over others. He raised the hypothesis that if the repeated activity in a presynaptic neuron leads to the firing of the postsynaptic neuron, then a lasting modification will occur in the synaptic structure, therefore the subsequent activity of this presynaptic neuron has a high probability of exciting the postsynaptic neuron, strengthening their connectivity (Hebb 1949). This occurs always when the activity of the two neurons exhibit a causal relationship with each other (Garraway et al. 2001; Rossignol and Frigon 2011).

From these evidences, the learning process promoted using self-modulating systems, such as biofeedback, seems to involve not only behavior but mainly structural neuronal reorganization (Sitaram et al. 2017). Nevertheless, current discussions are claiming that associative learning can also arise either from structural changes in neural connections and/or from new patterns of functional connectivity (Balasubramanian et al. 2017).

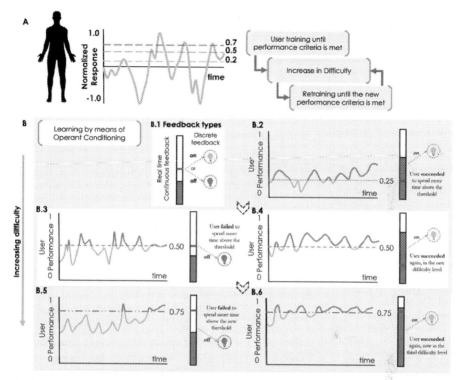

Fig. 3. Training protocol based on operant conditioning. The protocol is designed based on the rules of operant conditioning, which include progressive increase in difficulty (to increase specificity of response), contingent feedback on the proposed task (feedback which the user can relate with the recorded physiological activity), and a reward (which works as reinforcement mechanism). A) An example of a physiological activity, normalized between 0 and 1 for simplicity, comprising different target thresholds (0.25, 0.50, and 0.75). Here the protocol starts with a lower threshold, which is increased as the participant reaches the proposed goals, in order to increase the task difficulty. B) Examples of difficulty progression for a given task. Here we assume, for simplicity, that these time series represent an RMS amplitude of an EMG signal over time (i.e., training muscle contraction with increasing difficulty). In this protocol, the goal is to keep the lamp "on" for the most part of the trial, by maintaining the muscle activity above the threshold. On the right side of each graph, we see a representation of the equivalent time that the user spent on each state (on/off), and its success on the task. As we see, in the first case, a minimum level of contraction was found to be satisfactory, that is, the threshold that the patient needs to reach is very low and, as soon as he surpasses this target, the lamp lights up as a reinforcement. In the second and third cases, given that the patient reached the proposed goals with the previous threshold, the next level of difficulty is presented progressively.

7 Clinical Applicability of Biofeedback

Given this contextualization about the system, protocol, and mechanisms underlying the learning process involved in a biofeedback approach, as can be seen, there are innumerable possibilities and health conditions in which biofeedback training can be used and bring benefits, therefore this review choose to emphasize applicability in specific sensorimotor and cognitive conditions.

Studies show that ADHD is one of the most prevailing cognitive disorders among children (Willcutt 2012). They are normally diagnosed around the age of 7 years. It can be characterized as a spectrum disorder since it contains different levels of severity: inattentive, hyperactive/impulsive, and combined (Lofthouse et al. 2012). The conventional treatment is based on psychostimulant medications that in some cases can cause side effects, like weight loss, insomnia, and nausea (Rabipour and Raz 2012). For those who do not adapt themselves to pharmaco-treatment, the adoption of neurofeedback training can work as a complementary therapy (Hodgson et al. 2014). Most children with ADHD present abnormal EEG, exhibiting a great amount of slow-wave activity and a diminished amount of fast-wave activity mainly in the frontal lobe. This common pattern across ADHD patients has been used as the basis for neurofeedback indication as a viable intervention for this condition (Vernon et al. 2004) since these patterns can be self-modulated. Due to this characterization, most of the protocols favor EEG-brain theta wave inhibition and the enhancement of low beta activity (Lofthouse et al. 2012). Findings indicate that after neurofeedback training, patients present better performance on intelligence tests and control of attention (Heinrich et al. 2007).

Post-traumatic stress disorder is another disorder that has been treated using neurofeedback protocols. It can be described as a disorder that appears when a strong and particular event causes overactivation fight-flight responses that persist, even after the danger is ended (American Psychiatric Association). According to the National Institute of Mental Health, the symptoms include re-experiencing the traumatic event (e.g., rethinking over and over) or avoidance of situations that remind the trauma, with an increase of physical distress in both situations (National Institute of Mental Health). The current PTSD treatments include the conjugation of psychotherapy and medication and recent findings indicate that neurofeedback could be effective as well (Reiter et al. 2016). The neurofeedback protocol used to treat PTSD is known as alpha–theta brainwave neurofeedback therapy (BWT), which basically focuses on reinforcement of those waves. Peniston and Kulkosky (1991) conducted a study on Vietnam-war veterans diagnosed with PTSD and found that training with BWT decreases the suffering/illness scores on clinical scales (e.g., depression, hysteria, and paranoia) compared to traditional drug treatment.

For patients with SCI or stroke, the goal of neuro/biofeedback rehabilitation is to promote the self-modulation of physiological signals that support neural network reorganizations (Seáñez-González et al. 2016). In this way, muscle signals (recorded by EMG) can be used to estimate joint angles and intensity of contraction in conjunction with neural signals (recorded by EEG), and the integration of these signals potentially can be used to control an exoskeleton or external device. This protocol was tested in healthy subjects and a person with cervical SCI (with visual feedback) and showed to be promising for the use in the rehabilitation and the daily life of people with very limited motor function (Kawase et al. 2017). VR and AR platforms are also an alternative to create immersive, interactive, and motivational protocols, increasing the involvement of patients with the therapy and optimizing the rehabilitation procedure (Carelli et al. 2017). In a study with

SCI patients, the subjects used their upper body movements (captured by inertial sensors), not affected by the lesion, to control a virtual cursor and simultaneously visual feedback was provided. They were able to remap their residual motor skills into efficient control patterns, learning to use their own body to control the cursor and a wheelchair in a virtual environment. After training, significant improvements in their motor and also in their brain structure performance was observed (Seáñez-González et al. 2016). Recent evidence also demonstrates that patients with SCI may have a realistic illusion of walking on different surfaces (sand, paved streets, and grass), as well as experiencing virtual leg movements during different stages of gait and still assimilate virtual members with part of their own body. This was made through a protocol in which an exoskeleton was controlled by EEG signals associated with visual feedback conjugated with the vibro-tactile stimulus, applied on the patient's arms, to represent the different textures of the floor and the phases of the gait cycle (Shokur et al. 2016).

In a research conducted with people with chronic stroke a clinical trial conducted by Frolov et al. (2017), where patients trained to self-modulate their EEG SMR activities by imagining a hand movement with visual and kinesthetic feedback, demonstrated positive effects on functionality of the upper limbs (Frolov et al. 2017). A systematic review by Stanton et al. (2017), pointed out that the use of biofeedback as a rehabilitation component in people with stroke history is increasing, particularly to improve lower limb performances. These authors concluded that biofeedback training is more effective for this application compared to conventional therapy, but that the long-term effects are not yet clear (Stanton et al. 2017).

With respect to the use of biofeedback in rehabilitation for amputee people, the main goal is to improve motor control and provide somatosensory feedbacks that replace the natural information lost, after amputation. This can be performed through a proper activation of the preserved sensory systems. The feedback, in this case, can be invasive, applied directly to the peripheral nerves associated to sensory-motor paths (Farina and Aszmann 2014), directly to the brain (Tabot et al. 2015), or non-invasively through tactile stimuli on the skin (Hellman et al. 2015). The study of myoelectric prostheses (EMG-controlled), providing also sensory feedback to the user, has been very promising in the last years (Peerdeman et al. 2011) since this type of biofeedback can improve prosthesis use and facilitate embodiment (Antfolk et al. 2013). A study demonstrated that it is possible to improve force control in a predictive and accurate way, in which EMG signals were used to control an upper limb prosthesis, with a corresponding feedback of the range movement and grip strength (both provided by visual feedback on a screen) (Dosen et al. 2015; Schweisfurth et al. 2016). Štrbac et al. (2017) proposed a protocol by which people with upper limb amputation could control prosthesis from EMG activity. In this prosthesis, force sensors provided information about the force exerted and allowed the delivery of visual (on computer screen) and electrotactile feedback during the task of grasping an object.

8   Final Considerations

This narrative review gets together different knowledge about biofeedback: system components, from the recording of physiological activity, extraction of characteristics, real-time processing and the feedback provided, to discuss the bases of system construction, training protocol designs and possible underlying mechanisms to learning self-modulation. Finally, we indicate promising clinical applications in cognitive and sensorimotor rehabilitation.

In the current scenario, despite the numerous studies in this area, there is still a wide spectrum to be explored regarding the applicability of training with self-regulation systems. Most studies are still basic, as case reports, requiring more studies with randomized controlled clinical trials to assess and identify real clinical benefits, in specific populations.

In addition, some questions still need to be better understood. For instance, for a given condition, is there an optimal window for applying this training? What is the "dose", how many sessions are needed, and for how long? Are functional and neurophysiological outcomes immediate and/or permanent? Are the underlying mechanisms the same in different application protocols and contexts?

However, even with many questions to be answered, the use of the training with biofeedback systems is increasingly present in clinical practice, becoming a very valuable and promising therapeutic tool for health professionals, which can help countless people with different dysfunctions or disabilities, improving their functionality and quality of life.

Acknowledgements. National Institute for Translational Neuroscience (MCTI/CNPq/Faperj).

Funding:. "Conselho Nacional de Desenvolvimento Científico e Tecnológico" and "Coordenação de Aperfeiçoamento de Pessoal de Nível Superior – CAPES"

Conflict-of-Interest Statement:. The authors declare that they have no conflict of interest.

References

Amadio, A.C., et al.: Introdução à biomecânica para análise do movimento humano: descrição e aplicação dos métodos de medição. Rev. Bras. Fisioter. 3(2), 41–54 (1999)

American Psychiatric Association: What Is Post Traumatic Stress Disorder? (2017). https://www.psychiatry.org/patients-families/ptsd/what-is-ptsd. Accessed 17 Dec 2019

Antfolk, C., Alonzo, M.D., Rosén, B., Lundborg, G.: Sensory feedback in upper limb prosthetics. Expert Rev. Med. Devices 10(1), 45–54 (2013)

Anzai, Y.: Pattern Recognition and Machine Learning. Elsevier (2012)

Armagan, O., Tascioglu, F., Oner, C.: Electromyographic biofeedback in the treatment of the hemiplegic hand: a placebo-controlled study. Am. J. Phys. Med. Rehabil. 82(11), 856–861 (2003)

Azuma, R.: Tracking requirements for augmented reality. Commun. ACM 36(7), 50–51 (1993)

Balasubramanian, K., Vaidya, M., Southerland, J., Badreldin, I., Eleryan, A., Takahashi, K., et al.: Changes in cortical network connectivity with long-term brain-machine interface exposure after chronic amputation. Nat. Commun. 8(1), 1–10 (2017)

Basmajian, J.V, De Luca, C.J.: Muscles Alive: Their Functions Revealed by Electromyography, vol. 5 (1985). Williams & Wilkins Baltimore

Benabid, A.L., et al.: An exoskeleton controlled by an epidural wireless brain–machine interface in a tetraplegic patient: a proof-of-concept demonstration. Lancet Neurol. **18**(12), 1112–1122 (2019)

Bendtsen, L., Evers, S., Linde, M., Mitsikostas, D.D., Sandrini, G., Schoenen, J.: EFNS guideline on the treatment of tension-type headache - report of an EFNS task force. Eur. J. Neurol. **17**(11), 1318–1325 (2010)

Bensmaia, S.J., Miller, L.E.: Restoring sensorimotor function through intracortical interfaces: progress and looming challenges. Nat. Rev. Neurosci. **15**(5), 313–325 (2014)

Bentley, L.D., Duarte, R.V., Furlong, P.L., Ashford, R.L., Raphael, J.H.: Brain activity modifications following spinal cord stimulation for chronic neuropathic pain: a systematic review. Eur. J. Pain **20**(4), 499–511 (2016)

Bishop, C.M.: Pattern Recognition and Machine Learning. Springer (2006)

Blana, D., Kyriacou, T., Lambrecht, J.M., Chadwick, E.K.: Feasibility of using combined EMG and kinematic signals for prosthesis control: a simulation study using a virtual reality environment. J. Electromyogr. Kinesiol. **29**, 21–27 (2016)

Borresen, J., Lambert, M.I.: Autonomic control of heart rate during and after exercise. Sports Med. **38**(8), 633–646 (2008)

Bouton, C.E., et al.: Restoring cortical control of functional movement in a human with quadriplegia. Nature, 1–13 (2016)

Boyer, É.O., Bevilacqua, F., Susini, P., Hanneton, S.: Investigating three types of continuous auditory feedback in visuo-manual tracking. Exp. Brain Res. **235**(3), 691–701 (2016). https://doi.org/10.1007/s00221-016-4827-x

Buch, E., et al.: Think to move: a neuromagnetic brain-computer interface (BCI) system for chronic stroke. Stroke **39**(3), 910–917 (2008)

Budzynski, T.H., Stoyva, J.M.: An instrument for producing deep muscle relaxation by means of analog information feedback1. J. Appl. Behav. Anal. **2**(4), 231–237 (1969)

Bunderson, N.E.: Real-time control of an interactive impulsive virtual prosthesis. IEEE Trans. Neural Syst. Rehabil. Eng. **22**(2), 363–370 (2014)

Burton, G.: Non-neural extensions of haptic sensitivity. Ecol. Psychol. **5**(2), 105–124 (1993)

Buzsáki, G.: Rhythms of the Brain. In Rhythms of the Brain (2009). https://doi.org/10.1093/acprof:oso/9780195301069.001.0001

Buzsáki, G., Anastassiou, C.A., Koch, C.: The origin of extracellular fields and currents-EEG, ECoG, LFP and spikes. Nat. Rev. Neurosci. **13**(6), 407–420 (2012)

Buzsáki, G., Watson, B.O.: Brain rhythms and neural syntax: implications for efficient coding of cognitive content and neuropsychiatric disease. Dialogues Clin. Neurosci. **14**(4), 345 (2012)

Cho, H.Y., Kim, K., Lee, B., Jung, J.: The effect of neurofeedback on a brain wave and visual perception in stroke: a randomized control trial. J. Phys. Ther. Sci. **27**(3), 673–676 (2015)

Carelli, L., et al.: Brain-computer interface for clinical purposes: cognitive assessment and rehabilitation. Biomed. Res. Int. **2017**, 1695290 (2017)

Caria, A., et al.: Regulation of anterior insular cortex activity using real-time fMRI. Neuroimage **35**, 1238–1246 (2007)

Carvalho, R.: Brain - machine interface of upper limb recovery in stroke patients rehabilitation: a systematic review (2019). https://doi.org/10.1002/pri.1764

Castelnuovo, G., et al.: Psychological treatments and psychotherapies in the neurorehabilitation of pain: evidences and recommendations from the Italian consensus conference on pain in neurorehabilitation. Front. Psychol. **7**, 115 (2016)

Clifford, G.D.: Signal Processing Methods for Heart Rate Variability. Oxford University, Oxford (2002)

Cooke, S.F., Bear, M.F.: Stimulus-selective response plasticity in the visual cortex: an assay for the assessment of pathophysiology and treatment of cognitive impairment associated with psychiatric disorders. BPS **71**(6), 487–495 (2012)

Coyle, S., Ward, T., Markham, C., McDarby, G.: On the suitability of near-infrared (NIR) systems for next-generation brain-computer interfaces. Physiol. Meas. **25**(4), 815–822 (2004)

De Nunzio, A.M., et al.: Biofeedback rehabilitation of posture and weightbearing distribution in stroke: a center of foot pressure analysis. Funct. Neurol. **29**(2), 127–134 (2014)

Decharms, R.C.: Applications of real-time fMRI. Nat. Rev. Neurosci. **9**(9), 720–729 (2008)

DeCharms, R.C., et al.: Control over brain activation and pain learned by using real-time functional MRI. Proc. Natl. Acad. Sci. **102**(51), 18626–18631 (2005)

Ditunno, J.F., Young, W., Donovan, W.H., Creasey, G.: The international standards booklet for neurological and functional classification of spinal cord injury. Spinal Cord **32**, 70–80 (1994)

Dong, J.G.: The role of heart rate variability in sports physiology. Exp. Ther. Med. **11**(5), 1531–1536 (2016)

Donovan, L., Feger, M.A., Hart, J.M., Saliba, S., Park, J., Hertel, J.: Effects of an auditory biofeedback device on plantar pressure in patients with chronic ankle instability. Gait Posture **44**, 29–36 (2016)

Dosen, S., Markovic, M., Somer, K., Graimann, B., Farina, D.: EMG Biofeedback for online predictive control of grasping force in a myoelectric prosthesis. J. Neuroeng. Rehabil. **12**(1), 1–13 (2015)

Evans, J.W., Kundu, P., Horovitz, S.G., Bandettini, P.A.: Separating slow BOLD from non-BOLD baseline drifts using multi-echo fMRI. Neuroimage **105**, 189–197 (2015)

Farina, D., Aszmann, O.: Bionic Limbs: Clinical Reality and Academic Promises, vol. 6, no. (257), pp. 6–9 (2014)

Fazli, S., et al.: NeuroImage Enhanced performance by a hybrid NIRS – EEG brain computer interface. Neuroimage **59**(1), 519–529 (2012)

Felsinger, J.M., Gladstone, A.I., Yamaguchi, H.G., Hull, C.L.: Reaction latency (StR) as a function of the number of reinforcements (N). J. Exp. Psychol. **37**(3), 214 (1947)

Fetz, E.E.: Operant conditioning of cortical unit activity. Science **163**, 955–958 (1969)

Finley, W.W., Smith, H.A., Etherton, M.D.: Reduction of seizures and normalization of the EEG in a severe epileptic following sensorimotor biofeedback training: preliminary study. Biol. Psychol. **2**(3), 189–203 (1975)

Frolov, A.A., et al.: Post-stroke rehabilitation training with a motor-imagery-based brain-computer interface (BCI)-controlled hand exoskeleton: a randomized controlled multicenter trial. Front. Neurosci. **11**, 400 (2017)

Garraway, S.M., Hochman, S.: Modulatory actions of serotonin, norepinephrine, dopamine, and acetylcholine in spinal cord deep dorsal horn neurons. J. Neurophysiol. **86**(5), 2183–2194 (2001)

Giggins, O.M., Persson, U.M., Caulfield, B.: Biofeedback in rehabilitation. J. Neuroeng. Rehabil. **10**(1), 60 (2013)

Gomez-Pilar, J., Corralejo, R., Nicolas-Alonso, L.F., Alvarez, D., Hornero, R.: Assessment of neurofeedback training by means of motor imagery based-BCI for cognitive rehabilitation. In: 2014 36th Annual International Conference of the IEEE Engineering in Medicine and Biology Society, EMBC 2014, pp. 3630–3633 (2014)

Gordan, R., Gwathmey, J.K., Xie, L.: Autonomic and endocrine control of cardiovascular function. World J. Cardiol. **7**(4), 204–214 (2015)

Grice, G.R.: The relation of secondary reinforcement to delayed reward in visual discrimination learning. J. Exp. Psychol. **38**(1), 1 (1948)

Gruzelier, J.H.: Neuroscience and biobehavioral reviews EEG-neurofeedback for optimising performance. I: a review of cognitive and affective outcome in healthy participants. Neurosci. Biobehav. Rev. **44**, 124–141 (2014)

Gunkelman, J.D., Johnstone, J.: Neurofeedback and the brain. J. Adult Dev. **12**(2–3), 93–98 (2005)

Güntekin, B., Başar, E.: Review of evoked and event-related delta responses in the human brain. Int. J. Psychophysiol. **103**, 43–52 (2016)

Hayano, J.: Pitfalls of assessment of autonomic function by heart rate variability. J. Physiol. Anthropol. **2**, 1–8 (2019)

Heerink, W.J., Dorrius, M.D., Groen, H.J.M., Van Ooijen, P.M.A., Vliegenthart, R., Oudkerk, M.: Respiratory level tracking with visual biofeedback for consistent breath-hold level with potential application in image-guided interventions. Eur. Radiol. Exp. **2**(1), 1–9 (2018). https://doi.org/10.1186/s41747-018-0052-7

Heinrich, H., Gevensleben, H., Strehl, U.: Annotation: neurofeedback - train your brain to train behaviour. J. Child Psychol. Psychiatry **48**(1), 3–16 (2007)

Hejjel, L., Roth, E.: What is the adequate sampling interval of the ECG signal for heart rate variability analysis in the time domain? Physiol. Meas. **25**(6), 1405–1411 (2004)

Herderschee, R., Hay-Smith, E.C., Herbison, G.P., Roovers, J.P., Heineman, M.J.: Feedback or biofeedback to augment pelvic floor muscle training for urinary incontinence in women: shortened version of a Cochrane systematic review. J. Urol. **190**(6), 2169 (2013)

Hernando, A., et al.: Inclusion of respiratory frequency information in heart rate variability analysis for stress assessment. IEEE J. Biomed. Health Inform. **20**(4), 1016–1025 (2016)

Hochberg, L.R., et al.: Neuronal ensemble control of prosthetic devices by a human with tetraplegia. Nature **442**(7099), 164 (2006)

Hodgson, K., Hutchinson, A.D., Denson, L.: Nonpharmacological treatments for ADHD: a meta-analytic review (2014). https://doi.org/10.1177/1087054712444732

Hohmann, M.R., et al.: A cognitive brain–computer interface for patients with amyotrophic lateral sclerosis. Prog. Brain Res. **228**, 221–239 (2016)

Holm, H., et al.: Several common variants modulate heart rate, PR interval and QRS duration. Nat. Genet. **42**(2), 117–122 (2010)

Houghton, A., Gray, D.: Making Sense of the ECG: a Hands-On Guide. CRC Press (2008)

Hwang, H., Kwon, K., Im, C.: Neurofeedback-based motor imagery training for brain – computer interface (BCI). J. Neurosci. Methods **179**, 150–156 (2009)

Ivanov, P.C., Chen, Z., Hu, K., Stanley, H.E.: Multiscale aspects of cardiac control. Physica A **344**(3–4), 685–704 (2004)

Kaiju, T., et al.: High Spatiotemporal resolution ECoG recording of somatosensory evoked potentials with flexible micro-electrode arrays. Front. Neural Circ. **11**(April), 1–13 (2017)

Kandel, E., Schwartz, J., Jessell, T., Siegelbaum, S., Hudspeth, A.J.: Princípios de Neurociências-5. AMGH Editora (2014)

Karatsidis, A., et al.: Validation of wearable visual feedback for retraining foot progression angle using inertial sensors and an augmented reality headset. J. Neuroeng. Rehabil. **15**(1), 78 (2018)

Kawase, T., Sakurada, T., Koike, Y., Kansaku, K.: A hybrid BMI-based exoskeleton for paresis: EMG control for assisting arm movements. J. Neural Eng. **14**(1) (2017)

Kent, P., Laird, R., Haines, T.: The effect of changing movement and posture using motion-sensor biofeedback, versus guidelines-based care, on the clinical outcomes of people with sub-acute or chronic low back pain-a multicentre, cluster-randomised, placebo-controlled, pilot trial. BMC Musculoskelet. Disord. **16**(1), 1–19 (2015)

Keynan, J.N., et al.: Limbic activity modulation guided by fMRI-inspired EEG improves implicit emotion regulation. Biol. Psychiatry **80**, 490–496 (2016)

Kim, J.H., Jang, S.H., Kim, C.S., Jung, J.H., You, J.H.: Use of virtual reality to enhance balance and ambulation in chronic stroke: a double-blind, randomized controlled study. Am. J. Phys. Med. Rehabil. **88**(9), 693–701 (2016)

Konrad, P.: The ABC of EMG. Pract. Introduction Kinesiological Electromyogr. **1**(2005), 1–60 (2005)

Koralek, A.C., Jin, X., Long, J.D., Costa, R.M., Carmena, J.M.: Corticostriatal plasticity is necessary for learning intentional neuroprosthetic skills. Nature **483**(7389), 331–335 (2012)

Lee, B., Fung, A., Thrasher, T.A.: The effects of coding schemes on vibrotactile biofeedback for dynamic balance training in Parkinson's disease and healthy elderly individuals. IEEE Trans. Neural Syst. Rehabil. Eng. **26**(1), 153–160 (2018)

Lehrer, P.M., et al.: Biofeedback treatment for asthma. Chest **126**(2), 352–361 (2004)

Li, Z., Wang, X.-X., Liang, Y.-Y., Chen, S.-Y., Sheng, J., Ma, S.-J.: Effects of the visual-feedback-based force platform training with functional electric stimulation on the balance and prevention of falls in older adults: a randomized controlled trial. PeerJ **6**, e4244 (2018)

Liew, S.L., et al.: Improving motor corticothalamic communication after stroke using real-time fMRI connectivity-based neurofeedback. Neurorehabil. Neural Repair **30**(7), 671–675 (2016)

Lofthouse, N., Arnold, L.E., Hersch, S., Hurt, E., DeBeus, R.: A review of neurofeedback treatment for pediatric ADHD. J. Atten. Disord. **16**(5), 351–372 (2012)

Logothetis, N.K., Pauls, J., Augath, M., Trinath, T., Oeltermann, A.: Neurophysiological investigation of the basis of the fMRI signal. Nature **412**(6843), 150 (2001)

De Luca, C.J.: Electromyography. Encyclopedia of Medical Devices and Instrumentation, pp. 98–109. John Wiley Publisher (2006)

Schweisfurth, M.A., Markovic, M., Dosen, S., Teich, F., Graimann, B., Farina, D.: Electrotactile EMG feedback improves the control of prosthesis grasping force. J. Neural Eng. **13**(5), 056010 (2016)

Ma, C.Z.H., Wan, A.H.P., Wong, D.W.C., Zheng, Y.P., Lee, W.C.C.: A vibrotactile and plantar force measurement-based biofeedback system: paving the way towards wearable balance-improving devices. Sensors **15**(12), 31709–31722 (2015)

Ma, C.Z., Zheng, Y., Lee, W.C.: Topics in Stroke Rehabilitation Changes in gait and plantar foot loading upon using vibrotactile wearable biofeedback system in patients with stroke. Top. Stroke Rehabil. **9357**, 1–8 (2017)

Ma, J., Zhang, Y., Cichocki, A., Matsuno, F.: A novel EOG / EEG hybrid human-machine interface adopting eye movements and ERPs. Appl. Rob. Control **9294**(c), 1–14 (2014)

Mattia, M., Sanchez-Vives, M.: Unraveling brain modularity through slow oscillations. In: Corinto, F., Torcini, A. (eds.) Nonlinear Dynamics in Computational Neuroscience. PSS, pp. 17–31. Springer, Cham (2019). https://doi.org/10.1007/978-3-319-71048-8_2

Mayer, K., Blume, F., Wyckoff, S.N., Brokmeier, L.L., Strehl, U.: Neurofeedback of slow cortical potentials as a treatment for adults with attention deficit-/hyperactivity disorder. Clin. Neurophysiol. **127**(2), 1374–1386 (2016)

Mcguire, L.M.M., Sabes, P.N.: Sensory transformations and the use of multiple reference frames for reach planning. Nat. Publ. Group **12**(8), 1056–1061 (2009)

Merzenich, M.M., Nelson, R.J., Stryker, M.P., Cynader, M.S., Schoppmann, A., Zook, J.M.: Somatosensory cortical map changes following digit amputation in adult monkeys. J. Comp. Neurol. **224**(4), 591–605 (1984)

Mihara, M., et al.: Near-infrared spectroscopy-mediated neurofeedback enhances efficacy of motor imagery-based training in poststroke victims: a pilot study. Stroke **44**(4), 1091–1098 (2013)

Mihara, M., Miyai, I.: Review of functional near-infrared spectroscopy in neurorehabilitation. Neurophotonics **3**(3), 031414 (2016)

Mizuno, H., Tsujiuchi, N., Koizumi, T.: Forearm motion discrimination technique using real-time EMG signals. In: Proceedings of the Annual International Conference of the IEEE Engineering in Medicine and Biology Society, EMBS, pp. 4435–4438 (2011)

Moleiro, M.A., Cid, F.V.: Effects of biofeedback training on voluntary heart rate control during dynamic exercise. Appl. Psychophysiol. Biofeedback **26**(4), 279–292 (2001)

Morgan, M.L., Deangelis, G.C., Angelaki, D.E.: Article multisensory integration in macaque visual cortex depends on cue reliability. Neuron **59**(4), 662–673 (2008)

Morrison, M.M.: Inertial Measurement Unit. Google Patents (1987)

Murphy, D.P., et al.: Electroencephalogram-based brain-computer interface and lower-limb prosthesis control: a case study. Front. Neurolo. **8**(DEC), 1–8 (2017)

Murta, T., Leite, M., Carmichael, D.W., Figueiredo, P., Lemieux, L.: Electrophysiological correlates of the BOLD signal for EEG-informed fMRI. Hum. Brain Mapp. **36**(1), 391–414 (2015)

Nagai, Y., Jones, C.I., Sen, A.: Galvanic skin response (GSR)/Electrodermal/Skin conductance biofeedback on epilepsy: a systematic review and meta-analysis. Front. Neurol. **10**(April), 1–8 (2019)

National Institute of Mental Health: Post-Traumatic Stress Disorder (2019). https://www.nimh. nih.gov/health/topics/post-traumatic-stress-disorder-ptsd/index.shtml. Accessed 17 Dec 2019

Naros, G., Naros, I., Grimm, F., Ziemann, U., Gharabaghi, A.: Reinforcement learning of self-regulated sensorimotor β-oscillations improves motor performance. Neuroimage **134**, 142–152 (2016)

Neblett, R.: Surface Electromyographic (SEMG) biofeedback for chronic low back pain. Healthcare **4**(2), 27 (2016)

Neske, G.T.: The slow oscillation in cortical and thalamic networks: mechanisms and functions. Front. Neural Circuits **9**, 1–25 (2016)

Neuper, C., Scherer, R., Wriessnegger, S., Pfurtscheller, G.: Motor imagery and action observation: modulation of sensorimotor brain rhythms during mental control of a brain-computer interface. Clin. Neurophysiol. **120**(2), 239–247 (2009)

Hebb, D.O., Hebb, D.O.: The Organization of Behavior, vol. 65. Wiley, New York (1949)

Hellman, R.B., Chang, E., Tanner, J., Helms Tillery, S.I., Santos, V.J.: A robot hand testbed designed for enhancing embodiment and functional neurorehabilitation of body schema in subjects with upper limb impairment or loss. Front. Hum. Neurosci. **9**, 26 (2015)

Nolan, R.P., et al.: Heart rate variability biofeedback as a behavioral neurocardiac intervention to enhance vagal heart rate control. Am. Heart J. **149**(6), 1137.e1-1137.e7 (2005)

Őri, Z., Monir, G., Weiss, J., Sayhouni, X., Singer, D.H.: Heart rate variability: frequency domain analysis. Cardiol. Clin. **10**(3), 499–533 (1992)

Orndorff-Plunkett, F., Singh, F., Aragón, O.R., Pineda, J.A.: Assessing the effectiveness of neurofeedback training in the context of clinical and social neuroscience. Brain Sci. **7**(8), 1–22 (2017)

Pavlov, I.P.: Conditioned Reflexes. Oxford University Press, Oxford (1927)

Peerdeman, B., Boere, D., Witteveen, H., Huis, R.: Myoelectric forearm prostheses: state of the art from a user-centered perspective. J. Rehabil. Res. Dev. **48**(6), 719–738 (2011)

Peniston, E.G., Kulkosky, P.J.: Alpha-theta brainwave neurofeedback for Vietnam veterans with combat-related post-traumatic stress disorder. Med. Psychother. **4**(1), 47–60 (1991)

Petrini, F.M., et al.: Enhancing functional abilities and cognitive integration of the lower limb prosthesis. Sci. Transl. Med. **11**(512) (2019)

Pfurtscheller, G., Brunner, C., Schlögl, A., Lopes da Silva, F.H.: Mu rhythm (de)synchronization and EEG single-trial classification of different motor imagery tasks. Neuroimage **31**(1), 153–159 (2006)

Pfurtscheller, G., et al.: 15 Years of BCI research at Graz University of Technology: current projects. IEEE Trans. Neural Syst. Rehabil. Eng. **14**(2), 205–210 (2006)

Rabipour, S., Raz, A.: Brain and cognition training the brain: fact and fad in cognitive and behavioral remediation. Brain Cogn. **79**(2), 159–179 (2012)

Acharya, U.R., Joseph, K.P., Kannathal, N., Lim, C.M., Suri, J.S.: Heart rate variability: a review. Med. Biol. Eng. Compu. **44**(12), 1031–1051 (2006)

Ramos-Murguialday, A., et al.: Brain–machine interface in chronic stroke rehabilitation: a controlled study. Ann. Neurol. **74**(1), 100–108 (2013)

Rao, S.S.C.: Biofeedback therapy for constipation in adults. Best Pract. Res. Clin. Gastroenterol. **25**(1), 159–166 (2011)

Reaz, M.B.I., Hussain, M.S., Mohd-Yasin, F.: Techniques of EMG signal analysis: detection, processing, classification and applications. Biol. Proced. Online **8**(1), 11–35 (2006)

Reiter, K., Andersen, S.B., Carlsson, J.: Neurofeedback treatment and posttraumatic stress disorder: effectiveness of neurofeedback on posttraumatic stress disorder and the optimal choice of protocol. J. Nerv. Ment. Dis. **204**(2), 69–77 (2016)

Richard, D., et al.: NeuroImage assessment of the cerebral cortex during motor task behaviours in adults: a systematic review of functional near infrared spectroscopy (fNIRS) studies. Neuroimage **54**(4), 2922–2936 (2011)

Riener, R., Lünenburger, L., Colombo, G.: Human-centered robotics applied to gait training and assessment. J. Rehabil. Res. Dev. **43**(5), 679 (2006)

Robertson, J.V., Hoellinger, T., Lindberg, P., Bensmail, D., Hanneton, S., Roby-Brami, A.: Effect of auditory feedback differs according to side of hemiparesis: a comparative pilot study. J. Neuroeng. Rehabil. **6**(1), 1–11 (2009)

Rossignol, S., Frigon, A.: Recovery of locomotion after spinal cord injury: some facts and mechanisms. Annu. Rev. Neurosci. **34**, 413–440 (2011)

Sarasola-Sanz, A., et al.: A hybrid-BMI based on EEG and EMG activity for the motor rehabilitation of stroke patients. In: IEEE International Conference on Rehabilitation Robotics, pp. 895–900 (2017)

Schenck, C., Kesar, T.M.: Effects of unilateral real-time biofeedback on propulsive forces during gait. J. Neuroeng. Rehabil. **14**(1), 1–10 (2017)

Schultz, A.E., Kuiken, T.A.: Neural interfaces for control of upper limb prostheses: the state of the art and future possibilities. PM and R **3**(1), 55–67 (2011)

Seáñez-González, I., et al.: Body-machine interfaces after spinal cord injury: rehabilitation and brain plasticity. Brain Sci. **6**(4), 1–19 (2016)

Shokur, S., et al.: Assimilation of virtual legs and perception of floor texture by complete paraplegic patients receiving artificial tactile feedback. Sci. Rep. **6**(May), 1–14 (2016)

Skinner, B.F.: The Behavior of Organisms: An Experimental Analysis. Appleton-Century-Crofts, New York (1938)

Silverthorn, D.U.: Fisologia Humana: uma abordagem integrada. Porto Alegre: Artmed (2010)

Silvoni, S., et al.: Tactile event-related potentials in amyotrophic lateral sclerosis (ALS): implications for brain-computer interface. Clin. Neurophysiol. **127**(1), 936–945 (2016)

Sitaram, R., et al.: Closed-loop brain training: the science of neurofeedback. Nat. Rev. Neurosci. **18**(2), 86–100 (2017)

Stern, J.M.: Atlas of EEG Patterns. Lippincott Williams & Wilkins (2005)

Štrbac, M., et al.: Short-and long-term learning of feedforward control of a myoelectric prosthesis with sensory feedback by amputees. IEEE Trans. Neural Syst. Rehabil. Eng. **25**(11), 2133–2145 (2017)

Sober, S.J., Sabes, P.N.: Flexible strategies for sensory integration during motor planning. Nature Neuscience **8**(4), 490–497 (2005)

Stanton, R., Ada, L., Dean, C.M., Preston, E.: Biofeedback improves performance in lower limb activities more than usual therapy in people following stroke: a systematic review. J. Physiother. **63**(1), 11–16 (2017)

Sterman, M.B., Wyrwicka, W., Roth, S.: Electrophysiological correlates and neural substrates of alimentary behavior in the cat. Ann. N. Y. Acad. Sci. **157**(2), 723–739 (1969)

Sterman, M.B.: Basic concepts and clinical findings in the treatment of seizure disorders with EEG operant conditioning. Clin. EEG Neurosci. **31**(1), 45–55 (2000)

Sterman, M.B., Egner, T.: Neurofeedback treatment of epilepsy: from basic rationale to practical application. Expert Rev. Neurother. **6**(2), 247–257 (2006)

Studer, P., et al.: Slow cortical potential and theta/beta neurofeedback training in adults: effects on attentional processes and motor system excitability. Front. Hum. Neurosci. **8**, 1–13 (2014)

Sturma, A., Hruby, L.A., Prahm, C., Mayer, J.A., Aszmann, O.C.: Rehabilitation of upper extremity nerve injuries using surface EMG biofeedback: protocols for clinical application. Front. Neurosci. **12**, 1–11 (2018)

Tabot, G.A., Kim, S.S., Winberry, J.E., Bensmaia, S.J.: Restoring tactile and proprioceptive sensation through a brain interface. Neurobiol. Dis. **83**, 191–198 (2015)

Tatum, W.O., et al.: American clinical neurophysiology society guideline 7: guidelines for EEG reporting. Neurodiagnostic J. **56**(4), 285–293 (2016)

Timofeev, I.: Neuronal plasticity and thalamocortical sleep and waking oscillations. Progress Brain Res. **193**(c), 121–144 (2011)

Shusterman, V., Barnea, O.: Sympathetic nervous system activity in stress and biofeedback relaxation. IEEE Eng. Med. Biol. Mag. **24**(2), 52–57 (2005)

Vaid, S., Singh, P., Kaur, C.: EEG signal analysis for BCI interface: a review. In: 2015 Fifth International Conference on Advanced Computing & Communication Technologies, pp. 143–147 (2015)

Valdés, B.A., Van der Loos, H.F.M.: Biofeedback vs. game scores for reducing trunk compensation after stroke: a randomized crossover trial. Top. Stroke Rehabil. **25**(2), 96–113 (2018)

Van Drongelen, W.: Signal Processing for Neuroscientists. Academic Press (2018)

Vernon, D., Frick, A., Gruzelier, J.: Neurofeedback as a treatment for ADHD: a methodological review with implications for future research. J. Neurother. **8**(2), 53–82 (2004)

Wahbeh, H., Oken, B.S.: Peak high-frequency HRV and peak alpha frequency higher in PTSD. Appl. Psychophysiol. Biofeedback **38**(1), 57–69 (2013)

Walker, J.E.: Anxiety associated with post traumatic stress disorder—the role of quantitative electro- encephalograph in diagnosis and in guiding neurofeedback training to remediate the anxiety. Biofeedback **37**(2), 67–70 (2003)

Watanabe, T., Sasaki, Y., Shibata, K., Kawato, M.: Advances in fMRI real-time neurofeedback. Trends Cogn. Sci. **21**(12), 997–1010 (2017)

Weber, E., Köberl, A., Frank, S., Doppelmayr, M.: Predicting successful learning of SMR neurofeedback in healthy participants: methodological considerations. Appl. Psychophysiol. Biofeedback **36**(1), 37–45 (2011)

West, C.K., Gibson, J.J.: The senses considered as perceptual systems. J. Aesthetic Educ. **3**(1), 142 (1969)

World Health Organization: Stroke and Cerebrovascular Disorders: Neurological Implications (1995)

Willcutt, E.G.: The prevalence of DSM-IV attention-deficit/hyperactivity disorder: a meta-analytic review. Neurotherapeutics **9**(3), 490–499 (2012)

Wolpaw, J.R., McFarland, D.J., Neat, G.W., Forneris, C.A.: An EEG-based brain-computer interface for cursor control. Electroencephalogr. Clin. Neurophysiol. **78**(3), 252–259 (1991)

World Health Organization: What do we know about disability? (2011). http://www.who.int/dis abilities/world_report/2011/report/en/s

World Health Organization (WHO): Er Health for All Better People Health With for Disability All People With Disability, pp. 1–32 (2015)

Wyler, A.R., Robbins, C.A., Dodrill, C.B.: EEG operant conditioning for control of epilepsy. Epilepsia **20**(3), 279–286 (1979)

Wyrwicka, W., Sterman, M.B.: Instrumental conditioning of sensorimotor cortex EEG spindles in the waking cat. Physiol. Behav. **3**(5), 703–707 (1968)

Xie, P., Chen, X., Ma, P., Li, X., Su, Y.: Identification method of human movement intention based on the fusion feature of EEG and EMG. In: Proceedings of the World Congress on Engineering, vol. 2, July 2013

Yoo, J.W., Lee, D.R., Cha, Y.J., You, S.H.: Augmented effects of EMG biofeedback interfaced with virtual reality on neuromuscular control and movement coordination during reaching in children with cerebral palsy. NeuroRehabilitation **40**(2), 175–185 (2017)

Yoo, S.S., et al.: Increasing cortical activity in auditory areas through neurofeedback functional magnetic resonance imaging. NeuroReport **17**(12), 1273–1278 (2006)

Yucha, C., Montgomery, D.: Evidence-Based Practice in Biofeedback and Neurofeedback. Wheat Ridge, CO: AAPB (2008)

Zapała, D., et al.: The impact of different visual feedbacks in user training on motor imagery control in BCI. Appl. Psychophysiol. Biofeedback **43**(1), 23–35 (2017). https://doi.org/10.1007/s10484-017-9383-z

Zich, C., Debener, S., Kranczioch, C., Bleichner, M.G., Gutberlet, I., De Vos, M.: Real-time EEG feedback during simultaneous EEG-fMRI identifies the cortical signature of motor imagery. Neuroimage **114**, 438–447 (2015)

Movement-Related Electroencephalography in Stroke Patients Across a Brain-Computer Interface-Based Intervention

Juan C. Castro-Aparicio[1] (iD), Ruben I. Carino-Escobar[2] (iD),
and Jessica Cantillo-Negrete[2(✉)] (iD)

[1] Universidad Nacional Autónoma de México, 04510 Mexico City, Mexico
[2] Instituto Nacional de Rehabilitación Luis Guillermo Ibarra Ibarra, 14389 Mexico City, Mexico
jcantillo@inr.gob.mx

Abstract. Stroke is a clinical condition that can cause a long-term disability due to hemiparesis. Experimental interventions such as Brain-Computer Interfaces (BCI) could be part of rehabilitation strategies. However, recovery mechanisms are not fully understood. For this reason, and with the purpose of understanding how changes in cortical activity after upper limb rehabilitation interventions are associated with clinical recovery, this study compares the patterns of cortical activation across a BCI-based intervention during the motor intention (MI) and feedback (passive movement) intervals of the trials performed by stroke patients. Moreover, it evaluates the correlation between subjects' cortical activity with the clinical outcome. The cortical activity of 10 patients showed activations in regions of the somatosensory cortex during both MI and passive movement, with significant differences across the intervention in alpha and beta activations. Particularly, compensatory mechanisms involving the unaffected hemisphere could be hypothesized. Therefore, MI and passive movement's neural correlates are promising biomarkers of stroke recovery that deserve further attention.

Keywords: Neurorehabilitation · Brain-computer interfaces · Electroencephalography

1 Introduction

In the United States, each year approximately 795,000 people experience a new or recurrent stroke, this clinical condition is a leading cause of severe long-term disability [1]. Motor impairment of the upper limb is one of the most disabling and prevalent consequences, occurring in 73%–88% first time stroke survivors and in 55%-75% of chronic stroke patients [2]. The need for the development of more effective therapies for this motor impairment becomes evident once it is taken into consideration that after six months of the stroke onset, only 35% of patients recover enough hand motor function to be able to use it in activities of the daily living [3].

Therapies that increase stroke patients' neuroplasticity have shown potential for improving functionality and motor control of the affected limbs. Specifically, interventions based on robotic assistive devices are a promising emergent field that has

P. R. d. A. Ribeiro et al. (Eds.): LAWCN 2021, CCIS 1519, pp. 215–224, 2022.
https://doi.org/10.1007/978-3-031-08443-0_13

demonstrated the capability to target the underlying physiology of neuroplasticity [3]. Brain-computer interfaces (BCI) are also a potential tool for neurorehabilitation since they allow efferent central nervous system communication and can act as a decoder of user intentions for the control of assistive robotic devices [4]. BCI are comprised by several elements, namely signal acquisition, signal preprocessing, feature extraction, feature selection, classification, and feedback (external devices) [4].

It is important to consider that the implementation of BCI for motor rehabilitation after stroke have important challenges, mainly because cortical activation of brain regions in the sensorimotor cortex during motor intention (MI) of the affected hand is reduced, especially in those patients with cortical or mixed (both cortical and subcortical) lesions [5, 6]. Even so, patients with paralysis of the upper limb can still elicit a power increase or decrease in alpha and beta frequencies during MI, this phenomenon is described as event related desynchronization or synchronization (ERD/ERS) [7]. It is therefore reasonable to hypothesize that implementing these paradigms is a practical way to target neuroplasticity with the purpose of improving the rates of recovery in patients with upper limb motor impairment.

On the other hand, brain rhythms could provide biomarkers for recovery of upper limb motor function in stroke [8, 9]. However, electroencephalography (EEG) is not usually measured during patients' conventional treatment. Therefore, BCI-based therapies provide the opportunity to explore EEG-based biomarkers of upper limb motor function in stroke. Since in healthy subjects, passive movement elicits cortical activations similar to those of actual movement [10], it would also be reasonable to hypothesize that a possible biomarker in stroke patients would be the similarity between cortical activations during passive movement provided by a BCI controlled robotic device with activations during MI.

The purpose of this study is to analyze the cortical activations of stroke patients during MI tasks with the paralyzed hand and passive movement, across an intervention comprised by a BCI therapy plus conventional therapy. As well as exploring their application as recovery markers by evaluating their correlation with the change in motor function across these rehabilitation interventions measured with a clinical scale.

2   Materials and Methods

2.1   Patients

This study includes data from 10 stroke patients recruited in the National Institute of Rehabilitation "Luis Guillermo Ibarra Ibarra". All patients read and signed an informed consent approved by the Ethics Committee, and the study itself was approved by the Institute's Research Committee. Patients were between 2 and 10 months since onset of ischemic stroke [11], as confirmed through neuroimaging studies by a neurologist. Before stroke, patients were right-handed and had no history of neurological lesions or significant alterations in attention and memory according to the neuropsychological test NEUROPSI [12]. All patients presented adequate understanding of instructions and capability to give informed consent. Clinical assessment and physiological measurements were also performed as part of a larger longitudinal study. In this work, only the Fugl-Meyer Assessment for Upper Extremity (FMA-UE) is presented.

2.2 Intervention

Each patient underwent an intervention comprised by BCI-based therapy plus conventional therapy, provided sequentially, so that each patient would receive both therapies in a randomized order. Conventional therapy was performed by the same rehabilitation therapist for all patients. It consisted of activities to improve the affected upper limb's fine and gross motor skills, sensitivity function, muscle strength, motor coordination, as well as neurofacilitation techniques. Conventional and BCI therapy sessions had a duration of 30 to 40 min and lasted 4 weeks with 3 sessions per week.

For each BCI session, patients were instructed to sit in a comfortable armchair in a sound-attenuated room, with the same illumination conditions and at the same time of the day, with a computer monitor placed approximately at 1.5m in front of them. Each session consisted of 3 runs of 20 trials. The trials' time structure is based on the Graz paradigm [13]. They began with an initial 3 s resting period in which patients observed a white cross on the computer screen. The patient was notified that the task was about to begin by a loud beeping sound at the 2 s mark. After the initial resting period, at the 3 s mark, the MI period of the task began. An arrow pointing to the direction of the patient's paralyzed hand appeared on the screen and disappeared after 1.5 s, after which the screen turned black for 3.5 s, during this period patients were instructed to continuously attempt a spherical grasp on a baseball located in their hand. Afterwards, at the 8 s after the trial's onset, the screen turned grey for 4 s, during this period discrete feedback was provided by means of a robotic hand orthosis. To finalize the trial and to prevent habituation, the screen turned blue for a period of 3 to 5 s, during which patients could blink, move, and rest. A depiction of the trials' time structure is shown in Fig. 1A.

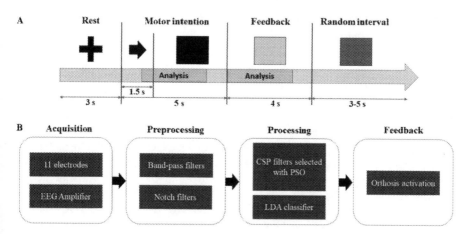

Fig. 1. A) Trial structure of each session of BCI-based therapy. B) General stages and components of the BCI system.

2.3   BCI System

The acquisition stage of the BCI system consisted of a g.USBamp biosignal amplifier from g.tec and an electrode cap with 11 g.LADYbird active electrodes placed in the F3, F4, Fz, P3, P4, Pz, C3, C4, Cz, T3 and T4 positions of the international 10–20 system, placing the ground electrode in the AFz position and the reference electrode in the right earlobe. The EEG signal was acquired with 24 bits of resolution and a sampling rate of 256 Hz.

The processing stage of the BCI consisted of offline and online phases. In the offline phase, data from each trial were filtered in 6 frequency bands (8–12, 12–16, 16–20, 20–24, 24–28 and 28–32 Hz) using 30th order FIR filters and a notch filter. Spatial filters were then computed by applying the Common Spatial Patterns (CSP) algorithm to these filtered signals, which resulted in 66 features (11 channels times 6 frequency bands). Particle Swarm Optimization (PSO) was consequently used to select the minimum number of features that allowed the best classification between the rest (REST) and the MI condition, using Linear Discriminant Analysis (LDA). The output of this processing stage were the coefficients of CSP and LDA, and the subject-specific frequency bands selected using PSO. EEG data from the last session of therapy was used for the offline phase.

The online phase of the BCI processing stage was comprised by the classification of 1-s windows of each trial (Fig. 1A) as either REST or MI. For this classification to be performed, EEG data was filtered in the frequency bands that were selected in the offline stage. Then it was spatial filtered with the offline computed CSP coefficients, and lastly it was classified with LDA. If two of the three processed 1 s MI windows (4.5–7.5 s of the trial time structure) were correctly classified as MI, then a Bluetooth command activated the robotic orthosis providing passive movement feedback to patients at the 8th s of the trial. A detailed description of the BCI can be found in the work of Cantillo-Negrete et al. [14]. A visual depiction for the overall BCI system is found in Fig. 1B.

2.4   EEG Signal Acquisition

The main variable in the present work consisted of the frequency features extracted from the EEG data, which was obtained in three time periods from each patient. The first acquisition period, referred to as baseline period, took place before the interventions. The baseline period was followed by the first intervention period, after which data was analyzed, called post-therapy1. This would be followed by the remaining therapy modality and the second post-therapy acquisition period after this second intervention (post-therapy2). The order in which each patient received conventional and BCI system-based therapy modalities was randomized.

For baseline measurements, data was obtained in a similar manner as described in Sect. 2.2, however, feedback was not recorded in baseline trials (there was no activation of the robotic orthosis, since it was an introductory session), so that only rest and MI time intervals were acquired. For both the first and second post-therapy periods, trials were comprised by rest, MI, and feedback time intervals.

2.5   EEG Signal Processing

Each patient's raw EEG data was preprocessed using two notch filters at 60 Hz and 120 Hz, a low-pass filter at 32 Hz, a high-pass filter at 4 Hz, as well as a common average reference (CAR) spatial filter to reduce reference placement effects. Preprocessed and segmented signals were visually inspected and the trials with excessive noise where manually eliminated. Time-frequency features were obtained for each trial and EEG channel using Morlet wavelet transform [15]. ERD/ERS was computed for each trial by subtracting averaged power from the 3 s time interval that comprised the rest condition from the trial's power during MI and dividing it by the rest condition's averaged power and finally, multiplying the result by 100. For the patients with right hemisphere lesions, right hemisphere electrodes were interchanged with left hemisphere electrodes, so that all patients' EEG channels would represent information from the same affected and unaffected hemisphere. Therefore, the affected hemisphere's (AH) cortical activity is shown over the left hemisphere's channels and unaffected hemisphere's (UH) cortical activity is shown over the right channels. Grand averaged brain topographic activity was computed for each session in two frequency bands: alpha from 8 to 13 Hz and beta from 14 to 30 Hz.

2.6   Statistical Analysis

ERD/ERS data were analyzed with a non-parametric cluster-based permutation test in the time-frequency domain to determine statistical significance while addressing the multiple comparison problem [16]. The averaged ERD/ERS values from baseline, post-therapy1, and post-therapy2 were compared, as well as the MI (4–7 s) and feedback (8–11 s) intervals from post-therapy1 and post-therapy2. Comparisons were performed separately for alpha and beta frequency bands.

To analyze the relation between ERD/ERS data and the clinical outcomes, correlation was determined between the clinical recovery (as defined by the change in the FMA-UE score between the end and the onset of the whole intervention) with ERD/ERS values in each therapy period as well as in both frequency bands.

In each comparison between ERD/ERS data, t-tests were conducted for each time-frequency data point, while spearman tests were performed to determine the correlation between ERD/ERS data and clinical recovery. Clusters were then constructed from each time-frequency significant t-value map ($p < 0.05$). Afterwards all the positive or negative t-values within the clusters were summed to obtain cluster-level t-scores. Clusters were then compared to a permutation distribution constructed from the largest cluster t-scores obtained using 1,000 permutations of data points between each comparison. Cluster-level p-values were obtained by calculating a probability density function on the values obtained during the iterations. The cluster-level p-values with a magnitude lower than 0.05 were considered significant. All computations were performed using the MATLAB® 2019 software from MathWorks and the Fieldtrip toolbox version 20200406.

3 Results

3.1 Patients' Clinical Assessment

For the 10 patients, clinical and demographical information was as follows: half of the patients were female, the youngest patient was 43 years old and the oldest was 85, mean age was 59.9 years (SD ± 12.8); laterality of hemisphere lesion was equally distributed with half of the patients' lesions localized in the left hemisphere and for the others in the right; the mean of the clinical recovery was 5.4 scale's points (SD ± 8.4). A total of 8 patients had a lesion limited to the subcortical area, one in the cortical and one had a lesion pertaining both cortical and subcortical areas. Eight of the patients had a high impairment of the upper limb motor function according to the scores of the FMA-UE.

3.2 ERD/ERS Brain Topographic Maps

Grand averaged ERD/ERS topographical maps are shown in Fig. 2, separated by frequency band (alpha and beta) and time interval (MI and feedback). For the baseline and the post-therapy1, the central UH and AH showed a desynchronization tendency, as well as synchronization in sagittal electrodes Cz and Pz in the alpha band, during MI. In post-therapy1 patients also elicited desynchronization in central regions in the AH and UH during feedback. In post-therapy 2 central regions of the UH and frontal regions of both hemispheres showed desynchronization, in both alpha and beta, during MI and feedback.

3.3 ERD/ERS Comparisons

Results of the statistical comparisons are shown in the plots marked by letters in Fig. 2. Significant differences were observed between the feedback of post-therapy1 and post-therapy2, in central sagittal, frontal, and temporal regions of the UH, in alpha (Fig. 2A). Significant differences were also observed between MI and feedback in post-therapy1 with more pronounced ERD elicited during MI in the frontal AH and central UH in beta (Fig. 2B).

3.4 Comparison Between Clinical Recovery and ERD/ERS

The clinical recovery for all 10 patients between the beginning and end of interventions is shown in Fig. 3A. The correlation between the clinical recovery and the ERD/ERS is shown in Fig. 3B. Significant correlations were only detected between the post-therapy2 ERD/ERS and the clinical recovery during passive movement, specifically in the sagittal electrodes, as well as the central and posterior electrodes of the unaffected hemisphere in the beta frequency band.

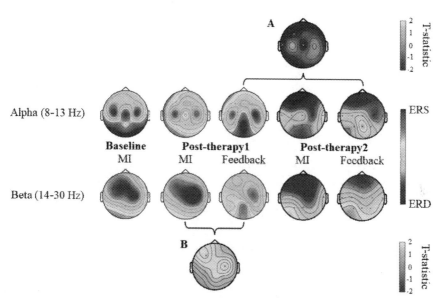

Fig. 2. Grand averaged ERD/ERS topographic maps during MI (4–7 s) and feedback (8–11 s) intervals for each evaluation period and cluster analysis of ERD/ERS results. Affected hemispheres are shown left on each topographical map and unaffected hemispheres are shown right. **A.** Differences between post-therapy1 and post-therapy2 in the feedback interval (8–11 s) in the alpha frequency band. **B.** Differences between the MI (4–7 s) and feedback (8–11 s) intervals in post-therapy1 in the beta frequency band. Differences with p ≤ 0.05 are marked with (x), comparisons with p ≤ 0.01 are marked with (*).

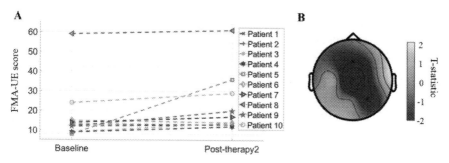

Fig. 3. Clinical recovery in all patients and its correlation with the grand-averaged ERD/ERS map corresponding to the alpha frequency band (8–13 Hz) and feedback period (8–11 s).

4   Discussion

Before the intervention most patients had a severe upper limb motor impairment as measured with the FMA-UE. After the intervention 8 patients presented an increase in FMA-UE scores, implying that neuroplasticity processes occurred during this period. Therefore, these neuroplasticity processes could have been reflected in cortical activation changes. In alpha, bilateral cortical activations were observed during MI and robotic feedback, at baseline and at post-therapy1, implying that patients engaged their AH and UH for performing motor tasks. In post-therapy2 cortical activations differed from those observed at baseline and post-therapy1, probably due to neuroplasticity effects of the intervention across a longer period of rehabilitation. These bilateral activations have been described as a compensatory mechanism in stroke patients with a significantly affected motor function [17]. In beta, activations were more pronounced in the UH across the intervention. Furthermore, a significant correlation between the unaffected hemisphere and clinical recovery was also found. Although the role of the UH is still unclear in stroke, it has been hypothesized that BCI therapies that increase the engagement of the UH during MI could improve motor function by enhancing compensatory recovery mechanisms [18]. Also important, is that recovery was associated with cortical activations elicited during passive hand movement, and not during MI. Most studies have focused in analyzing MI cortical activity, but the literature regarding the role of passive movement with relation to motor recovery is more limited. While it has been proposed that passive movement shows smaller ERD as a marker of cognitive engagement than the execution of an active motor task [19], it has also been found that active and passive movement show no difference in classification performance of motor imagery [20]. This highlights the potential of analyzing neuroplasticity processes during motor-related tasks to describe recovery biomarkers.

Significant cortical activation differences between MI and feedback (passive movement) were only observed in post-therapy1, but not in post-therapy2. This could be explained by the neuroplasticity driven by the rehabilitation intervention. Since it allowed patients to elicit cortical activations during MI, that were more similar to the ones elicited during passive movement, only after patients had received both interventions. It has been reported that in healthy subjects, passive movement resembles actual executed movement [10]. Therefore, it can be hypothesized that if patients' cortical activations in beta during MI are similar to those observed during passive movement, then cortical activations might be closer to those of a healthy subject, thus, being a possible marker of recovery. Specially, since these activations were only observed in the beta frequency band, because there is an association of beta with propagation of information between the primary motor cortex, and its efferent structures and the muscles [21].

Significant activation differences were observed during passive movement provided by the robotic orthosis (BCI feedback) between post-therapy2 and post-therapy1. These activations were in frontal and temporal regions of the AH, and in the central sagittal area. This could imply a higher involvement of the AH and interhemispheric coupling during motor-related information processing. Therefore, a higher recruitment of preserved neuronal tissue in the AH, coupled to an increase in callosal pathway activation during passive movement, could also be a marker of stroke recovery. This is important since most studies have reported EEG biomarkers during MI [8, 9], but not during passive movement, showing a promising route for increasing the understanding of brain recovery mechanisms in stroke.

It is also important to acknowledge the inherent limitations of this study. As with any EEG protocol, there is a limited spatial resolution, which is a factor for the low regional specificity of the previously discussed findings. The averaging between subjects can induce certain bias in the qualitative analysis of results. However, the non-parametric cluster permutation test allowed to assess quantitative differences in cortical activations, without a significant bias due to the distribution of data. The sample of 10 patients could have restricted the potential biomarkers identified in this study, to a population of severely affected stroke patients. However, cortical activations during MI and passive movement elicited by a robotic device, could provide valuable insights for neuroplasticity mechanisms during BCI and other experimental interventions.

Data Availability
The EEG data used to support the findings of this study are restricted by the National Institute of Rehabilitation "Luis Guillermo Ibarra Ibarra" ethics committee to protect patient privacy. Data are available from Dr. Jessica Cantillo-Negrete for researchers who meet the criteria for access to confidential data.

Acknowledgement. The authors would like to thank all the patients that participated in this study. This work was supported by Consejo Nacional de Ciencia y Tecnología (CONACYT) with grant number SALUD-2018–02-B-S-45803.

Conflicts of Interest. The authors declare that they have no conflicts of interest.

References

1. Virani, S.S., Ma, J., Alonso, A., et al.: Heart disease and stroke statistics – 2021 update. Circulation **143**, 254–743 (2021)
2. Lawrence, E.S., Coshall, C., Duunderwentndas, R., et al.: Estimates of the prevalence of acute stroke impairments and disability in a multiethnic population. Stroke **32**, 1279–1284 (2001)
3. Dobkin, B.H.: Rehabilitation after stroke. N. Engl. J. Med. **352**(16), 1677–1684 (2005)
4. Wolpaw, J.R., Birbaumer, N., McFarland, D.J., Pfurtscheller, G., Vaughan, T.M.: Brain–computer interfaces for communication and control. Clin. Neurophysiol. **113**(6), 767–791 (2002)
5. Lopez-Larraz, E., Ray, A.M., Figueiredo, T.C., Bibián, C., Birbaumer, N., Ramos-Murguialday, A.: Stroke lesion location influences the decoding of movement intention from EEG. In: 39th Annual International Conference of the IEEE Engineering in Medicine and Biology Society (EMBC), pp. 3065–3068 (2017)
6. Müller-Putz, G., Schwartz, A., Pereira, J., Ofner, P.: From classic motor imagery to complex movement intention decoding. In: Brain-Computer Interfaces: Lab Experiments to Real-World Applications, pp 39–70 (2016)
7. Pfurtscheller, G., Brunner, C., Schlögl, A., Lopes da Silva, F.H.: Mu rhythm (de)synchronization and EEG single-trial classification of different motor imagery tasks. Neuroimage **31**(1), 153–159 (2006)
8. Carino-Escobar, R.I., Carrillo-Mora, P., Valdés-Cristerna, R., et al.: Longitudinal analysis of stroke patients' brain rhythms during an intervention with a brain-computer interface. Neural Plast. **2019**, 1–11 (2019)
9. Mane, R., Chew, E., Phua, K.S., et al.: Prognostic and Monitory EEG-biomarkers for BCI upper-limb stroke rehabilitation. IEEE Trans. Neural Syst. Rehabil. Eng. **27**(8), 1654–1664 (2019)
10. Szameitat, A.J., Shen, S., Conforto, A., Sterr, A.: Cortical activation during executed, imagined, observed, and passive wrist movements in healthy volunteers and stroke patients. Neuroimage **62**(1), 266–280 (2012)

11. Jung, H.-Y.: Rehabilitation in subacute and chronic stage after stroke. In: Lee, S.H. (ed.), Stroke Revisited: Diagnosis and Treatment of Ischemic Stroke, pp. 351–360, Springer, Singapore (2017). https://doi.org/10.1007/978-981-10-1424-6_33

12. Ostrosky-Solis, E., Gómez-Pérez, A., Ardilla, M., Rosselli, E., Matute, E., Pineda, D.: Batería Neuropsicológica Neuro PSI Atención y Memoria, 6 a 85 años, Bookstore (2003)

13. Pfurtscheller, G., Neuper, C.: Motor imagery and direct brain-computer communication. Proc. IEEE **89**(7), 1123–1134 (2001)

14. Cantillo-Negrete, J., Carino-Escobar, R.I., Carrillo-Mora, P., Elias-Vinas, D., Gutierrez-Martinez, J.: Motor imagery based brain-computer Interface coupled to a robotic hand orthosis aimed for neurorehabilitation of stroke patients. J. Healthcare Eng. **2018**, 1–10 (2018). ArticleID 1624637

15. Tallon-Baudry, C., Bertrand, O., Delpuech, C., Pernier, J.: Oscillatory γ-band (30–70 Hz) activity induced by a visual search task in humans. J. Neurosci. **17**(2), 722–734 (1997)

16. Graimann, B., Huggins, J., Levine, S., Pfurtscheller, G.: Visualization of significant ERD/ERS patterns in multichannel EEG and ECoG data. Clin. Neurophysiol. **113**(1), 43–47 (2002)

17. Ward, N.S., Brown, M.M., Thompson, A.J., Frackowiak, R.S.: Neural correlates of motor recovery after stroke: a longitudinal fMRI study. Brain **126**(11), 2476–2496 (2003)

18. Kawai, R., Markman, T., Poddar, R., et al.: Motor cortex is required for learning but not for executing a motor skill. Neuron **86**(3), 800–812 (2015)

19. Park, W., Kwon, G.H., Kim, D.-H., Kim, Y.-H., Kim, S.-P., Kim, L.: Assessment of cognitive engagement in stroke patients from single-trial EEG during motor rehabilitation. IEEE Trans. Neural Syst. Rehabil. Eng. **23**(3), 351–362 (2015)

20. Kaiser, V., Kreilinger, A., Müller-Putz, G.R., Neuper, C.: First steps toward a motor imagery based stroke BCI: new strategy to set up a classifier. Front. Neurosci. **5**, 1–10 (2011). Article 86

21. Aumann, T.D., Prut, Y.: Do sensorimotor β-oscillations maintain muscle synergy representations in primary motor cortex? Trends Neurosci. **38**(2), 77–85 (2015)

Resting-State Exaggerated Alpha Rhythm from Subthalamic Nucleus Discriminates Freezers from Non-freezers Phenotypes in Parkinson's Disease: Possible Association to Attentional Circuits

Arnaldo Fim Neto[1,2](✉) 📵, Maria Sheila Guimaraes Rocha[3] 📵,
Luiz Ricardo Trajano[1] 📵, Julia Baldi de Luccas[1,2] 📵, Bruno Leonardo Bianqueti[1,2] 📵,
Tiago Paggi de Almeida[4] 📵, Fábio Godinho[1,5,6] 📵, and Diogo Coutinho Soriano[1,2] 📵

[1] Center of Engineering, Modeling and Applied Social Sciences, Federal University of ABC,
São Bernardo do Campo, Brazil
fim.arnaldo@gmail.com
[2] Brazilian Institute of Neuroscience and Neurotechnology, Campinas, São Paulo, Brazil
[3] Department of Neurology, Hospital Santa Marcelina, São Paulo, São Paulo, Brazil
[4] Department of Cardiovascular Sciences, University of Leicester, Leicester, UK
[5] Medicine School, University of Sao Paulo, Sao Paulo, Brazil
[6] Department of Functional Neurosurgery, Santa Marcelina Hospital, São Paulo, São Paulo,
Brazil

Abstract. Parkinson's disease (PD) is the second most prevalent neurodegenerative disorder. Currently, PD represents a complex "circuitopathy" involving the cortex, thalamus, basal ganglia, and associated locomotor networks. Freezing of gait (FOG) is a typical symptom affecting around 50% of advanced PD patients with a massive impact on their mobility, safety, and life quality. The unpredictable occurrence of this symptom outlines a problem of significant relevance in PD treatment. The understanding of the electrophysiological phenomena underlying cortical and subcortical structures should prompt treatment solutions. Despite the phasic nature of FOG, it is reasonable to argue that FOG patients may present specific dysfunctional motor circuit oscillations, as mentioned above. Subthalamic nucleus (STN) beta (8–35 Hz) local field potential (LFP) power correlates with rigidity and bradykinesia. A few works have analyzed its spectral characteristics under FOG and non-FOG (n-FOG) groups. This work presents a spectral analysis of the STN-LFP during rest (lying) concerning 37 recordings during surgery for deep brain stimulation (DBS) electrode implantation from 23 PD patients: 14 of whom presented with FOG (FOG group), and nine had not the clinical phenomenon (n-FOG group). FOG patients showed higher STN-LFP alpha (8–15 Hz) activity when compared to n-FOG patients. This feature marginally correlated with the FOG clinical score. We hypothesized that exaggerated alpha activity might be

---

F. Godinho and D. C. Soriano—Co-Senior Authors

P. R. d. A. Ribeiro et al. (Eds.): LAWCN 2021, CCIS 1519, pp. 225–232, 2022.
https://doi.org/10.1007/978-3-031-08443-0_14

linked to a deficit in attention and executive circuit underpinning the FOG manifestation. These findings may contribute to newer electrophysiological biomarkers for the FOG phenomenon and, therefore, new hypotheses and interventions concerning this disabling motor symptom.

Keywords: Parkinson's disease · Subthalamic nucleus · Freezing of gait

1 Introduction

Parkinson's disease (PD) is an idiopathic neurodegenerative disorder that progressively deteriorates the patient's autonomy and quality of life. It is a complex "circuitopathy" associated with dysfunctional neuronal oscillations within the corticobasal–thalamo-cortical (CBGTC) loop. The disease affects 1–3% of the worldwide population older than 60 years old [1]. PD patients disclose non-motor (sleep, sensory, cognitive, and autonomic) and motor symptoms such as tremor, rigidity, bradykinesia, and gait disturbances [1]. Freezing of gait is a specific and disabling motor symptom, which typically causes falls and mobility restrictions in the advanced PD population. Conceptually, FOG is [2] "a brief, episodic absence or marked reduction of forwarding progression of the feet despite the intention to walk." Due to its functional complexity, sudden and unpredictable occurrence, the electrophysiological mechanisms underlying FOG are still far from being elucidated, making it challenging to define an appropriate treatment [3, 4].

Despite its phasic nature, it is reasonable to assume that FOG relies on a dysfunctional CBGTC loop and on locomotor networks alterations that increase the probability of its acute condition, which implies gait freezing. Indeed, the connection among the central brain regions involved in locomotion control is altered in FOG patients compared to those without FOG and healthy subjects [3, 5]. Some results show that the communication between the subthalamic nucleus and supplementary motor area (SMA) is impaired [5] in FOG patients compared to the n-FOG ones. The worse integrative information among the circuits that perform motor planning, posture adjustments, cognitive decision, and visual perception underlies FOG episodes.

Subthalamic DBS has been established as an alternative strategy to alleviate PD motor symptoms [6]. Undoubtedly, STN-DBS effectively relieves PD patients' motor complaints, mainly tremor, rigidity, and bradykinesia. Nevertheless, DBS efficacy concerning FOG is far from a consensus [3, 4], which has motivated the quest for more precise electrophysiological markers and anatomical targets for gait disturbances [7]. Recently, exaggerated synchrony of alpha/beta rhythms obtained from basal ganglia local field potentials (LFP) was described as a candidate biomarker of FOG [8–10]. However, the STN-LFP spectral composition remains unclear in such patients during the rest, i.e., in the initial condition for the upcoming demand of selective movement or attention [11, 12]. The spectral features during the transition during rest, particularly within the period between motor preparation and the type of motor execution was yet observed for cortical structures. Notably, in the FoG phenotype, disconnection between attentional and lower limb movement preparation is attributed to a lack of event-related desynchronization in beta band sustained by a dysfunction in communication between sensorimotor areas and STN [13]. During upper limb freezing, elevated beta bandpower was computed in transition tapping period to freezing event compared to regular finger tapping [14]. Indeed, the understanding of the altered electrophysiological rhythms during anticipatory movement may contribute to unravel new biomarkers that either discriminate the FOG phenotypes or even predict the FOG event.

In the present work, we present a detailed spectral comparison concerning 37 STN-LFP recordings (24 FOG *vs.* 13 n-FOG) from 23 patients submitted to DBS neurosurgery during lying. We observed an increased alpha rhythm in FOG patients. These results may contribute to the proposal of new electrophysiological FOG biomarkers and, therefore, new target variables for DBS.

2 Materials and Methods

2.1 Patients

Either UPDRS or MDS-UPDRS evaluated motor and non-motor scores during practical OFF and ON-medication states one month before surgery by a movement disorders neurologist (MR). The study included twenty-nine patients diagnosed with moderate to advanced idiopathic PD with severe motor fluctuations or dyskinesias. The patients were classified in FOG and n-FOG groups according to their performance on the FOG questionnaire [14]. The FOG-Questionnaire evaluated the presence of daily FOG. The presence of clinical FOG was defined if the score was at least ≥ 3 on question 3 or 4, or if the examiner observed freezing of gait during motor evaluation. The n-FOG did not present FOG episodes during the assessment of gait initiating, stepping, and turning and scored below three on either question on the FOG questionnaire. Six patients were excluded due to excessive anxiety during surgery and poor quality of intraoperative recordings, resulting in 23 patients: 14 FOG and nine n-FOG. The local ethics committee approved this study, and all patients gave prior written consent (CAAE: 62418316.9.2004.0066 registered in "Plataforma Brasil": http://conselho.saude.gov.br/plataforma-brasil-conep?view=default).

2.2 Surgery

The surgical procedure was previously reported [16]. We performed a digital fusion of stereotactic tomography (CT) with non-stereotactic 1.5T magnetic resonance imaging (MRI) to target the dorsolateral STN. Microelectrode recordings (MER) acquired the STN-LFP through a set of three parallel 1 MΩ impedance tungsten microelectrodes (microTargeting® electrodes, FHC, Greenville, MA, USA). Action potentials were amplified (1000 -fold), filtered (0.3–10 kHz, notch filtered at 60 Hz), and digitally stored (Lead Point - Medtronic, Minneapolis, MN, USA). The sensorimotor sector of STN was identified by an increase in the background noise amplitude besides the irregular activity of neurons. The ventral extremity of quadripolar electrodes was placed at the ventral border of the STN defined by MER (3389 model - Medtronic, Minneapolis, MN, USA). Before electrodes implanting, the STN-LFP signals were acquired and sampled at 24 kHz, bandpass filtered (1–200 Hz), and recorded at lying for 60 s. Fourteen patients received bilateral implanting (10 FOG and four n-FOG), while nine patients received unilateral implanting (4 FOG and five n-FOG), providing 37 STN-LFP recordings (24 FOG and 13 n-FOG). All patients were in practical off-condition during the surgery, as they did not receive levodopa treatment for 12 h at least.

2.3 Signal Processing

STN-LFP signals were exported and post-processed in Matlab 2018b. Signals (in μV) were downsampled to 1 kHz (decimation method), followed by notch filtering at 60 Hz and at their harmonics, bandpass filtering (6th order Butterworth filter, 2–200 Hz). Each observation was z-scored normalized, leading to adimensional (ad.) time-series. This last procedure preserves the spectral shape and the power distribution along the frequency spectrum, defining a more robust framework for inter signal comparisons [13]. The frequency bandwidth (i.e., 2–200 Hz) included the main LFP sub-bands: theta (4–8 Hz), alpha (8–15 Hz), low beta (15–25 Hz), high beta (25– 35 Hz), beta (15–35 Hz) and gamma (35–200 Hz). Results concerning beta and beta division in low and high bands were shown here, given the possible functional role of such division.

The spectral composition of FOG and n-FOG patients were performed through Welch periodogram considering power spectral density (PSD) estimation [13]. Sixty seconds of the z-normalized STN-LFP for each patient were Hamming windowed (4 s) with 50% of overlap followed by a square of the magnitude estimates of the discrete Fourier transform whereas averaging considering all windows, which implies a spectral resolution of 0.25 Hz. The STN-LFP bandpower (in ad.^{2}) was obtained by evaluating the area under the PSD curve, considering each of the LFP rhythms aforementioned.

2.4 Statistical Analysis

STN-LFP bandpower was presented as mean and standard deviation (SD). D'Agostino's test confirmed normal distribution. Comparison of mean bandpower between FOG and n-FOG groups was computed by unpaired t student in case of normality. Otherwise, the nonparametric Mann-Whitney test was carried out. The correlation coefficients (ρ) between bandpower and FOG scores were evaluated considering the whole population without phenotypic categorization. Pearson's correlation was performed for normal distribution, and Spearman's coefficient was used otherwise.

3 Results

Figure 1 illustrates the Welch periodograms of STN-LFP in logarithmic scale (dB/Hz). PSD for FOG and n-FOG groups are shown under rest. Visual inspection may clarify that PSD amplitude is differed between groups within the alpha-low beta band.

Table 1 and Figure 2 summarize the quantitative analysis for group comparison (FOG in red and n-FOG in blue) concerning classical STN-LFP bandpower rhythms for the phenotypes. No significant differences were found for: theta ($p = 0.283$; unpaired t student test - Fig 2A); beta ($p = 0.503$; unpaired t student test - Fig 2C); low beta ($p = 0.673$; unpaired t student test - Fig 2D), high beta ($p = 0.477$; Mann Whitney test - Fig 2E) and gamma ($p = 0.714$; unpaired t student test - Fig 2F). Alpha bandpower was

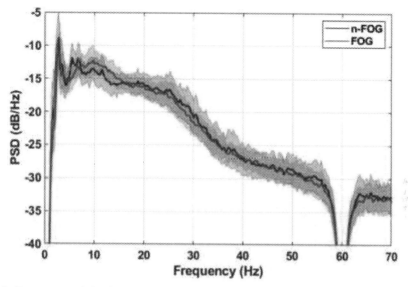

Fig. 1. Power spectral density (PSD - dB/Hz) for FoG and n-FOG groups under rest conditions. Visual inspection suggests that PSD is higher in the FOG group in the alpha and low beta band (8–15 Hz). Data are expressed as mean ± SD.

Table 1. Mean bandpower (area under the PSD curve) for FOG and n-FOG phenotypes within a specific range of bands, including the theta (4–8 Hz), alpha (8–15 Hz), low beta (15–25 Hz), high beta (25–35 Hz), beta (15–35 Hz) and gamma (35–200 Hz). The values of the bandpower are presented as mean ± standard deviation (SD) for 37 recordings in 24 FOG and 13 n-FOG phenotypes.

	FOG (N = 24)	n-FOG (N = 13)
Theta	0.164 ± 0.039	0.188 ± 0.071
Alpha	0.331 ± 0.087	0.248 ± 0.089
Low beta	0.238 ± 0.059	0.249 ± 0.087
High beta	0.085 ± 0.042	0.103 ± 0.066
Beta	0.319 ± 0.078	0.347 ± 0.135
Gamma	0.069 ± 0.031	0.073 ± 0.040

significantly different between phenotypes ($p = 0.011$; unpaired t student test; Fig 2B), being increased for FOG patients.

Finally, we assessed correlations between STN-LFP bandpower and fog score (Fig. 3). It was found negative, though not significant, correlation of theta ($\rho = -0.051$; $p = 0.983$), high beta ($\rho = -0.265$; $p = 0.286$), beta ($\rho = -0.078$; $p = 0.756$) and gamma ($\rho = -0.280$; $p = 0.259$) with fog score. Low beta was weakly positively

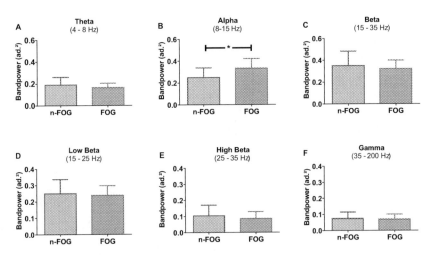

Fig. 2. Mean bandpower for STN-LFP bands as theta, alpha, low beta, high beta, beta, and gamma for FOG and n-FOG phenotypes under rest. *p < 0.05.

correlated with FOG score ($\rho = 0.098$; $p = 0.697$). In contrast, alpha was positively correlated with such symptom ($\rho = 0.315$; $p = 0.202$).

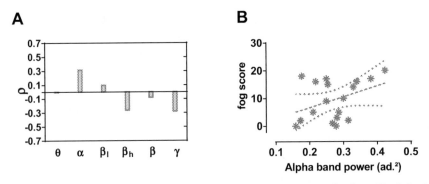

Fig. 3. (A) Correlation between fog score and STN-LFP bandpower as the theta (θ), alpha (α), low beta (β_l), high beta (β_h), beta (β) and gamma (γ). (B) Correlation between alpha bandpower and fog score.

4 Discussion

The "circuitopathy" underlying the FOG is still a matter of intense debate [3, 4]. It is unclear the electrophysiological correlates underlying this debilitating symptom in PD. Efforts to support the prediction of early kinematic abnormalities preceding the FOG event have emerged, pointing to the requirement for a better understanding of the underlying neurophysiological phenomenon. Herein, we observed exaggerated alpha oscillations at resting state in FOG patients compared to those without FOG.

Previously, Syrkin-Nikolau et al. [10] showed increased alpha activity in patients who presented FOG during walking and FOG episodes. Additionally, alpha bandpower in STN-LFP has been associated with attention and executive domains in frontal cortical and premotor areas [17]. In terms of executive disfunction, PD patients with FOG present conflict-resolution deficit, fail to prevent hasty decisions to move under unfamiliar environment, and, subsequently, a higher probability of triggering FOG [3, 4]. An electroencephalography-based study in PD patients [12] showed increased alpha oscillations and gamma amplitude cross-talking regarding the attention circuit. This crosstalk contributes to a functional discordance between top-down (voluntary and goal-directed allocation of attention to perform movement) and bottom-up (a circuit breaker when stimulus-driven attracts attention), affording the anti-kinetic activity. Although the work did not categorize the patients into FOG and n-FOG phenotypes, the study provided a possible mechanistic hypothesis for the phenomenon.

Another critical hallmark concerns the role of beta activity. Admittedly, beta rhythm suppression associates with the facilitation of continuous movement sequences [18]. Nevertheless, we did not find any significant differences across FOG and n-FOG patients groups concerning this rhythm or associated sub-bands. Some previous studies reported different results concerning beta bandpower in PD according to the presence of FOG. For instance, both [8] and [9] reported increased bandpower for the low and high beta band during walking, respectively. In this case, the movement condition may play a critical role in justifying the discrepancy from our results.

Finally, our results provide evidence that despite the phasic nature of the FOG phenomenon, there is a functional difference between FOG and n-FOG PD patients at rest condition in the CBGTC circuit, at the STN level, associated with increased LFP alpha power. This increased alpha rhythm may be related to dysfunctional behavior and the synchronism with attentional/higher-order cognitive networks. It may outline an essential marker for pharmacological or electrical intervention, which requires careful attention.

Acknowledgments. AFN thanks the CAPES (grant n. 33144010015P8, 2019/1814368) for the financial support. DCS thanks FAPESP (2013/07559 3; 2019/09512–0) and CNPq (n. 306298/2020–1).

References

1. Mc Gregor, M.: Circuit mechanisms of Parkinson's disease. Neuron **101**, 1042–1056 (2019)
2. Giladi, N., et al.: Motor blocks in Parkinson's disease. Neurology **42**, 333–339 (1992)
3. Marquez, J.B., et al.: Neural correlates of freezing of gait in Parkinson's disease: an electrophysiology mini-review. Front. Neurol. **11**, 1–12 (2020)
4. Gao, C., Lie, J., Tan, Y.: Freezing of gait in Parkinson's disease: pathophysiology, risk factors, and treatments. Transl. Neurodegeneration **9**(12), 1–12 (2020)
5. Fling, B.W., et al.: Functional reorganization of the locomotor network in Parkinson patients with freezing of gait. PLoS ONE **9**(6), 1–12 (2015)
6. Benabid, A.L.: Deep brain stimulation for Parkinson's disease. Curr. Opin. Neurobiol. **13**(6), 696–706 (2003)

7. Rocha, M.S.G., et al.: Fields of forel brain stimulation improves levodopa-unresponsive gait and balance disorders in Parkinson's disease. Neurosurgery **89**(3), 450–459 (2021)
8. Singh, A., Plate, A., Kammermeier, S., Mehrkens, J.H., Ilmberger, J., Bötzel, K.: Freezing of gait-related oscillatory activity in the human subthalamic nucleus. Basal Ganglia **3**(1), 25–32 (2013)
9. Toledo, J.B.: High beta activity in the subthalamic nucleus and freezing of gait in Parkinson's disease. Neurobiol. Dis. **64**, 60–65 (2014)
10. Syrkin-Nikolau, J., et al.: Subthalamic neural entropy is a feature of freezing of gait in freely moving people with Parkinson's disease. Neurobiol. Dis. **108**, 288–297 (2017)
11. Sadaghiani, S., et al.: Intrinsic connectivity networks, alpha oscillations, and tonic alertness: a simultaneous electroencephalography/functional magnetic resonance imaging study. J. Neurosci. **30**, 10243–10250 (2010)
12. Yoo, H.B., et al.: The functional alterations in top-down attention streams of Parkinson's disease measured by EEG. Nat. Sci. Rep. **8**, 10609 (2018)
13. Giladi, N., et al.: Validation of the freezing of gait questionnaire in patients with Parkinson's disease. Mov. Disord. **4**(5), 655–661 (2009)
14. Tar, C., et al.: Attention modulation during motor preparation in Parkinsonian freezers: a time frequency EEG study. Clin. Neurophysiol. **127**(12), 3506–3515 (2016)
15. Scholten, M., et al.: Transitions between repetitive tapping and upper limb freezing show impaired movement-related beta band modulation. Clin. Neurophysiol. **10**, 2499–2507 (2020)
16. Godinho, F., et al.: Spectral characteristics of subthalamic nucleus local field potentials in Parkinson's disease: Phenotype and movement matter. Eur. J. Neurosci. **53**, 2804–2818 (2021)
17. Horn, A., et al.: Toward an electrophysiological "Sweet Spot" for deep brain stimulation in the subthalamic nucleus. Hum. Brain Mapp. (2017)
18. Joundi, R.A., et al.: Persistent suppression of subthalamic beta-band activity during rhythmic finger tapping in Parkinson's disease. Clin. Neurophysiol. **124**, 565–573 (2013)

Effect of Hand Dominance When Decoding Motor Imagery Grasping Tasks

Katrine Linnea Nergård[1]([✉]) [ID], Tor Endestad[2,3] [ID], and Jim Torresen[1,3] [ID]

[1] Department of Informatics, University of Oslo, Oslo, Norway
katrner@uio.no
[2] Department of Psychology, University of Oslo, Oslo, Norway
[3] RITMO, University of Oslo, Oslo, Norway

Abstract. Discriminating between different motor imagery tasks within the same limb is challenging because of the proximity of their spatial representations on the motor cortex. Overcoming this challenge would largely increase the number of control dimensions and pave the way for more practical brain-computer interfaces (BCIs). This paper explores how hand dominance affects classification performance when decoding different motor imagery tasks completed with the same hand. This aspect has, to the best of our knowledge, not been presented in the literature before. The performance was also evaluated to see if acceptable accuracies for real-life applications could be reached without handcrafted features. EEG signals were collected from nine subjects performing the same set of imagery grasping tasks with both dominant and non-dominant hand. The signals were analyzed using traditional state-of-the-art methods, such as filterbank common spatial patterns (FBCSP) and Tangent Space (TS), in addition to well-validated convolutional neural networks designed for limited data. Automatic channel selection according to a Riemannian geometry criterion before classification improved discrimination. Variation in performance when using dominant versus non-dominant hand was found for all the subjects. To establish whether these differences are statistically significant, or to identify trends, more data is required. Five out of nine subjects achieved accuracies above 70% for classification within the same hand without using tailored features.

Keywords: BCI · EEG · Motor imagery · Machine learning

1 Introduction

A brain-computer interface (BCI) is a system that translates brain activity into commands for an interactive application. Many application areas can be revolutionized, such as control of assistive technologies for severely motor-impaired users, rehabilitation for stroke patients, gaming devices, and adaptive human-computer interfaces reacting to the user's mental state. Brain activity is often captured using electroencephalography (EEG), and there is a growing interest in the commercialization of EEG products for BCI applications. Several new

P. R. d. A. Ribeiro et al. (Eds.): LAWCN 2021, CCIS 1519, pp. 233–249, 2022.
https://doi.org/10.1007/978-3-031-08443-0_15

electrode headsets designed for speed, ease of use, comfort, and mobility in real-world environments have entered the market in the last few years.

The various control signals that can be employed in a BCI system are divided into different paradigms. Motor imagery (MI) signals are generated when imagining a motor task. Research has confirmed that imagining a movement activates the same area in the brain as when physically generating the movement [23]. This study will be limited to EEG-based BCIs following the motor imagery paradigm. Promising results have been obtained for distinguishing between the MI tasks of body parts with separated spatial representations on the motor cortex. The number of commands that can be decoded corresponds to the number of MI tasks that the BCI system can distinguish. The ability to discriminate between finer motor tasks with close-by cortical representations would vastly increase the number of available commands and hence the functionality of such a BCI. This paper aims to serve as a stepping stone towards increasing the number of available commands.

There are several challenges to overcome in the development of more practical BCIs. EEG signals are noisy and non-stationary, and the data is highly complex. Also, the statistical distribution of MI data is highly variable across subjects, runs, and sessions. Therefore a calibration process with hand-engineered feature extraction techniques has traditionally been necessary to achieve acceptable performances by the classifier [18]. Emerging deep learning techniques have, however, shown great promise in tackling these challenges. These techniques do not rely on hand-engineered features and can merge feature extraction, selection, and classification. Sometimes they require no preprocessing and can potentially be used to build subject-independent systems with no calibration time, when dealing with highly complex data. The literature shows that convolutional neural networks (CNNs) have been the most popular choice, but advantages compared to traditional EEG processing approaches remain unverified [26].

An MI EEG dataset was collected for this study. The main objective was to determine whether finer motor tasks within the same hand are easier to classify when imagined with the dominant hand compared to the non-dominant one. A secondary goal was to investigate whether such finer motor tasks on a single limb could reach acceptable performance criteria to pass as additional commands in a practical BCI. There is a consensus in the field that the required accuracy level for real-world application is around 70% [6,13,16]. Current state-of-the-art algorithms in conventional machine learning were explored and compared to novel, promising EEG-tailored convolutional neural networks. Different data augmentation- and feature selection techniques were also experimented with.

2   Materials and Methods

In a traditional MI EEG-based system, signal processing is carried out by the following steps. First, raw EEG data is collected and usually preprocessed to some degree to remove noise or artifacts. Then features are extracted, and, in some systems, the most salient features are selected before classification. Finally, the classifier attempts to decode the motor imagery task performed by the user.

2.1 Data Acquisition

Both the literature [25,30] and the available datasets online reveal that the vast majority of the existing MI EEG-based BCI systems have focused on differentiating between left hand, right hand, feet, and tongue. These tasks have been shown to produce significant and discriminative changes in the EEG signals relative to background EEG [11]. The classification of tasks like these has been widely documented, yielding good accuracy performances. The task of discriminating the motor imagery of different movements within the same limb, however, has proven challenging [10,21]. The challenge arises because these motor tasks activate regions that have very proximate representations on the motor cortex area of the brain, all on the same hemisphere. To date, few studies have addressed this problem. The studies that have [9,10,17,32], however, show promising results, demonstrating the possibility of utilizing EEG signals to decode single-limb MI tasks. Nevertheless, in these studies, the motor imagery task was conducted on one side only. The effect of hand dominance was not considered, which is the focus of this study.

The work of D. Zapala et al. [33], has evaluated the effect of handedness on one simple left-hand/right-hand motor imagery task. Differences in performance between dominant and non-dominant hands for subjects with the same handedness is not discussed in Zapala's work. The results of the study show that lateralization of the sensorimotor rhythm (SMR) during a motor imagery task is different for right and left-handed subjects. Those who were left-handed presented lower accuracy compared to the right-handed subjects in a single BCI session. The SMR suppression in the alpha band (8–13 Hz) was weaker during mental simulation of left-hand movements. Consequently, the authors suggest that the individual differences in hand dominance should be considered in the user's training to improve BCI control. In another study by C. Marques-Chin et al. [20], the main objective was to identify specific hand movements from electroencephalographic activity. The effect of hand dominance was discussed, and four participants performed an experiment using both their dominant and non-dominant hands. When comparing the results, the authors found no significant difference in the average classification accuracy. The research was limited to motor execution, and additional recording devices such as an optical sensor and a sensor glove were included.

In our study, a custom dataset was created to explore the effect of hand dominance when decoding tasks within the same hand, where participants imagined different grasps, using both dominant and non-dominant hand. Grasp types are divided into two main categories: precision and power. In a power grasp, all fingers and palms are activated. In a precision grasp, only the tip of the thumb and opposing finger(s) are used. To ensure that the collected MI data was informative and high-quality, the experimental setup followed the principal guidelines provided by H. Cho et al. [8]. Nine right-handed, non-impaired subjects, aged between 25 and 60 participated in the EEG experiment. Five of the subjects were female and four were male. None of them had any previous experience with BCIs. Before the experiment began, the subjects were instructed to imagine the kinesthetic, not the visual experience, during the motor imagery period. As reported in the work of C. Stinear et al. [31], kinesthetic MI modulates more corticomotor excitability than visual MI does.

The cue-based protocol consisted of four different motor imagery/executory tasks, namely the imagination/execution of a left-hand cylindrical grasp (class 1), left-hand pinch grasp (class 2), right-hand cylindrical grasp (class 3), and right-hand pinch grasp (class 4). Each session comprised of four motor imagery runs. One run consisted of 40 trials (10 for each of the four possible classes) in a pseudorandom order, yielding a total of 160 trials per session. Two additional runs of motor execution (ME) were also collected in each session to be used in an experiment combining MI and ME data. Since motor imagery is more tiring than execution, a combination of the two could potentially increase the amount of useful data that can be collected each session.

Throughout the experiments, the subjects were seated comfortably in an armchair in front of a computer screen, see Fig. 1. Each trial lasted eight seconds. A fixation cross appeared on the screen at the beginning of a trial ($t = 0$ s). After three seconds, a visual cue in the form of an image (corresponding to one of the four classes) appeared and stayed on the screen for two seconds, followed by a blank screen for three consecutive seconds. This cue prompted the subjects to perform the corresponding motor imagery/execution task. The subjects were asked to carry out the task until the fixation cross reappeared from the screen at $t = 8$ s. The protocol is illustrated in Fig. 2. After each run, the participants were asked to rest while seated to avoid fatigue.

Fig. 1. Experimental setup.

The EEG data was recorded with the BioSemi ActiveTwo system, sampled at 1024 Hz Hz. The code for visual stimuli and trigger point collection was written in

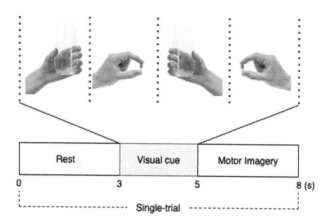

Fig. 2. Illustration of tasks and experimental protocol of a single trial.

Matlab, using the Psychophysics Toolbox extensions [7]. A 64-channel montage was used, based on the international 10–20 system.

2.2   Data Processing

The raw EEG-data was preprocessed and analyzed using MNE-Python [12]. To provide a realistic picture of performance, minimal preprocessing was applied on all subjects, and there was no tailoring for specific subjects. First, potential power line noise 50 Hz (Europe) was removed with notch filtering. Then a high-pass filter with a cutoff frequency 2 Hz was applied to the data to remove baseline drift.

Before feature extraction or classification, the raw data was divided into 3D arrays consisting of time-locked trials, called epochs. The epochs were then bandpass filtered to select the band(s) defined by the algorithm that was used before being downsampled to 128, in accordance with the MNE software's best practice [12]. Bad epochs were automatically rejected by defining a threshold of 800e-6V for peak-to-peak amplitude and flat signal detection.

The choice of trial segment was [0.5–2.5] seconds post cue, which is a window that is widely used in literature [14, 19, 24, 27]. Before any channel or feature selection was applied, each trial was shaped with a size of (64, 256), i.e., 64 channels, and 256 samples in a two-second window with a sampling frequency of 128. Preliminary analysis of the data revealed that the motor imagery induced activity repression was clearly most prominent in this time segment, further supporting this choice of window. Using epochs that start 0.5 s after cue onset also avoids classifying responses evoked by the visual cue.

The data was scaled and normalized to zero mean and unit variance using the function z-score. By using this function, the convergence time was reduced. The built-in function 'Scaler' in MNE was used, which scales each channel using mean and standard deviation computed across all of its time points and epochs. Due to scaling sensitivity in deep learning, the data was multiplied with 1e6.

New data examples can be artificially generated to reduce overfitting and allow the use of more complex deep learning models. This technique is called data augmentation and can lead to better generalization abilities and increased stability and accuracy. Two approaches were tested in this study, sliding window augmentations and reuse of downsampled data. Two different overlaps were used for the sliding window: 0.1 and 0.5 s. With a 0.1 s overlap, one trial was expanded to five highly correlated trials formed by the moving windows of [0.3–2.3], [0.4–2.4], [0.5–2.5], [0.6–2.6] and [0.7–2.7]. An overlap of 0.5 s, gave the following segments: [0.5–2.5], [1.0–2.0], [1.5–3.5], [2.0–4.0] and [2.5–4.5]. The latter segments were less correlated than the first ones and utilized the full trial. The size of the data set was increased by five times with both overlaps. When reusing downsampled data, the data could be augmented eight times. The original sampling frequency was 1024 Hz Hz, and the data was downsampled by a factor of 8 128 Hz.

2.3 Feature Extraction, Selection, and Classification

Riemannian geometry classifiers (RGCs) and filter bank common spatial patterns (FCSPs) are considered the standard for several BCI problems, including motor imagery [18]. When evaluating the performance of novel deep learning networks, FCSPs are the algorithms to compare to. Deep learning methods are currently lagging in performance for BCI, given the limited available training data. It is assumed that a considerable amount of data is required for EEG signals, due to their high dimensionality. Shallow networks do, however, show promise. The methods that were used in this study are presented in the following subsections.

Channel Selection. Both manual selection and automatic selection of channels were employed. All eight neighboring electrodes of both C3 and C4 were selected in the manual selection, including C3 and C4. These channels are located on the sensory-motor cortex, where distinctive activity can be expected when performing/imagining different hand movements.

In addition, an automatic channel selection was made based on a Riemannian geometry criterion. For each class, a centroid is estimated, and the channel selection is based on the maximization of the distance between centroids. This is done by a backward elimination, where the electrode that carries the less distance is removed from the subset at each iteration [3].

Filter Bank Common Spatial Patterns. The Common Spatial Patterns (CSP) algorithm is considered a standard tool in the repertoire of oscillatory activity-based BCIs. It has won multiple competitions for decoding EEG, such as BCI competition IV and datasets 2a and 2b. Simply put, CSP finds spatial filters where the variance of the filtered signal is maximal for one class and minimal for the other. Maximizing this difference between the classes leads to optimized discriminant band-power features. However, CSP also has some limitations, as it is not robust to noise and non-stationarity and is prone to overfitting when the amount of training data is small. To make CSP more stable and robust, a variant called Filter Bank CSP (FBCSP) was introduced [1,2]. In this method, the EEG signals are first filtered in multiple frequency bands using a filter bank. After filtering, the CSP algorithm is used on each of the bands to optimize the spatial filters. Here both spatial and spectral information is exploited, using band power features from relevant frequency bands.

The implementation of FBCSP followed the description in V. J. Lawhern et al. [14]. First, the EEG signal was bandpass filtered into nine non-overlapping filter banks with a step size 4 Hz, starting 4 Hz. Hence the following banks were created: 4–8 Hz, 8–12 Hz, 12–16 Hz, 16–20 Hz, 20–24 Hz, 24–28 Hz, 28–32 Hz, 32–36 Hz, and 36–40 Hz. Second, four CSP filters were trained with a one-versus-rest strategy, using Ledoit wolf regularization for each filter bank. This gives a feature vector with a total of 36 features, four CSP filters times nine filter banks, for each trial. Third, an elastic-net logistic regression classifier was trained, with a penalty $\alpha = 0.95$. Finally, the trained classifier was applied to the test set through cross-validation.

Tangent Space Projection. Tangent Space followed by Logistic Regression (TSLR) is a Riemannian geometry classifier. The same preprocessing as for the other methods was applied, except the bandpass filtering 4 Hz 30 Hz. Then covariance matrices were computed and mapped into the Riemannian manifold using the pyRiemann software [4,5]. Finally, the matrices were projected onto the tangent space before LR classification.

Convolutional Neural Networks. Three well-validated convolutional neural networks were implemented; EEGNet [24], DeepConvNet [28] and ShallowConvNet [28]. Specifically, the EEGNet-8,2 version was used, where 8 and 2 denote the number of temporal and spatial filters to be learned, respectively. The temporal kernel length was set to 32 samples to account for the data being high-pass filtered 4 Hz. The implemented model was fit using the Adam optimizer, with default parameters, minimizing the categorical cross-entropy loss function. The drop-out rate was set to 0.5 due to the limited amount of training data. The maximum number of training iterations (epochs) was set to 500, and early stopping was enabled, saving the model weights, which produced the lowest validation set loss. This is a compact CNN architecture intended for EEG-based BCIs, with the aim of being applicable across several different BCI paradigms, working well with limited data, and producing neurophysiologically interpretable features.

The DeepConvNet architecture is inspired by successful computer vision architectures, aiming to create a model that can extract a wide range of features, not restricted to specific feature types. Finally, the ShallowConv network is inspired by the FBCSP pipeline, specifically tailored to decode band power features. The transformations performed by FBCSP are similar to the transformations of the ShallowConvNet.

2.4   Experiments

First, data from BCI competition IV 2a was classified with all the mentioned classifiers, and these results were compared to those of V. J. Lawhern et al. [14] to verify that the algorithms were implemented correctly. The hyperparameters and preprocessing methods were kept the same, and the results were in line with the compared study.

When investigating the effect of hand-dominance, the right-hand (dominant) grasps were separated from the left-hand (non-dominant) grasps during the experiments, making each of them a binary classification problem. The number of class samples per subject was thereby reduced from 160 (4 classes × 10 trials × 4 runs) to 80 (2 classes × 10 trials × 4 runs). The case where all left-hand precision and power grasps are isolated will be referred to as the LH-LH case (non-dominant). Similarly, the case where all right-hand precision and power grasps are isolated will be referred to as the RH-RH case (dominant).

The following experiments were conducted for both cases, using all the five models - FBCSP, TSLR, EEGNet, ShallowConvNet, and DeepConvNet.

1. Motor imagery data for all subjects, cross-validated on every run. This will be referred to as the baseline experiment.
2. Sliding window augmented motor imagery data for all subjects, cross-validated on every run.
3. Motor imagery data augmented by reusing downsampled data for all subjects, cross-validated on every run.
4. Motor imagery and executory data for all subjects, cross-validated on every run. The number of class samples per subject increased from 80 to 120 since two additional runs were added.
5. Manual channel selection before feature extraction or classification.
6. Riemannian automatic channel selection algorithm before feature extraction or classification.

Inter- or intra-subject classification has an impact on the performance. Models trained on the data of a single subject (intra-subject) have less variability to account for and often lead to better performances. However, the data available for such models is limited. With multiple subjects included (inter-subject), the model sees more data. This study was limited to intra-subject classification.

The validation procedure can also impact the performance. Using different subjects for training and testing may lead to lower performance but applies to real-life scenarios. In the experiments of this study, Kfold cross-validation was used, where the folds comprised of the various runs of the given subject. Consequently, with four runs per subject, the number of folds was four. When motor execution and imagery were combined, the number of folds was six, reflecting the total number of runs. The random state was kept the same for all experiments to ensure a proper comparison. For evaluation, one fold was set aside and not included in the training. Performance may be overrated if measures are estimated through cross-validation on training data [18].

The evaluation metric of choice was accuracy, the most widely used evaluation criteria in BCI research. The classes should be balanced when using this metric, meaning there should be the same number of samples for each class, as is the case in this study. It is also important to note that the accuracy of a random classifier is already 100% divided by the number of classes. For example, if there are two classes, there is a 50% chance of correct classification, given balanced classes [29].

The software and hardware used for these experiments were:

- Programming language: Python3
- Signal processing library: MNE-python 0.23.0.
- Traditional baselines: MNE-python 0.23.0 and scikit-learn 0.24.
- Deep learning library: Keras and TensorFlow 2.
- Hardware: Nvidia RTX3090 GPU.

3   Results and Discussion

In this section the results of all relevant experiments are summarized. The accuracies of the LH-LH and RH-RH classification problems averaged across all folds and subjects are summarized in Tables 1 and 2, respectively. For simplicity, only the best performing augmentation technique has been included. This technique was sliding window augmentation with an overlap of 0.1s, providing a five times increase in the amount of data. Only motor imagery data was used when experimenting with augmentation and channel selection.

Table 1. LH-LH case (non-dominant hand): accuracies averaged across all subjects and all folds. Best performing experiment marked in bold for each model.

Experiment	FBCSP	TSLR	EEGNet	ShallowConvNet	DeepConvNet
Motor imagery data only	54.17	56.04	53.85	54.48	49.69
Motor imagery + Motor executory	53.86	55.54	55.39	55.33	**53.65**
Sliding window augmentation	52.48	55.25	54.12	54.60	50.19
Manual channel selection (18 chns)	53.44	49.69	53.65	52.60	50.42
Riemann channel selection (16 chns)	59.27	60.52	53.02	54.69	52.60
Riemann channel selection (8 chns)	**61.34**	**61.81**	**55.00**	**57.40**	52.40

Table 2. RH-RH case (dominant hand): accuracies averaged across all subjects and all folds. Best performing experiment marked in bold for each model.

Experiment	FBCSP	TSLR	EEGNet	ShallowConvNet	DeepConvNet
Motor imagery data only	53.33	52.50	53.12	53.85	51.56
Motor imagery + Motor executory	57.59	57.45	54.48	56.25	49.34
Sliding window augmentation	53.63	53.98	53.67	54.02	50.71
Manual channel selection (18 chns)	52.50	53.75	53.65	55.31	52.19
Riemann channel selection (16 chns)	60.83	61.35	55.94	57.19	51.46
Riemann channel selection (8 chns)	**63.88**	**65.14**	**57.40**	**57.40**	**53.33**

In the baseline experiment, where only motor imagery data is included, most models yielded an average accuracy close to chance. TSLR performed best in the LH-LH case (non-dominant), with a 56.04% accuracy score. This score is 3.54% points better than what was obtained with the same model for the RH-RH case (dominant). Interestingly, adding motor executory data increases performance up to 4.95% points for the conventional methods in the RH-RH case, surpassing LH-LH. The LH-LH case was unaffected by additional motor executory data. The increase in data also slightly enhances the performance of all the neural networks except DeepConvNet in the RH-RH case. A drawback of including executory data is that it can be challenging for motor-impaired people. However, from an inter-subject perspective, the potential data increase that follows a combination of MI and ME is an appealing aspect to explore further. Sliding window augmentation did not improve performance for any of the models, and neither did manual channel selection.

The average accuracies across subjects for almost all the experiments are, in general, very close to chance. The exceptions are the Riemann channel selection experiments, which increase the performance by 12.64% points for the best performing model, compared to the baseline experiment (TSLR, RH-RH case). In this case, the number of channels is reduced from 64 to 8 before being fed to the classifier, thereby reducing dimensionality. Because of the promising results of Riemann channel selection performance, especially with eight channels, this experiment will be further reviewed by analyzing the performance of the individual subjects. The results of the Riemann channel selections are presented in Tables 3 and 4.

Riemann geometry and FBCSP outperform all convolutional neural networks for most subjects. There is high variability in performance among the participants for all models. Three subjects (4, 5, and 7) reached the 70% threshold with

Table 3. LH-LH case (non-dominant hand), with Riemann channel selection, 8 channels: accuracies of individual subjects averaged over all folds. Scores above 70% marked in bold.

Subj.	FBCSP	TSLR	EEGNet	ShallowConvNet	DeepConvNet
1	48.75	46.25	47.50	52.50	45.00
2	60.00	50.00	60.00	56.25	50.00
3	65.00	67.50	57.50	58.75	55.00
4	**71.25**	65.00	58.75	62.50	45.00
5	61.25	**70.00**	46.25	58.75	50.00
6	61.25	61.25	48.75	56.25	50.00
7	**73.75**	**75.00**	66.25	66.25	57.50
8	52.50	53.75	52.50	57.50	50.00
9	58.75	67.50	55.00	57.50	58.75
Avg	60.63	60.31	55.00	57.40	52.40

Table 4. RH-RH case (dominant hand), with Riemann channel selection, 8 channels: accuracies of individual subjects averaged over all folds. Scores above 70% marked in bold.

Subj.	FBCSP	TSLR	EEGNet	ShallowConvNet	DeepConvNet
1	65.00	61.25	51.25	53.75	55.00
2	**73.75**	**78.75**	**72.50**	**72.50**	61.25
3	**76.25**	**78.75**	**76.50**	58.75	55.00
4	53.75	55.00	58.75	45.00	47.50
5	65.00	67.50	50.00	62.50	51.25
6	56.25	58.75	55.00	52.50	53.75
7	62.50	66.25	58.75	58.75	55.00
8	57.50	62.50	50.00	57.50	52.50
9	65.00	57.50	52.50	57.50	56.25
Avg	63.23	64.06	57.40	57.40	53.33

their non-dominant hand, and two subjects (2 and 3) reached it with their dominant hand. Interestingly, the same subjects did not reach these levels with both dominant and non-dominant hand, indicating that there was indeed a difference in performance with regards to the that hand-side was used for the imagery task.

It should be noted that what hand-side performs better seemingly depends on two factors. One being the subject performing the task. Subject 2 achieved 28.75% points higher accuracy when using their dominant hand, compared to using to their non-dominant. This result is contrary to subject 7, where the non-dominant hand yielded 11.25% points better accuracy than the dominant one. The second factor that affects performance is the classifier that was used. Subjects 5 and 9 received better scores for RH-RH imagery when classified with FBCSP, but poorer when using TSLR. For the remaining subjects, which side performed better was consistent across the models.

Figure 3 compares the average FBCSP classification score and standard deviation for both dominant and non-dominant hands. In this case, six out of nine subjects reached their highest obtained accuracy with their dominant hand. Similarly, Fig. 4, compares the results of TSLR. Using TSLR, only four out of nine performed better with their dominant hand. For two of the subjects the best-performing hand-side depended on the classification model. Hence no clear trends with regards to which side tends to yield better performances can be identified. Additional data collection and studies are necessary, where more participants complete both the dominant and non-dominant hand experiments multiple times across several sessions.

For one subject, the difference between the hand-sides was statistically significant (t-test, p = 0.006). This was subject 7, using the TSLR classifier. The small sample sizes for each subject make it difficult to draw any relevant conclusion regarding the statistics.

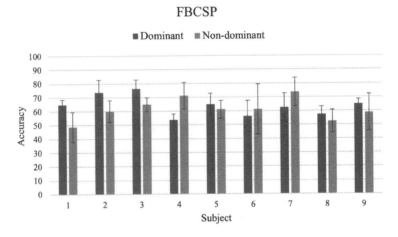

Fig. 3. Accuracy scores for dominant and non-dominant hand, using FBCSP. Error bars denote the standard deviation of the folds.

Regarding within-hand classification and real-world application, five out of the nine subjects reached decoding accuracies above the required threshold (70%) for at least one of their hands. The results indicate that same-limb motor imagery has the potential to be utilized in a BCI system, providing additional commands to external devices. It should, however, be noted that in an additional experiment where all four classes were considered, the accuracy dropped significantly. The four-class system did not pass the minimum threshold, emphasizing that

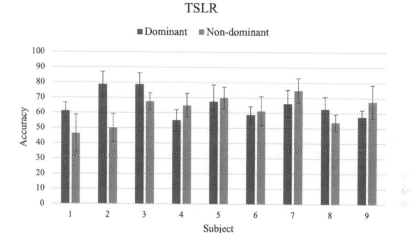

Fig. 4. Accuracy scores for dominant and non-dominant hand, using TSLR. Error bars denote the standard deviation of the folds.

increasing the number of commands is challenging, and more research is necessary.

It is also clear that differences in subject-wise performance are a challenge. In an experiment by M. Lee et al. [15], 30% of the subjects were not able to achieve more than 70% decoding accuracy when using an MI-based BCI. BCI illiteracy is a proposed condition wherein users of BCI technology fail to reach proficiency in using it within a standard training period [22]. The condition is a challenge in MI BCI systems, because it means that not everyone can use them. The subjects who did not achieve accuracy above the threshold in any of the experiments could suffer from BCI illiteracy.

The performance also varies within trials, runs, and sessions. The classification accuracy is usually at its peak around the chosen window segment in this study, i.e., 0.5 to 2.5. In later stages of the trials, the classification accuracy often decreases. Subjects losing concentration towards the end of the task could be the cause of this performance decrease. When collecting data for this study, it was commented that the motor imagery runs were particularly tiring compared to the executory ones.

3.1 Future Work

Collecting more data to potentially identify trends as to which hand-side usually performs better is an enticing next step following this study. The ability to control an SMR-BCI is closely linked to handedness [33], and it would be interesting to explore whether the difference in performance between dominant and non-dominant hand depends on the handedness of the subject. To research this, data from both right-handed and left-handed participants would need to be collected.

There are also many ways to further explore the existing dataset beyond the scope of this work. Models pre-trained on open relevant datasets can be used for transfer learning, aiming for better initialization or regularization. Pre-training could perhaps enhance the performance of the neural networks especially. Several other models, feature extraction, and feature selection techniques can be tested to potentially improve performance.

There is a shifting focus in the BCI field from inter-subject analysis to intra-subject analysis. It would be exciting to examine this aspect further, as such a system would require no training from the user, and the amount of available training data would be substantially increased. Further understanding of the extracted features would also be helpful in the investigation of novel classification methods, specifically focused on single-limb classification. Structural and functional differences are known to exist within the cortical sensorimotor networks with respect to the dominant vs. non-dominant hand.

4   Summary and Conclusion

One critical limitation of current BCI applications is the lack of usability, mainly due to the small number of available classes for decoding, leaving room for few commands. In this study, the aim was to contribute in a direction toward more commands. To this end, the study sought to determine whether hand-dominance has an effect when classifying imagery movements within the same limb. Another objective was to investigate to what extent finer motor tasks by a single limb can reach acceptable performance criteria to pass as additional commands in a BCI. To achieve these objectives, an EEG dataset with nine right-handed participants was collected. The participants performed an identical set of grasping tasks with both their dominant and non-dominant hands. Current algorithms in traditional machine learning, such as FBCSP and Riemannian geometry, were implemented and compared to novel, promising, EEG-tailored convolutional neural networks. Different data augmentation and feature selection techniques were be explored in various experiments.

Channel selection according to a Riemannian geometry criterion before feature extraction or classification improved discrimination. None of the scores averaged across all subjects reached the required accuracy level of 70%. Some of the individual subjects in the study did, however. The best scores were 75.00% for grasps imagined by the non-dominant hand and 78.75% for grasps performed by the dominant hand. BCI illiteracy could have caused some of the subjects not to reach accuracy levels above the required minimum to be deployed in a BCI application.

For all the subjects, one of the sides provided higher accuracy decoding levels than the other, indicating that what hand was used mattered for the result. Which side depended on both the subject and the classifier. To identify a trend or establish whether the differences are statistically significant, more data is required. The results of this study should be viewed as an exploratory report of potential classification differences when the same experiments are performed by both dominant and non-dominant hand. Further research on the topic is encouraged.

Acknowledgments. This work is partially supported by The Research Council of Norway as a part of the Predictive and Intuitive Robot Companion (PIRC) project under grant agreement 312333 and through its Centres of Excellence scheme, RITMO with project No. 262762. The authors would also like to thank Rahul Omprakash Agrawal and Henrik Eijsink for assistance with the lab and useful discussions.

References

1. Ang, K.K., et al.: Filter bank common spatial pattern algorithm on BCI competition IV datasets 2a and 2b. Front. Neurosci. **6** (2012). ISSN: 1662-453X. https://doi.org/10.3389/fnins.2012.00039. https://www.frontiersin.org/articles/10.389/fnins.2012.00039/full#B1. Accessed 06 Sept 2021
2. Ang, K., et al.: Filter Bank Common Spatial Pattern (FBCSP) in braincomputer interface. In: Proceedings of the International Joint Conference on Neural Networks, p. 2397. July 2008. https://doi.org/10.1109/IJCNN.2008.4634130
3. Barachant, A.: MEG decoding using Riemannian Geometry and Unsupervised classification (2014)
4. Barachant, A., et al.: Classification of covariance matrices using a Riemannian-based kernel for BCI applications. Neurocomputing **112**, 172–178 (2013). https://doi.org/10.1016/j.neucom.2012. https://hal.archives-ouvertes.fr/hal-00820475. Accessed 06 Oct 2021
5. Barachant, A., et al.: Multiclass brain-computer interface classification by Riemannian geometry. IEEE Trans. Biomed. Eng. **59**(4), 920–928 (2012). https://doi.org/10.1109/TBME.2011.2172210. https://hal.archives-ouvertes.fr/hal-00681328. Accessed 06 Oct 2021
6. Blankertz, B., et al.: The berlin brain-computer interface: non- medical uses of BCI technology. Front. Neurosci. **4** (2010). ISSN: 1662-4548. https://doi.org/10.3389/fnins.2010.00198. https://www.ncbi.nlm.nih.gov/pmc/articles/PMC3002462/. Accessed 13 June 2021
7. Brainard, D.H.: The psychophysics toolbox. Spat. Vis. **10**(4), 433–436 (1997). ISSN: 0169-1015
8. Cho, H., et al.: A step-by-step tutorial for a motor imagery-based BCI, pp. 445–460 (2018)
9. Edelman, B.J., Baxter, B., He, B.: EEG source imaging enhances the decoding of complex right-hand motor imagery tasks. IEEE Trans. Bio-Med. Eng. **63**(1), 4–14 (2016). ISSN: 1558-2531. https://doi.org/10.1109/TBME.2015.2467312
10. Ge, S., Wang, R., Yu, D.: Classification of four-class motor imagery employing single-channel electroencephalography. PLOS ONE **9**(6), e98019 (2014). ISSN: 1932-6203. https://doi.org/10.1371/journal.pone.0098019. https://journals.plos.org/plosone/article?id=10.1371/journal.pone.0098019. Accessed 18 May 2021
11. Graimann, B., Allison, B., Pfurtscheller, G.: Brain–computer interfaces: a gentle introduction. In: Graimann, B., Pfurtscheller, G., Allison, B. (eds.) Brain-Computer Interfaces: Revolutionizing Human-Computer Interaction. The Frontiers Collection, pp. 1–27. Springer, Heidelberg (2010). ISBN: 978-3-642-02091-9. https://doi.org/10.1007/978-3-642-02091-9_1. Accessed 13 June 2021

12. Gramfort, A., et al.: MEG and EEG data analysis with MNEPython. Front. Neurosci. **7** (2013). ISSN: 1662–453X. https://doi.org/10.3389/fnins.2013.00267. https://www.frontiersin.org/articles/10.3389/fnins.2013.00267/full. Accessed 9 June 2021

13. Kübler, A., et al.: Brain-computer communication: self-regulation of slow cortical potentials for verbal communication. Arch. Phys. Med. Rehabil. **82**(11), 1533–1539 (2001). ISSN: 0003–9993. https://doi.org/10.1053/apmr.2001.26621

14. Lawhern, V.J., et al.: EEGNet: a compact convolutional network for EEG-based brain-computer interfaces. J. Neural Eng. **15**(5), 056013 (2018). arXiv: 1611.08024. ISSN: 1741–2560, 1741–2552. https://doi.org/10.1088/1741-2552/aace8c. Accessed 10 June 2021

15. Lee, M.-H., et al.: EEG dataset and OpenBMI toolbox for three BCI paradigms: an investigation into BCI illiteracy. GigaScience **8**(5) (2019). ISSN: 2047–217X. https://doi.org/10.1093/gigascience/giz002. Accessed 15 June 2021

16. Li, A., et al.: Towards paradigm-independent brain computer interfaces, pp. 1–6 (2020). https://doi.org/10.1109/BCI48061.2020.9061657

17. Liao, K., et al.: Decoding individual finger movements from one hand using human EEG signals. PLOS ONE **9**(1), e85192 (2014). ISSN: 1932–6203. https://doi.org/10.1371/journal.pone.0085192. https://journals.plos.org/plosone/article?id=10.1371/journal.pone.0085192. Accessed 18 May 2021

18. Lotte, F., et al.: A review of classification algorithms for EEG-based braincomputer interfaces: a 10 year update. J. Neural Eng. **15**(3), 031005 (2018). ISSN: 1741–2552. https://doi.org/10.1088/1741-2552/aab2f2

19. Lotte, F.: Signal processing approaches to minimize or suppress calibration time in oscillatory activity-based brain-computer interfaces. Proc. IEEE **103**, 871–890 (2015). https://doi.org/10.1109/JPROC.2015.2404941

20. Marquez-Chin, C., Atwell, K., Popovic, M.R.: Prediction of specific hand movements using electroencephalographic signals. J. Spinal Cord Med. **40**(6), 696–705 (2017). ISSN: 1079–0268. https://doi.org/10.1080/10790268.2017.1369215. https://www.ncbi.nlm.nih.gov/pmc/articles/PMC5778933/. Accessed 18 May 2021

21. Navarro, I., Hubais, B., Sepulveda, F.: A comparison of time, frequency and ICA based features and five classifiers for wrist movement classification in EEG signals. In: 2005 IEEE Engineering in Medicine and Biology 27th Annual Conference, pp. 2118–2121, January 2005. ISSN: 1558–4615. https://doi.org/10.1109/IEMBS.2005.1616878

22. Padfield, N., et al.: EEG-based brain-computer interfaces using motor-imagery: techniques and challenges. Sensors (Basel Switzerland) **19**(6) (2019). ISSN: 1424–8220. https://doi.org/10.3390/s19061423. https://www.ncbi.nlm.nih.gov/pmc/articles/PMC6471241/. Accessed 13 June 2021

23. Pfurtscheller, G., Neuper, C.: Motor imagery activates primary sensorimotor area in humans. Neurosci. Lett. **239**(2), 65–68 (1997). ISSN: 0304–3940. https://doi.org/10.1016/S0304-3940(97)00889-6

24. Riyad, M., Khalil, M., Adib, A.: MI-EEGNET: a novel convolutional neural network for motor imagery classification. J. Neurosci. Methods **353**, 109037 (2021). ISSN: 0165–0270. https://doi.org/10.1016/j.jneumeth.2020.109037. https://www.sciencedirect.com/science/article/pii/S016502702030460X. Accessed 20 May 2021

25. Rodríguez-Bermúdez, G., García-Laencina, P.J.: Automatic and adaptive classification of electroencephalographic signals for brain computer interfaces. J. Med. Syst. **36**(Suppl 1), S51–63 (2012). ISSN: 0148–5598. https://doi.org/10.1007/s10916-012-9893-4

26. Roy, Y., et al.: Deep learning-based electroencephalography analysis: a systematic review. J. Neural Eng. **16**(5), 051001–051001 (2019). ISSN: 1741–2560. https://doi.org/10.1088/1741-2552/ab260c

27. Sakhavi, S., Guan, C., Yan, S.: Parallel convolutionallinear neural network for motor imagery classification. In: 2015 23rd European Signal Processing Conference (EUSIPCO), pp. 2736–2740. IEEE, Nice, August 2015. https://doi.org/10.1109/EUSIPCO.2015.7362882. http://ieeexplore.ieee.org/document/7362882/. Accessed 14 June 2021

28. Schirrmeister, R.T., et al.: Deep learning with convolutional neural networks for EEG decoding and visualization. Hum. Brain Mapp. **38**(11), 5391–5420 (2017). ISSN: 1097-0193. https://doi.org/10.1002/hbm.23730. https://onlinelibrary.wiley.com/doi/abs/10.1002/hbm.23730. Accessed 15 June 2021

29. Schlogl, A., et al.: Evaluation criteria for BCI research, p. 66 (2007)

30. Schlögl, A., et al.: Characterization of four-class motor imagery EEG data for the BCI-competition 2005. J. Neural Eng. **2**(4), L14–22 (2005). ISSN: 1741-2560. https://doi.org/10.1088/1741-2560/2/4/L02

31. Stinear, C., et al.: Kinesthetic, but not visual, motor imagery modulates corticomotor excitability. Exp. Brain Res. Experimentelle Hirnforschung. Expérimentation cérébrale **168**, 157–164 (2006). https://doi.org/10.1007/s00221-005-0078-y

32. Yong, X., Menon, C.: EEG classification of different imaginary movements within the same limb. PLoS ONE **10**(4) (2015). ISSN: 1932–6203. https://doi.org/10.1371/journal.pone.0121896. https://www.ncbi.nlm.nih.gov/pmc/articles/PMC4382224/. Accessed 18 May 2021

33. Zapała, D., et al.: The effects of handedness on sensorimotor rhythm desynchronization and motor-imagery BCI control. Sci. Rep. **10** (2020). ISSN: 2045–2322. https://doi.org/10.1038/s41598-020-59222-w. https://www.ncbi.nlm.nih.gov/pmc/articles/PMC7005877/. Accessed 15 May 2021

Kinematic Responses as a Control Strategy to Visual Occlusion

Carlos Eduardo Campos[1,2,6(✉)] ⓘ, Cíntia de Oliveira Matos[1] ⓘ,
Lucas Cléopas Costa da Silva[3] ⓘ, Paulo Rogério de Almeida Ribeiro[3] ⓘ,
Crislaine Rangel Couto[1,4] ⓘ, Suziane Peixoto dos Santos[5] ⓘ,
and Herbert Ugrinowitsch[1] ⓘ

[1] Universidade Federal de Minas Gerais-UFMG, Belo Horizonte, Minas Gerais, Brazil
carloscampos@uit.br, herbertu@ufmg.br
[2] Universidade de Itaúna, Itaúna, Minas Gerais, Brazil
[3] Universidade Federal Do Maranhão-UFMA, São Luís, Maranhão, Brazil
paulo.ribeiro@ecp.ufma.br
[4] Instituto Metodista Izabela Hendrix, Belo Horizonte, Brazil
[5] Universidade Federal Do Triângulo Mineiro-UFTM, Uberaba, Minas Gerais, Brazil
suziane.peixoto@uftm.edu.br
[6] Escola de Formação de Oficiais EFO-PMMG, Belo Horizonte, Minas Gerais, Brazil

Abstract. The neuron motor system has the ability to update the control strategy according to the environment. Intercepting a moving object is a task that can provide and study this ability. The aim of this study is to determine the performance and the control strategy on visual occlusion perturbation to intercepting moving targets. Sixteen subjects (24.4 ± 5.32 years old; 12 males and 4 females) were recruited. The experiment was carried out with a familiarization and an experimental phase where the participants managed a Physical Effector Machine (PEM) synchronized with a Virtual Interception Task (VIT). During the familiarization phase, participants learned the movement time (200 to 250 ms). In the experimental phase participants performed under two different conditions: Perturbation condition (PC), which corresponds to the target occlusion for 75 ms and 300 ms before expected movement onset and Control condition (CC) where there was no occlusion. In both conditions, the target moved at a constant velocity (145 cm.s^{-1}). The results were analysed from the kinematics Movement time (MT), Relative time to peak velocity (%tPV), Correction Numbers (CN) and Spatial absolute-error (AE). The statistics were run by non-parametric Mann Whitney test to verify differences between CC and PC. The results showed a higher AE for PC than CC condition [$U_{(159)} = 16.738$; $p = .01$; $r = .43$]. For the TM, %tPV and NC there were no differences between conditions. Our findings allowed us to conclude that the occlusion affected the performance accuracy but the control strategy to intercepting seemed to be similar in both conditions.

Keyword: Motor control · Feedback mechanism · Interceptive task

C.E. Campos, C.O. Matos, L.C.C. Silva, P.R.A. Ribeiro, C.R. Couto, S.P. Sontos and H. Ugrinowitsch–These authors contributed equally to this work.

P. R. d. A. Ribeiro et al. (Eds.): LAWCN 2021, CCIS 1519, pp. 250–262, 2022.
https://doi.org/10.1007/978-3-031-08443-0_16

1   Introduction

Interceptive moving targets involve accurately hitting an object in movement and at an exact location [1]. Hitting tasks require short and fast movement of the intercepting effector, such as a hand or a device [2]. Since intercepting moving targets involve many variables, it is usual to find studies using a single-degree of freedom task to investigate temporal and amplitude movement constraints on performance accuracy and control strategies to infer how the motor control system works [1, 3, 4].

Practicing a single-degree of freedom intercept task in a predictable context [4–6] improves movement control and performance based on kinematic information such as target velocity [2, 7]. Results using kinematics have shown the motor control strategy regarding the movement time (MT), target distance and velocity [1], target size and temporal precision [8] and even changes in control during learning [6]. For example, the relative time to peak velocity (%tPV) increases with learning under predictable context.

On the other hand, intercepting moving targets under unpredictable contexts is more difficult or even impossible, depending on the unpredictability [9, 10]. Facing unpredictable changes on target speed of initiated or ongoing movements requires corrections that depend on the available time to make the necessary changes to the previously sent control and demanding a higher level of visual information processing [9, 11]. The processing of visual sensory pathways, in unpredictable conditions, engages feedback mechanisms involving visual organs and brain circuitry to translate input information into output (i.e., movement) [12, 13]. Since the eye distance to the brain is short, retinal processing of visual input takes ~ 30 ms [14]. The continuous brain processing takes ~ 60–75ms that corresponds to visuomotor brain integration until initiating the volunteer muscle response [15, 17]. The kinematic response changes (e.g., velocity changes) take at least 200ms after initiation of voluntary muscle response to be visualized [2, 11–18]. It seems that kinematic response changes could be an efficient tool to observe and understand the strategies and control mechanisms in interceptive actions.

Evidence for corrections of interceptive actions can be provided from the kinematic response changes, such as velocity and acceleration [2]. In this sense, kinematic responses could be inferred as a strategy to use feedforward control, when the subject waits for the target to be as near as possible to the strike zone before starting the interception action [4]. On the other hand, anticipation of the peak velocity could be inferred as a strategy that gives more time for the subject to use feedback control and make possible corrections [10–15]. In addition, this anticipation strategy can be observed under unpredictable contexts, which means anticipation to the tPV and perceived inflections on the acceleration curves (e.g., valleys greater than 2% of the peak). These valleys are considered corrections in function of the velocity deceleration after peaks on velocity curves [2, 19]. Even if that kinematic analysis could be used to describe the motor control and strategies of interception tasks, this method has been little used to infer the control mechanisms involved in the interception of moving targets [6, 19, 20]. Furthermore, to our knowledge, no paper has yet been found to explain the computational analysis that allows the explanation of control strategy on visual occlusion perturbation using %tPV and the inflexions on the acceleration curves.

The aim of the present study is to determine the performance and the control strategy on visual occlusion perturbation through kinematic responses as %tPV and the acceleration inflections to infer the control mechanisms used to intercept moving targets. We expected that the PC would disrupt and reduce the performance of interceptive actions. Also, we expected that the control strategy in PC will be different to the CC.

2   Methods

2.1   Participants

Sixteen subjects (24.4 ± 5.32 years old; 12 males and 4 females) were recruited, and each one had written informed consent to participate voluntarily in this study. All participants were healthy and self-declared as right-handed preference and normal or corrected-to-normal vision. The procedures were approved by the Institutional Review Board of Universidade Federal de Minas Gerais (protocol 24754819.6.0000.5149), in conformity with the ethical standards established in the 1964 Declaration of Helsinki, amended in 1989, on the participation of human subjects in research.

2.2   Instruments and Task

The task involved virtual and physical element (Fig. 1) and required an Intel® Core™ i5 3.60 GHz, a projector (Epson PowerLite77c) a Virtual Interception Task (VIT) and a Physical Effector Machine (PEM). The VIT and PEM involved physical staffs (Juliana Buére, Jonathan Ferreira, Carlos Campos, Crislaine Couto, Cintia Matos & Herbert Ugrinowitsch, UFMG, Belo Horizonte, Brazil) and data acquisition was performed using Labview® (National Instruments Corporation, Austin/TX, USA). The data were processed using MatLab® (The Mathworks Co, Natick, MA).

The PEM is composed of a linear nylon guide (rail) of 100 cm (length) vs 10 cm (width) vs 4 cm (height), and abs premium physical effector attached on a linear guide Magnetic Transducer (BTL6-A110-M0400) Balluff® with precision in μm and a steel chair fixed on the floor (Fig. 1). The kinematic acquisition variables (position-time) were acquired at 200 Hz. For acquisition and transformation of the kinematic data, an A/D Board DAC-NIUSB-6009 National Instruments® was used.

To perform the VIT, participants sat down on a chair parallel to the attached linear guide where the elbow was supported according to the arm anthropometric dimensions. Participants were requested to intercept a virtual moving target (6 × 5 cm blue rectangle) using a virtual effector (4 × 5 cm green rectangle) within the width of the target and inside the limits of the strike zone. From the first appearance on the projection right side, the virtual target traveled 210 cm from right to left perpendicularly to the target rail. Then, the participant moved the physical effector flexing the shoulder and extending the elbow until the strike zone.

Participants were asked to perform the interceptive action in a range of 200–250 ms movement time (MT), since this range characterizes a ballistic movement and provide sufficient time to make corrections after the movement's onset [5], enabling the use of different mechanisms to control [6].

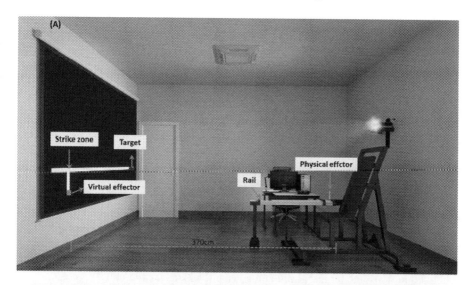

Fig. 1. Illustration of the experimental setup. (**a**) represents the virtual interception task (VIT) machine, including the virtual horizontal rail (304 cm) and the moving target (blue rectangle). A virtual effector (green rectangle) synchronized with the physical effector machine would be moved (30 cm) on the vertical rail and hit the target into the strike zone. (**b**) Represents the end position and visual feedback. The physical effector was moved forward along the virtual vertical rail until the strike zone. The zoomed detail represents the visual feedback available to participants after each trial. The dimensions are not to scale.

2.3 Study Design

The experiment was carried out with a familiarization and an experimental phase. During the familiarization phase, participants performed the movement time ranging from 200–250 ms for six trials in a row, which was adopted as performance criteria of movement time (MT) learning. The objective for the participants was to perform that specific MT, which was sufficient to pre-program and make corrections after the onset of the movement [5]. Furthermore, the movement time ensured that the control strategy observed at the end of the experiment was based on the participant's choice and not on the limitation of the task. In this phase, the target moved at a constant velocity of 130 cm.s^{-1}. Then, following a 5 min' break, the experimental phase began.

During the experimental phase, participants performed two different conditions with 10 attempts each. On perturbation condition (PC), the target had been occluded for 75 ms (i.e., the target projection disappeared), 300 ms before expected movement onset (See Fig. 2a), which corresponds to 250 ms before the target achieves the strike zone. On the other hand, on the control condition (CC) there was no perturbation (See Fig. 2b). In both conditions, the target moved at a constant velocity of 145 cm.s^{-1}.

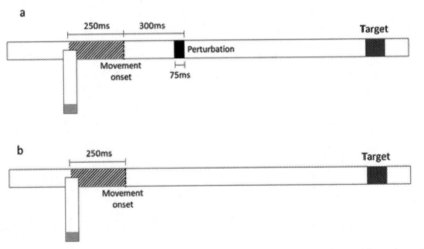

Fig. 2. Illustrations of the two experimental conditions. (**a**) illustrates the position where the target is occluded for 75 ms, 300 ms before the expected movement onset for PC. (**b**) illustrates the position where the target was expected to be before movement onset for CC.

2.4 Data Analysis

The data were obtained from LabView and processed using MatLab. The Movement Velocity (MV) and Movement Acceleration (MA) data for each participant were filtered with a dual pass second-order Butterworth filter with a cutoff frequency of 50 Hz [20]. From the MV we obtained the peak velocity and relative time to peak velocity (%tPV) using the *findpeaks* function. From the MA we extracted the acceleration peaks and valleys (e.g. inflexions on MA considered corrections) using a splitted signal. The splitted signal starts with an index before the maximum peak of the whole signal and goes until the end of the signal. The valleys of the splitted signal were found using *findpeaks* with the splitted signal inverted (- splitted). The calculated peaks and valleys were stored on vectors and for each index *i* a deviation was calculated as:

$$deviation[i] = 100 \times abs(peaks[i] - valleys[i])/valleys[i] \qquad (1)$$

For deviations greater than or equal to 2% a correction was counted up. This process was repeated for each trial of the participants to verify the existence and counter the corrections (CN).

2.5 Statistical Analysis

The effects of the two experimental conditions (CC and PC) were analysed from the kinematic variables (MT, %tPV and NC) as well as on spatial absolute-error (AE). The quantitative variables were expressed as means and standard deviations and to test the normality of the data distribution we run the Shapiro–Wilk test on Python. Since the data were not normally distributed the analysis was run by the non-parametric Mann Whitney test to verify possible differences between the CC and PC. In order to strengthen the inferences of the statistical results, Cohen's d correction was also performed calculating **r** [21]. All statistical analyzes were performed using Python and with a significance level of p < .05.

3   Results

The Mann Whitney test showed a higher AE for PC than CC condition [$U_{(159)} = 16.738$ p = .012; **r** = .43]. It seems that the occlusion condition perturbed the participants and imposed more difficulty to plan the interceptive movement (See Fig. 3).

Even though the statistical results comparing the kinematic variables TM, %tPV and NC did not show differences between experimental conditions (See Fig. 4), some individual participants' results behavior would provide interesting insights about the used control strategies. To present an explanation directed to the control strategy, we extracted the performance results of participants, from Fig. 4, who demonstrated a particular behavior that gave them any advantage during interception movements. The participants v2, v4, v7 and v16 showed specific and important behavior, which will be discussed in the next section.

4   Discussion

The aim of the present study was to determine the performance and the control strategy on visual occlusion perturbation using kinematic responses to infer the control mechanisms used for intercepting moving targets.

The first hypothesis was confirmed since the perturbation conditions (e.g. occlusion condition) disrupted and reduced the performance of interceptive actions. The performance reduction happens because during interceptive actions (See Fig. 2), the subject

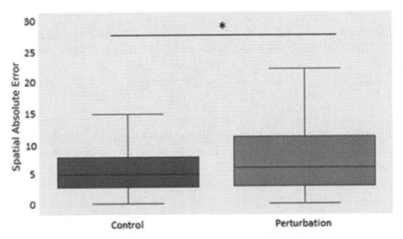

Fig. 3. Comparison of absolute error between CC and PC. *p < .05

needs to extract and use visual information from the environment (e.g. target displacement velocity) to guide movement planning [22, 23] and decide when to start the interceptive action. Some studies had already shown loss in the intercept rate when the target was occluded for 200 ms [24]. Since the disturbance is inserted, part of the information is suppressed and could not be used. After target occlusion ~30 ms will be spent by the retina [25, 26] to process the input (e.g. target disappearance) and ~75 ms to process and integrate visuomotor information according to the environment and the type of task [27]. In the present study, one of the experimental conditions was to intercept an occluded (for 75 ms) moving target 300 ms before the expected onset interceptive movement. The occlusion becomes a disturbance, since the time to initiate a voluntary action is ~100 ms [13, 28], and the resultant muscle strength produced, responsible for the desired interceptive movement, will spend ~ 100ms more [16, 29]. Thus, even if the task is known, the control of the first interceptive actions will lead to errors that will provide feedback for the next actions (e.g. motor planning), attenuating the occlusion effect and increasing performance [24, 30].

Once an error in the planning movement happens it is expected modifications on the movement using the feedback sources to achieve a greater performance. These modifications can be seen on the kinematics such as %tPV (See Fig. 4D) and inflexions on the acceleration curves represented by CN (See Fig. 4B). In order to modify the movement, enough time is necessary to perceive and compute the error as well as the time to replan and execute the action [31].

For the second hypothesis it was expected, during occlusion conditions, that subjects would make corrections due to suppression of information (e.g. PC), which could interfere in the desired action and consequently on quality of planning execution [27]. However, our second hypothesis was not confirmed, since no difference was found between both conditions.

Even though our general results did not show statistically significant differences, on either the %tPV or on the NC, comparing the two experimental conditions, an *ad hoc* analysis, shown in Fig. 5 and Fig. 6, gives strong indications for that phenomenon and

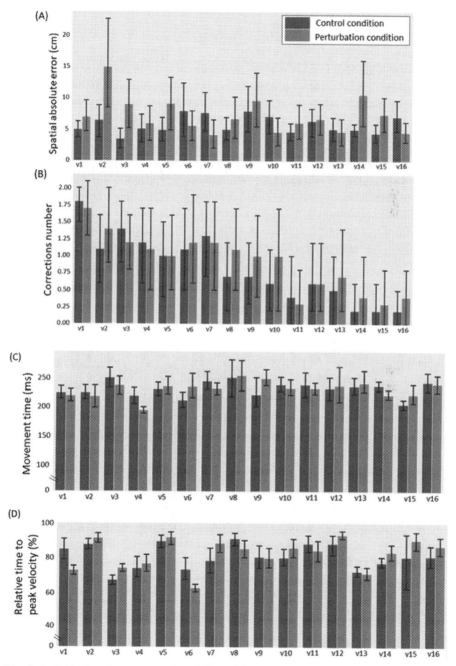

Fig. 4. Individual performance results of all participants comparing the spatial AE, %tPV, MT and NC between CC and PC conditions. (**a**) represents the spatial AE; (**b**) represents the NC; (**c**) represents the MT; and (**d**) represents the %tPV. The black bars represent the estimate of mean standard error.

highlights the necessity of including individual analysis for better understanding or, at least, to indicate how the motor system uses the mechanisms involved on the interception of moving targets, since several researches have shown that motor control and learning do not follow the same aways for all human beings [6, 8, 11–28]. Moreover, to be successful in an interceptive task, the subject needs to extract and use relevant visual information from the environment such as the direction, velocity of the target and its exact position to move one of the arms or moving an effector to intercept a moving target. Figure 5 shows the performance of five participants in the environment predictable control condition (e.g. CC). The performance is represented by average of Spatial AE (cm), %tPV and NC. It is a crucial aspect to understand the direct relationship between %tPV and the NC. The participants who spent less time to achieve the peak velocity had more time to apply corrections to maintain or increase the performance. The anticipation of peak velocity has been shown as a strategy that could [1] give more time to make any change on the movement using the feedback sources [2, 31, 32]. Conversely, when the relative time to peak velocity is close to the end of movement, there is no chance of making any change [2, 3, 11].

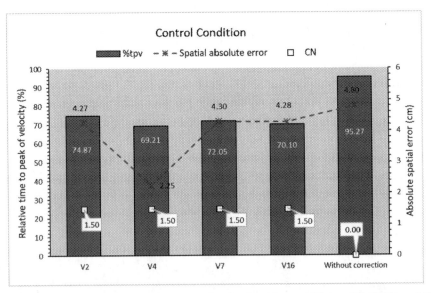

Fig. 5. Mean of 4 attempts of participants v2, v4, v7, v16 exemplifying AE, %tPV and CN performances and profile of AE and %tPV performance in attempts without corrections on control condition.

Figure 6 shows the performance of the same five participants in the Perturbation condition that the environment is unpredictable. The performance is represented by average of Spatial AE (cm), %tPV and NC. Note that the behavior is similar to that of the control condition. The anticipation of the peak velocity becomes more evident as a good control strategy. Izawa et al. [33] demonstrate that to anticipate the peak velocity brings more time to use feedback and possible corrections. Furthermore, this strategy in an unpredictable environment has been shown as a good candidate to infer the control mechanism used by the neural motor system [6, 33]. Since the correction number increases while the time to peak velocity decreases, it is plausible to affirm that the motor control system uses the feedback mechanism to adjust the interceptive action after the perturbation provoked by occlusion. It has been shown that when the %tPV happens near the beginning of the movement this strategy enables the neuro motor system to make corrections until the end of the movement [2]. In this case, the movement is controlled using a feedback mechanism [11, 34] and indicates that the neuro motor system anticipates the peak velocity, as a strategy, to gain more time to perform corrections.

Conversely, in both conditions participants who presented time to peak velocity close to the end of interceptive movements (e.g. 95.27 and 94.47% respectively) could not make any corrections. Furthermore, their spatial AE in the perturbation condition is more than double compared to the performance of the other participants. In this case, the neuromotor system seems to use the mechanism of preprogramming the motor output [2, 6].

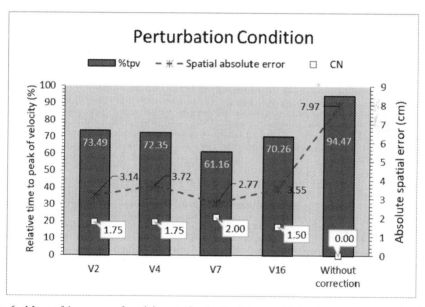

Fig. 6. Mean of 4 attempts of participants v2, v4, v7, v16 exemplifying AE, %tPV and CN performances and profile of AE and %tPV performance in attempts without corrections on perturbation condition.

5   Conclusion

In summary, according to our first hypothesis the results demonstrated that the occlusion, as a manipulation of visual information, can significantly affect the performance accuracy to intercept moving targets. Even though our second hypothesis was not confirmed, the methods chosen and the results obtained gave us enough information to infer about the control strategies using kinematic features. From a behavioral perspective, our last analysis gives a useful way to observe motor behavior and more specifically the control strategy. From a neurobiological perspective the kinematic variables used in our methods seems to be useful, since the visual sensory control presents a remarkable behavior in function of the context environment. The major challenge for the following research is to make sure that the analysed kinematic response could support the actual visual and somatosensory neural substrates.

Acknowledgements. This study was financed in part by the Coordenação de Aperfeiçoamento de Pessoal de Nível Superior – Brazil (CAPES) – Code 001 (Universidade Federal de Minas Gerais).

References

1. Tresilian, J.R., Lonergan, A.: Intercepting a moving target: effects of temporal precision constraints and movement amplitude. Exp. Brain Res. **2**(142), 193–207 (2002). https://doi.org/10.1007/s00221-001-0920-9
2. Tresilian, J.R., Plooy, A.: Systematic changes in the duration and precision of interception in response to variation of amplitude and effector size. Exp. Brain Res. **171**(4), 421–435 (2006). https://doi.org/10.1007/s00221-005-0286-5
3. Marinovic, W., Plooy, A.M., Tresilian, J.R.: The time course of direction specification in brief interceptive actions. Exp. Psychol. **57**(4), 293–300 (2010). https://doi.org/10.1027/1618-3169/a000034
4. Marinovic, W., Plooy, A., Tresilian, J.R.: The time course of amplitude specification in brief interceptive actions. Exp. Brain Res. **188**, 275–288 (2008). https://doi.org/10.1007/s00221-008-1360-6
5. Marinovic, W., Wallis, G.: Visual attention affects temporal estimation in anticipatory motor actions. Exp. Brain Res. **212**, 613–621 (2011). https://doi.org/10.1007/s00221-011-2772-2
6. Couto, C.R., et al.: Enhanced performance stabilization increases performance variability in a virtual interception task. Percept. Mot. Skills **128**(1), 546–559 (2020). https://doi.org/10.1177/0031512520954959
7. Fiehler, K., Brenner, E., Spering, M.: Prediction in goal-directed action. J. Vis. **18**(9), 1–21 (2019). https://doi.org/10.1167/19.9.10
8. Tresilian, J.R. Oliver, J.. Carrol, T.J.: Temporal precision of interceptive action: differential effects of target size and speed. Exp. Brain Res. **163**, 425–438 (2003). https://doi.org/10.1007/s00221-002-1309-0
9. Richter, S., Jansen-Osmann, P., Konczak, J., Kalveram, K.: Motor adaptation to different dynamic environments is facilitated by indicative context stimuli. Psychol. Res. **68**(4), 245–251 (2004). https://doi.org/10.1007/s00426-003-0140-y
10. Zago, M., Bosco, G., Maffei, V., Iosa, M., Ivanenko, Y.P., Lacquaniti, F.: Internal models of target motion: expected dynamics overrides measured kinematics in timing manual interceptions. J. Neurophysiol. **91**, 1620–1634 (2004). https://doi.org/10.1152/jn.00862.2003
11. Zago, M., Joseph Mcintyre, J., Patrice Senot, P., Lacquaniti, F.: Visuo-motor coordination and internal models for object interception. Exp. Brain Res. **192**, 571–604 (2009). https://doi.org/10.1007/s00221-008-1691-3
12. Smeets, J., Brenner, E.: Fast corrections of movements with a computer mouse. Spatial Vis. **16**(3), 365–376 (2003)

13. Franklin, D.W., Wolpert, D.M.: Specificity of reflex adaptation for task-relevant variability. J. Neurosci. **28**(52), 14165–14175 (2008). https://doi.org/10.1523/JNEUROSCI.4406-08.2008
14. Jin, J., Wang, Y., Lashgari, R., Swadlow, H.A., Alonso, J.-M.: Faster thalamocortical processing for dark than light visual targets. J. Neurosci. **31**(48), 17471–17479 (2011). https://doi.org/10.1523/JNEUROSCI.2456-11.2011
15. Cross, K.P., Cluff, T., Takei, T., Scott, S.H.: Visual feedback processing of the limb involves two distinct phases. J. Neurosci. **39**(34), 6751–6765 (2019). https://doi.org/10.1523/JNEUROSCI.3112-18.2019
16. Franklin, D.W., Franklin, S., Wolpert, D.M.: Fractionation of the visuomotor feedback response to directions of movement and perturbation. J. Neurophysiol. **112**(9), 2218–2233 (2014). https://doi.org/10.1152/jn.00377.2013
17. Scott, S.H., Cluff, T., Lowrey, C.R., Takei, T.: Feedback control during voluntary motor actions. Current Opinion of Neurobiology **33**, 85–94 (2015). https://doi.org/10.1016/j.conb.2015.03.006
18. Reichenbach, A., Thielscher, A., Peer, A., Bülthoff, H.H., Bresciani, J.P.: A key region in the human parietal cortex for processing proprioceptive hand feedback during reaching movements. Neuroimage **84**, 615–625 (2014). https://doi.org/10.1016/j.neuroimage.2013.09.024
19. Marinovic, W., Plooy, A.M., Tresilian, J.R.: The time course of direction specification in brief interceptive actions. Exp. Psychol. **57**(4), 292–300 (2010). https://doi.org/10.1027/1618-3169/a000034
20. Fialho, J.V.A.P., Tresilian, J.R.: Intercepting accelerated moving targets: effects of practice on movement performance. Exp. Brain Res. **235**(4), 1257–1268 (2017). https://doi.org/10.1007/s00221-017-4895-6
21. Cumming, G.: Cohen's d needs to be readily interpretable: comment on shieh. Behav. Res. Methods **45**(4), 968–971 (2013). https://doi.org/10.3758/s13428-013-0392-4
22. Merchant, H., Zarco, W., Prado, L., et al.: Behavioral and Neurophysiological Aspects of Target Interception. In: Sternad, D. (Org.), Progress in Motor Control, [S.l: s.n.], vol. 629, pp 201–220 (2009). https://doi.org/10.1007/978-0-387-77064-2, http://www.springerlink.com/index/10.1007/978-0-387-77064-2
23. Fooken, J., Yeo, S., Pai, D.K.: Spering: M.: Eye movement accuracy determines natural interception strategies. J. Vis **16**(14), 1–15 (2016). https://doi.org/10.1167/16.14.1
24. Marinovic, W., Plooy, A.M., Tresilian, J.R.: The utilization of visual information in the control of rapid interceptive actions. Exp. Psychol. **4**(56), 265–273 (2009). https://doi.org/10.1027/1618-3169.56.4.265
25. Churan, J., Kaminiarz, A., Schwenk, J.C.B., Bremmer, F.: Coding of interceptive saccades in parietal cortex of macaque monkeys. Brain Struct. Funct. **226**(8), 2707–2723 (2021). https://doi.org/10.1007/s00429-021-02365-x
26. Shadmehr, R.: Learning to predict and control the physics of our movements. J. Neurosci. **37**(7), 1663–1671 (2017). https://doi.org/10.1523/JNEUROSCI.1675-16.2016
27. Cluff, T., Crevecoeur, F., Scott, S.H.: A perspective on multisensory integration and rapid perturbation responses. Vision. Res. **110**, 215–222 (2015). https://doi.org/10.1016/j.visres.2014.06.011
28. Scott, S.H.: The computational and neural basis of voluntary motor control and planning. Trends Cogn. Sci. TiCS **16**(11), 541–549 (2012). https://doi.org/10.1016/j.tics.2012.09.008
29. Hayashi, T., Yokoi, A., Hirashima, M., Nozaki, D.: Visuomotor map determines how visually guided reaching movements are corrected within and across trials. E Neuro **3**(3), 1–13 (2016). https://doi.org/10.1523/ENEURO.0032-16.2016
30. Smeets, J.B.J., Martin, J., Brenner, E.: Similarities between digits' movements in grasping, touching and pushing. Exp. Brain Res. **203**(2), 339–346 (2011). https://doi.org/10.1007/s00221-010-2236-0

31. Elliott, D., Hansen, S., Grierson, L.E.M., Lyons, J., Bennett, S.J., Hayes, S.J.: Goal-directed aiming: two components but multiple processes. Psychol. Bull. **136**(6), 1023–1044 (2010). https://doi.org/10.1037/a0020958

32. Chua, R., Elliott, D.: Visual regulation of manual aiming. Hum. Mov. Sci. **12**(4), 365–401 (1993). https://doi.org/10.1016/0167-9457(93)90026-L

33. Izawa, J., Rane, T., Donchin, O., Shadmehr, R.: Motor adaptation as a process of reoptimization. J. Neurosci. **28**(11), 2883–2891 (2008). https://doi.org/10.1523/JNEUROSCI.5359-07.2008

34. Elliott, D., Binsted, G., Heath, M.: The control of goal-directed limb movements: correcting errors in the trajectory. Hum. Mov. Sci. **18**(2–3), 121–136 (1999). https://doi.org/10.1016/S0167-9457(99)00004-4

Author Index

Alberca, Lucas N. 101
Alves, Pedro Augusto Araujo da Silva de
    Almeida Nava 81
Alvim, Marina K. M. 155
Angonese, Alberto Torres 27

Barone, Dante 64
Barradas Filho, Alex Oliveira 81
Bianqueti, Bruno Leonardo 225
Borges, Fernando da Silva 119
Braz Junior, Geraldo 3

Campos, Brunno M. 155
Campos, Carlos Eduardo 250
Cantillo-Negrete, Jessica 215
Carino-Escobar, Ruben I. 215
Carlos, Bruna M. 155
Casqueiro, Gustavo Alves 27
Castellano, Gabriela 155
Castro-Aparicio, Juan C. 215
Cavalheiro, Esper 189
Contier, Ana Teresa 189
Cota, Vinícius Rosa 119, 132, 170
Couto, Crislaine Rangel 250

da Silva, Alexandra Miguel Raibolt 27
da Silva, Lucas Cléopas Costa 250
de Almeida, Tiago Paggi 225
de Luccas, Julia Baldi 225
de Oliveira, Alexandre César Muniz 48
de Oliveira, Cicero Joe Rafael Lima 48
Dias, Jade 15
Discacciati, Victor Rafael Pereira 132
dos Santos, Suziane Peixoto 250

Endestad, Tor 233

Faber, Jean 189
Fallico, Maximiliano 101
Fim Neto, Arnaldo 225
França, Keite Lira de Almeida 132

Gavernet, Luciana 101
Godinho, Fábio 225

Gomes Junior, Daniel Lima 3
Gomes, Paulo Gabriel Borralho 48
Gomez, David F. 64
Gori, Denis N. Prada 101

Lopez, Diego A. 64
Lopez, Manuel A. 64

Matos, Cíntia de Oliveira 250
Medeiros, Daniel de Castro 132
Menezes, Matheus Chaves 48
Moraes, Márcio Flávio Dutra 119, 132
Moreira, João Vitor da Silva 189
Muñoz, Dario S. 64

Nergård, Katrine Linnea 233
Nolasco, João D. 170

Oliveira, João Pedro Silva e 132
Oliveira, Walysson Carlos dos Santos 3

Pereira, Grace S. 132
Pinheiro, Daniel José Lins Leal 189

Ribeiro, Paulo Rogério de Almeida 48, 81,
    250
Rocha, Maria Sheila Guimarães 225
Rodrigues, Abner Cardoso 15
Rodrigues, Caio Maia 15
Rodrigues, Karina Aparecida 189
Rosa, Paulo Fernando Ferreira 27

Salas, Jaime A. Riascos 64
Santa, Jesús A. 64
Santos, Maikon L. 170
Soriano, Diogo Coutinho 225

Talevi, Alan 101
Terra, Heitor de Carvalho Barros 119
Torresen, Jim 64, 233
Trajano, Luiz Ricardo 225

Ugrinowitsch, Herbert 250

Printed in the United States
by Baker & Taylor Publisher Services